UBIZO

UBIZO

*a story of
coming home*

CHRISTA GUMEDE BUTHELEZI

Design and typesetting: HR Hegnauer
Editing: Maggie McReynolds, Un-Settling Books
Author's photo courtesy of Christa Gumede Buthelezi

Buthelezi, Christa Gumede
UBIZO: A Story of Coming Home
ISBN 979-8-9850405-0-0 digital edition
ISBN 979-8-9850405-1-7 paperback edition

Advance Praise

"At its core a story about the resilience and universality of the human spirit. While it is an artfully crafted memoir centering lasting effects of childhood trauma, the story is also a breathtaking tale of heartbreak, adventure, and finding peace in unexpected ways and places."

—Corinne Cunningham, author of *Farm Girl*

"A remarkable journey through adversity to authenticity."

—Sally Kay, author of *Reflexology Lymph Drainage: Illustrated Step by Step Guide to the Sally Kay Method*

"All of us dream, in some way, at some times, of escape from our current lives. What would happen if we were to hop on a plane, or a train, and go to a different spot, create a new life, and never return to everything we know? What we learn from this book is how interconnected we all are as humans. And how important it is to listen to our soul whispers."

—Cynthia Spencer, co-founder of *Stitch Your Art Out*

"A deeply personal story of one woman's journey that weaves together the universal themes of healing from trauma, searching for love (of self and others), and finding home, with a dash of magic thrown in. Alternately heartbreaking, compelling, and hopeful, I had a hard time putting it down."

—Alana Sheeren, Producer/Director, *Baby Ben Productions*

"I don't know traditional ceremonial ways, but feel, as I complete the last words of UBIZO, like I've just sat in healing ceremony. My heart feels tender and open. My body feels the deep stillness of having danced and sweated and cried. My feet feel planted on the Earth – in honest acknowledgement of the rocks and thorns here. My spirit feels expansive and clean. And I know the story – for Christa and for all of us – isn't over yet. It feels, in my heart, like the voices of ancestors whispering to each of us, "Keep going, dear one. It is beautiful. It is difficult. You are loved, and not alone."

—Kristin Noelle, founder of *Sacred Loom*

"A riveting, can't-put-it-down, story of how one American-born woman made her way from the darkness of childhood abuse to claiming the life she was meant for in South Africa with her Zulu soul family. In this brilliant book, Christa shows all of us that deep healing and a life of authenticity and belonging are available no matter what challenges must be overcome. Reading this story will draw you in and change you, inspiring you to say yes to pursuing the healing, and the life, that is meant for you as well."

—Nona Jordan, author of *Surf Lessons*

Life, they say, is best lived in good company – and I'm grateful for each and every one of the souls I've come to know in this life. Still, there are a few who I'd like to dedicate this book to:

For my parents – the ones who brought me to this world and gave me the experiences that allowed me to grow strong and wise, seeking better for me and for the world. And the ones who waited so patiently for me to come home, welcoming me without question and with so much love.

For my daughters and their daughters – may you each know your beauty, your strength, and how much you are loved every single day of your lives.

And for you, Khehla. You are the happily ever after, in ways I never could have imagined.

TABLE OF CONTENTS

Introduction

The words in this book are my own, gathered from wisps of memories, faded photographs, and journal entries along the path. As is true for most of our memories, they are captured through my own lens, and therefore are the truth as I know it, as I experienced it. Most names have been changed for privacy, yet the characters are intact and as I know them.

All opinions and ponderings about South Africa – and other places, for that matter – are my own as well. I've only been in this country for six years now, and I still have much to learn. My isiZulu, too, has a long way to go, so I've done my best here to honor the language, the culture, and the people of my adopted home.

I am the product, in many ways, of growing up in the United States – born as the civil rights movement was fully underway – though I've become aware as we edited this book that I've fully taken on South African and Zulu ways and attitudes. Much has changed in the American fabric of social justice in these last six years, and there is much, much more that needs to be addressed. The injustices and inequality people of color continue to face are both mindboggling and heartbreaking, all over the world, and to me personally on a very deep level. All of it done in the name of "race," a concept I believe is a social construct, one designed in the name of creating wealth by those who have colonized parts of the world that once thrived with their own indigenous cultures.

My life, from everyday events like standing in the grocery queue with my husband to the sharing of the stories in this book, is a practice in exploring the edges of healing the long-term effects of racism. It is simple yet powerful, to live our lives in accordance with ancient ways and to allow the love our family has for each other. It puts us in the way of hatred, yes, and yet it allows others to question what they were taught, no matter their color. For me, for us, and for many like us, that is the path to creating change in the long run.

After deep consideration, I am choosing here not to follow some American practices, such as capitalizing the word "black." It would be far easier to just go with the crowd on this one, but I believe that this sort of thing is only a Band-Aid, at best. It's too easy to hide behind such practices and think they solve the problem. They do not. We have far more work to do, all of us, to even begin to make things equitable. I've written and lived with the best of intentions, and I trust that the reader will allow the stories to unfold just as the lessons of my life have led me forward.

A bit of a warning for those easily triggered by stories of abuse or trauma: both are a significant part of my personal history and, therefore, of this book. While I don't wish to do harm to anyone, the stories from my childhood are an integral part of how I came to be who I am today. I doubt very much that I'd be here in KwaZulu-Natal, or doing any kind of healing work, if I had not gone through the difficult experiences I outline here. I've done my best to write about all of it as sensitively as possible, yet if it's hard for you to read that sort of story for any reason, you can safely skip chapters three through nine and still enjoy the rest of the book.

A few years after my arrival in South Africa, I was chatting with a dear friend in the US about life and how funny it is that we just never know what will happen. She, believing as I do in past lives and the like, said that she'd known many people living parallel lives with some degree of awareness – yet she'd never seen anyone else jump completely from one life to another. Perhaps that's the best explanation of all. I'll never know for sure. I've long since come to peace with the fact that, as human beings, we just don't get to understand fully. Not while we are on this Earth, anyway. Here in South Africa, as most tribal people were taught that white people do not have ancestors, my life as a *sangoma*, or practitioner of traditional African spirituality, is questioned constantly – and sometimes openly condemned. Yet as a fellow *sangoma* once said to me, do people really think I would choose this when I could be living a far more comfortable life in America? There is truth there, yes – but I would choose it again, in a heartbeat. It's been a huge adventure and an incredible gift, this calling. I have no regrets and look forward to whatever comes next.

I hope this book brings light to subjects that often remain in shadow, and serves as a reminder that we all belong, truly. Even better if it inspires someone to live their life fully and well, as the person they came to be rather than who they were told to be. In any case, I'm grateful for the opportunity to share all I've experienced, everything I've learned, and the extraordinary souls with whom I've walked this lifetime.

—Christa Gumede Buthelezi
Durban, KwaZulu-Natal
September 2021

Prologue

One sunny afternoon, I drove my little red rental car up a long, winding road through small farms to the top of a steep hill. There, the road seemed to end at a chain metal fence. Referring to my notes of the directions I'd been given, I took a left onto a gravel-strewn dirt road that led me directly into a thick forest.

The air cooled immediately as I drove past myriad ferns and lichen-covered rocks, between trees of all sorts. I recognized a few as some sort of wild banana and perhaps fig trees, but couldn't begin to identify them all. The little red car took the bumps and turns better than expected, thankfully, and eventually I came to a swing gate covered in all sorts of wood carvings – symbols of some sort, but not ones I recognized. I pushed the button, and almost immediately the gate swung open, and a small pack of large dogs spilled out. I was expected, yes, but no one seemed to have told them. I cracked my door open and looked up at the house for the first time. Strong and solid, made of stone I'd later be told was freed from the ground it was built on, yet not overbearing. There was a mural of low mountains done in tile over the huge garage and high archways over a small front porch lined with round stones.

Then, in that archway, I saw her. She was someone I'd found inspiring and somehow had been granted a rare interview with – provided I come early in the morning and stay only a couple hours. She had far better things to do, I understood, than entertain me.

She called off the dogs and, with a warm smile, graciously waved me out of the car and up the steps. Her voice was deep and resonant, a mellowed and gravelly version of my own. She greeted me with words I did not understand but that felt like a blessing being bestowed upon me.

I took my shoes off as she asked and tucked them under a woven bench in the front entry before following her into the house, the dogs close behind us. I was struck by the power of the artwork on the walls as we moved past the entry and into a large, open living space. The colors were rich and varied yet somehow worked with the vivid patterns of fabric on the windows, cushions strewn about everywhere, and the many natural artifacts – porcupine quills and feathers stuck here and there in beautiful vases and pots.

She was dressed in a cozy sweater and a flowy, nearly ankle-length skirt in a color-drenched pattern. There was a long power piece of a necklace, made from various crystals and stones, around her neck, nothing on her feet, and beaded bracelets on both wrists. Her hair was silver and braided to one side of her head, the tail end moving as she strolled into the sitting area in front of a huge stone fireplace. I'd heard that she was celebrating her 70th birthday, yet her face was nearly unlined, and her smile broad and youthful. She swayed as she walked, as a much younger woman might have, and there was a warmth along with the guardedness I'd been told to expect. She didn't often give interviews and had refused to allow a photographer to come along, saying she'd arrange for photographs herself, thanks very much.

Her laugh rang all the way up to the high, timbered ceilings as she noticed the awe-struck expression on my face. I was trying to take in all the paintings on the double-story walls, the smaller pieces propped up on windowsills, and the larger ceramic pieces, all hand-decorated, on the big, freeform wooden table just in front of a fire still glowing red against the early morning chill I'd felt at the entry. She asked that I call her Nona and settled herself into a huge leather chair, motioning that I should sit in the matching one adjacent to it. She assumed correctly that I had questions for her and assured me that she'd do her best to answer them all. Glancing at the long list in my open notebook, she gently and firmly reminded me that she only had an hour, ninety minutes at most.

We talked for a time. I tried to focus on the most critical queries so that I could weave together what I hoped would be a cover story, given the impact this place had already had on me. She explained that she'd been shooting photographs far longer than I'd been alive, since she was eleven years old in fact, and that she was perfectly capable of taking a "better than decent" self-portrait in one of the several mosaic-trimmed hanging mirrors she'd created and hung in her home.

I hoped all that was true and tried to keep her focused on my questions as she meandered off into story after story. Those stories were fascinating though, so mostly I found myself wandering along as we traveled the route she'd taken with her life. I discovered how she'd transformed from a shy, mistreated, and rather unhealthy child into this creative, wise, and witty creature with more self-assurance than I'd ever seen in an older woman. She seemed aware of all her own missteps along the way and yet singularly unbothered by them, considering it all learning ground. And fertilizer for the incredibly creative life she now lived in the middle of a magical, lush forest strewn with abstract sculptures of figures at once foreign and yet familiar to me.

I had moved off the chair and was sitting at her feet and petting one of her huge dogs, lost in the tale she was weaving, when suddenly she got up and asked me to follow her. As we approached the heavy wooden front door, she glanced at my feet and my rather delicate sandals and shook her head, pulling out a pair of Wellingtons just my size and urging me to put them on as she yanked her own flowered version of them onto her bare feet. Then she strode out onto the little front porch and pulled two beautifully carved walking sticks out of a large lapis blue glazed urn full of a variety of more sticks with different patterns decorating them. Thus equipped, she held onto my arm in a more familiar way than I'd expected.

We walked out the gate and down the dirt road until we came to a reverse fork marked by stacked stones. This road was clearly not driven much, as it was green with grasses waving a bit in the breeze. The day was heating up but it was still a bit cold as we passed under the shade of huge old trees with craggy bark and low-hanging branches.

Nona held onto me still in that companionable way, chatting about her favorite plants along the road, showing me flowers, and occasionally stopping to take her famous little shots of beauty with her phone. As we began to descend the hill, she pointed out herbs she used for medicine, plants that had been helping people for centuries. "The Earth," she said, "came with everything we need. There's no need for all the nonsense man has cooked up!"

We came to a little handwoven gate made of vines and branches, with small stone columns on either side. She swung it open and welcomed me to the fairy forest, the truly magical place she loved so well. And as we walked the narrow path single file, she showed me how to wield the walking stick, swinging it and tapping it against the ground from time to time so as to wake the snakes in time to allow them to move out of our way. I shuddered and her laugh rung out through the woods until she saw that I was actually excited rather than scared, a love of snakes being something we shared.

The birdsong was incredible as we moved further and further into the deep dark part of the forest. Bright feathers briefly showed themselves here and there. I tried to watch my footing, use the stick, and look for birds simultaneously, so I missed the change of scenery as the trees opened up, and we entered what can only be described as a sanctuary. Moss-lined, fern-strewn, flowering plant-laden, with light streaming in through far-reaching branches, it was clearly a haven for man and beast. Water sparkled in the small body of water to our left as a pair of big white birds I mistook as swans circled each other in the middle, and a tiny deer I'd never seen before sipped delicately at the lapping water on the opposite bank. Swallows of some sort dipped down into the water from time to time, and I fully expected a Disney soundtrack to start up at any moment. Or for Snow White and the seven dwarves to stroll by on their way to work, that didn't seem improbable either.

My host stood a small distance away, clearly amused by my slack jaw and wide-open eyes. She kneeled down and carefully plucked something from the ground, then pushed herself up with her stick, her ease once again belying her age. She carefully wrapped a small bouquet of the tiniest flowers I'd ever seen with a single blade of flat grass as she walked over to me, presenting them to me with a grin. Then she took me by the hand, and we walked very quietly and carefully over to a small glade at the foot of what she told me was an ironwood tree, one that had been there since long before we were even thought of. She then pointed up toward the sky.

I first thought she was showing me the pattern of the long branches against the blue sky, a fairly common theme in her well-known photography practice, but no – high above us was the biggest bird's nest I'd ever seen. When we were quiet and still for a few moments, the chirps of chicks could be heard. Judging from the sides of the enormous nest of woven branches and sticks, these chicks were clearly not yet nest-broken. White streaks nearly coated the sides. I watched in awe, Nona smiling broadly at me, as little beaks and tail feathers peeked out. And then, amazingly, two nearly full-feathered young eagles wobbled their way to the very outer edges of the nest, their talons flexing awkwardly and their bodies listing a bit from side to side. From time to time, they'd look down, then stretch their heads tall, glancing at each other.

As I watched them, I realized I wasn't breathing between the excitement and concern that they might fall. Then slowly, and in an almost synchronized way, they began to stretch their wings out from side to side. "Eagle ballet," Nona murmured, equally entranced, though I'm sure she'd seen it all before. We stood next to each other, nearly touching, mesmerized by all of it for some time.

While I'd hoped they might take flight, perhaps for the very first time, they were clearly not quite ready. Nona reflected back to our earlier conversation about the times in her life when she'd had to wait for things to unfold no matter how much she wanted to rush forward – and her theory that God and the ancestors must have much more important things to do than teach her patience. She pointed out that as big as these young birds were and as perfect as their wings looked, they were just not quite there. Like us, at so many points in life. We may feel we are equipped and ready to fly, yet often we push and exhaust ourselves, trying so hard to get wherever it is we think we must be when really it's just not time.

I breathed that lesson in as she looked up at the sky and then announced we must find our way back and let me be on my way. Looking at my watch, I realized that a few hours had flown by in this magic forest with this woman who seemed at once ancient and so engaged in life. I felt like I'd barely scratched the surface of her story yet had learned so much, and that something within me had changed too.

We walked up the hill with her holding onto my arm, and it was all I could do not to just wrap my arms around her the whole way up the hill. The walking sticks came in handy too, going in this direction – as grounded as I felt now, I was also very sleepy and content. The sun began to stream down on us as we climbed the grassy road and eventually arrived back where I'd parked my little car in what now seemed like a previous lifetime.

She hugged me goodbye and kissed the top of my head as if I were a young child, assuring me that she'd be available to answer any questions I might have once I was back in the office. And she sent me back down the fern and rock lined dirt road, waving as I went.

⚭ ⚭ ⚭

Time is a funny thing, isn't it? You never know when it will fold back on itself or stretch out further ahead of you.

Sometime in 2011, I was invited to imagine an interview with my future self in the year 2031. This exercise was part of a training I was doing, and I thought it was silly, to be honest. Yet what I "saw" that day has turned out to be a wildly accurate depiction of my life in 2021. I only wish I'd believed in this vision back then — it would have saved me a great deal of stress along the way and likely allowed me to enjoy the process far more. Had I had the courage all along to know deeply that this end game would come to pass, I can only imagine how much more fully I could have lived into my life along the way.

My vision of that interview plays out easily in my head now, like a movie, but back when I discussed it with my learning partner from the perspective of my 2011 self, I had so many questions. Where was this magical forest? The best guess I could take was somewhere in the Pacific Northwest, maybe even Canada. Africa never even crossed my mind, not in my wildest imagination. And what was that little body of water? Not exactly a pond and certainly not a lake — I didn't even know what a dam was when it was right in front of me.

Then there was this elderly — in terms of chronological years — woman who felt more alive and more in tune with herself and the world than anyone I'd ever met. She didn't seem at all limited or constrained by all she'd been through and even happily showed me her impressive scars — proudly and with laughter at all that the world had thrown at her. To be honest, I had a hard time imagining that this woman I so admired and so enjoyed could possibly be me in the future, though I sure was intrigued by her.

We impose such limits on ourselves, don't we? As much as I'd expanded the set of expectations my mother had for me – to be a legal secretary and focus on my career, since she'd always assured me no one would ever love me, I'd never had a really clear plan for my future. Over time, it had evolved in themes more than anything – to do good, to bring light to the world, to show compassion to myself and all beings. And to live a life that I didn't feel the need to take vacations from, to escape. How could those simple guidelines lead me to this wonderous place and allow me to mature in this magical way?

I eventually put it all far back in my mind, sure that it had all been a silly diversion, that life would turn out fine but not to expect all this. I didn't think of it again until 2020. The global pandemic had hit South Africa, where I'd been living for four years, and I had just received my permanent residency permit so I knew for the first time that I could stay. I was looking for a small farm to raise livestock and had no plans to leave the beautiful home I'd renovated in a small beach town north of Durban. Yet somehow one ad for an unusual property in the 1000 Hills area west of the city just kept popping up, so off I went to view it after my agent took a look and assured me it was a real find, something she thought I'd love to see.

I drove up that same hill from my vision in my Land Rover, then took the left at the metal fence. As I traveled the winding driveway, something in my throat began to loosen. I didn't say anything to the friend who went with me, but once we saw the mural over the garage and the high archway above the entry porch, its floor lined with stones, I knew. Déjà vu hit hard, and even though the interior of the house was filled to the brim with British-style plates and small framed pictures, along with more furniture than I could comprehend, it was that house. And it was that land, which I knew every foot of.

There was no doubt in my mind that I'd been there before, though it was only that evening that the actual memory of this "interview" I'd done with my future self came back fully. Within days, I had an accepted offer. And within months, I came home to the magic forest. It made little practical sense but when life gave me the opportunity to step into my dreams quite literally, what else could I have done?

Looking back, it's all pretty miraculous, the path that led me here. Let me tell you some of the stories.

One

In the beginning, I didn't know. I didn't know that not all people see souls. I didn't know that not all children dream of making medicine, of drawing light from the shadows, of bringing good to the world. I certainly didn't know that some of us land in hard places, in the beginning, in order to forge our strength in the fires of cruelty so that we can create empathy enough to last a lifetime.

All I knew was that I loved most to spend my days sitting under the big maple tree, shucking peas with my maternal grandmother while we spoke without uttering a single word, or listening to the voices of the spirits I knew loved me beyond reason as I pretended to cook up concoctions of herbs in the old potting shed. Dreaming of somehow finding my way to the place I felt was home though it seemed impossibly far away.

Then normal life took over, as it does. The voices were replaced with "education." My grandmother was unable to speak aloud anymore as she aged. And, as is true for many, alcohol and its friends became my medicine. I strove to create a life that fit the mold I was told would bring me happiness, one that would fulfill the dreams I'd always had of belonging.

Before I knew it, I was forty-nine years old, living on the northeast coast of what would turn out to be the wrong country, and reluctantly clothed in a glittery black gown with a plunging neckline. I was privileged, the wife of a prominent Beltway executive in Washington DC. And so I was in attendance at taping of the 2010 July 4th concert for the President one very steamy June weekend. This involved a post-rehearsal dinner for the performers on Saturday night and then a reception at the White House on Sunday before the actual concert at Ford's Theater, followed by a gala dinner at the National Building Museum on Sunday evening.

The little girl in me who'd grown up poor was a bit in awe of being at the White House. We were surrounded by Marines in highly pressed and polished dress uniforms and celebrities like Lionel Richie and Dick Van Dyke. I'd grown up watching *The Dick Van Dyke Show,* and Van Dyke was, as a result, my idea of the perfect father. To have spent time chatting with him that Saturday evening was something I will never forget. I fully expected that to be the highlight of the two-day Ford's Theater event. I was completely wrong.

On Sunday, as the reception at the White House began to wind down and those shiny Marines gently herded us downstairs to prepare for the short trip to the theatre for the actual concert, a colleague of my husband's began to tease me that while he wasn't Dick Van Dyke's new best friend, I'd never guess who he'd met. After I missed a few guesses, he blurted out that he'd shaken the hand of Archbishop Desmond Tutu – someone he knew I admired greatly. It turned out that Tutu was there to accept the Lincoln Medal later that night. His daughter, Mpho, was the minister at a church in nearby Alexandria, Virginia, and while he was sometimes in town, I'd never even caught a glimpse of him.

I immediately asked our friend where he'd met him, and he laughed and said he was in the men's room. While I was not above entering that inner sanctum at a concert or ball game, even I couldn't waltz in at the White House – could I? He must have been able to see my brain doing cartwheels trying to figure it out and took pity on me, saying that Tutu was in the lounge just outside, a place I was welcome to enter. I made my way quickly, concerned that we'd be hurried off to the theatre, a short drive across town, at any moment.

Luckily for me, he was still there. As I walked into the receiving room, I saw him graciously posing with small groups of guests clustered around him, as if he were a treasured doll. It struck me as strange that not one of them was really speaking with him, but rather smiling for the cameras, arms around his shoulders as he is physically quite a small man. I thought to myself that I'd much prefer to have even a brief conversation with this legend than to have a photograph of us without any connection. I'd followed the Archbishop's work in South Africa and his involvement in The Elders organization for decades, so it was quite unreal to witness him in person.

I stood, my ballgown-clad back against the wall several yards away from all the excitement, just observing. I was tired from the festivities of the night before and so let my mind drift and my eyes fall into soft focus. I have no idea how much time passed, but eventually I came back to myself, sensing someone moving toward me. I blinked several times until I was sure that it was Tutu himself walking in my direction. With only a wall behind me, I was confused about why he was approaching until he held out his hands to me and greeted me as an old friend, one he hadn't seen in a long time. I really couldn't imagine what he was thinking, who he had mistaken me for, but since there was no one else near me, I tried to focus on his words.

He asked me what my name was, "this time" (this time?) and laughed his wonderful laugh when I said Christa. "The perfect name for you, my dear, Christ – ah!" He enquired as to what I was doing with my time, and I told him about my work helping others heal from trauma. He replied that he must introduce me to his good friend Michael, that we were "pods in a pea" and would have much to discuss. Then, in his wonderful South African lilt, he asked a bit beseechingly, even apologetically, if he could bless me "here in this White House," as he hadn't been able to the last time we were together. Did I remember?

Did I remember? I could barely answer any of his questions. I was a little frozen and a lot in awe. All I could do was nod and agree and tell him that I was very happy to see him, too, and that yes, of course he could bless me.

And so he did. I don't remember any words, though another friend who'd joined us said later that she thought he'd used "both Christian and African words." What I do remember is being completely mesmerized by his finely woven purple shirt, the lines of the weave undulating in front of me as I kept my head bowed and eyes open, rather uncertain of the protocol for being blessed by a South African archbishop in the basement of the White House. Much as I had tried to learn all the Beltway rules, this had certainly not been included.

After he finished, he issued his version of the call: He asked me if I'd ever been to his home, to South Africa. I assured him that I knew where he lived and likely mumbled something about being a big fan of his work or something equally banal. I honestly don't know – I do recall him saying that I must, must come to South Africa. That I must come home, that it was time now, or would be soon.

When I said that I'd tried to visit a few times only to be diagnosed with cancer once and fall incredibly ill another time, he didn't seem surprised. He just held my hands – he had only let them go in order to bless me – and looked me in the eye, saying that I'd know when it was time. And that I should let him know, that if he and Mrs. Tutu were in town, I must come and have dinner with them, and if not – well, he'd make sure I was taken care of. And with that, he declared we must have a photo. So we walked over to the photographer and beamed at each other while he captured the moment.

Then it was over. He exacted a promise from me that I'd be in touch and let himself be pulled into the gathering crowd of well-dressed guests clamoring for a chance to have their pictures taken with the Archbishop. None of them knew what had just happened. I wasn't quite sure myself. I only knew that I'd been seen in a way no one had seen me before, and that it couldn't be undone. I stood there for a moment, allowing it all to sink in.

This much was clear, after this encounter – it was almost time to find my way home. This meeting, this man, woke in me all my old dreams, all that knowing, in a way that meant it was go time. There was, as I would see soon, no turning back. I knew that life was about to change, in very big ways, and while there was plenty of fear of the unknown, there was an even deeper calling to find out just what was ahead.

Two

I'm not sure when I knew for certain that I would end up in South Africa. That meeting with Tutu was certainly the catalyst to go, yes, yet there's no point in my memory when I didn't feel a connection, a longing to be there.

When I was as young as six or seven years old, all long bones and sharp angles and strawberry blonde bangs cut a bit too short to keep them out of my eyes, I spent hours on the rough plywood floor of my closet in the hundred-year-old New England house where we lived. Next to me, in a haphazard stack, I had a slightly musty collection of old *National Geographic* magazines bestowed upon me by my aunt and uncle, who went to each and every yard sale on the weekends to search for stock for their little antique shop. They were homebodies, both of them, and much preferred their inner world of historic treasures to anything modern – but they knew me well. I was, or would be as soon as I was able, a traveler.

After sorting through the pile and pulling out those with cover mentions of Africa, I'd linger over them, intent on finding my African friends in the images of the low mountains and the dust- and dirt-covered traditional houses. Lights off and flashlight in hand, I would settle in for a good, long visit, being careful not to wake my little sister Carrie in her bed just next to the closet.

Later, I'd climb in bed and dream of the place that felt so much like home, allowing myself to be transported in the only way I knew to the people I yearned so deeply to be with. I had no idea why, I just knew I'd somehow landed in the wrong place, that my feet belonged on that dusty, red-brown earth.

As a young girl growing up on Cape Cod, which had a mostly Caucasian population back then, I tended to run toward any people of color I spotted and hug them around the knees. Eagle People, I'd call them, not remembering or maybe not wanting to call them Negroes, as was common at the time. Or I'd call them Chocolate People, which might have made a little more sense. In any case, I was constantly looking around my mostly white world and trying to find those who felt like me, who felt like home.

I suppose it was adorable, really, except for the fact that I was born to two people who routinely used the N word and who were, I believe completely out of ignorance and fear, incredibly bigoted and prejudiced. My affinity for people of color was not encouraged by my family, to say the least, with the exception of my globe-trotting and much older cousin, Jack, who saw and nurtured my curiosity and open-mindedness always.

It would take decades before I actually got myself across the world and to the place I most wanted to be, to find the people I'd visited only in magazines, to come home, as Archbishop Tutu had urged me to do. Over that time, in the years just before I travelled to South Africa, I painted many images of mountains and local scenes I'd recognize once I reached Zululand, remarkable in their accurate depiction of a place I'd supposedly never visited. One felt particularly poignant: a landscape of traditional round houses with a sausage tree in the front, its blooms hanging in a way I thought was imaginary at the time. I'd later see plenty of them, often outside the homes of *sangomas* (traditional African healers). South Africa was, as Tutu intuited, always meant to be my home.

Let's address the elephant in the room from the very beginning, shall we? As a dear friend repeatedly points out, my life is not the norm in any way. The fact of the matter is that I am white. And all of my family here in South Africa, along with most of my friends, are black. A Zulu man I saw for a while showed his mother a photo of me for the first time. I was wearing a *doek,* or traditional head covering, and she assumed I was albino. In the scheme of things, that might have made more sense but no, I am garden-variety white. So in these times of so much racial tension and turmoil, I have – as I so often do – chosen to swim upstream.

While many of my white acquaintances – and yes, my friends – are just becoming aware of the depths of white privilege and misconceptions they carry, I've been in intensive training and deprogramming for nearly six years now. It's a constant learning and recalibrating that has become a given practice all day, every day, and I expect it will continue the rest of my life. I was programmed by 1960s and 1970s predominantly white America, so it's a given that there is much to shed and transform.

Sometimes, I end up educating others simply in the midst of day-to-day life. About a year after I moved to South Africa, I was involved in a horrible car crash after my tire blew out driving back from Durban. I ended up taking two tires off an eighteen-wheeler as I tried to avoid it, and most of the driver's side exterior off my Prado too. No one understood how I survived, and there was a great deal of thanking God and saying the Devil is a liar – a much-used term here meaning that God (and right and the truth) always wins. I ended up meeting with a few large Zulu church groups just to show them that I was truly ok.

I had refused to go to the "white" hospital an hour and a half drive away and instead spent the wee hours of that morning at the local mountain one that serves a predominantly black population and where I was well-known as an advocate for community patients. This caused much consternation among the church groups. I explained that if I had died in the accident, the doctors at that mountain hospital, Bethesda, could have transplanted my heart into any one of their dark-skinned bodies, if needed. This declaration was met with utter disbelief and a whole lot of exclamations of *"Haybo"* and *"Nkosi yami"* – meaning, roughly, "You're joking" and "My God."

And then, once they thought about it, there was a great deal of acceptance, of recognizing this truth. Of course my white heart would make their bodies run, as we all bleed the same red. Your body, too, for that matter. Think about it. If you put a Toyota engine in a Land Rover Discovery, it won't work. Yet my heart could do the job in any one of their bodies. So how are we different, really? Except in all the ways that make each of us unique – and beautiful.

I know I'm not black and I never will be – at least not in this lifetime. I don't "act black" or "talk black" – both of which are more American than South African practices, anyway. Just as when I was a child, I am still truly more comfortable in the company of people of color, which has more to do with my heart and core beliefs than anything else. Do I say inane things sometimes, still? Yes. Of course. And I see others doing the same and cringe routinely too, trying to stay compassionate and kind and maybe point out the fallacy or conditioning, when possible. I innately know that there are far fewer differences between us than there are similarities. Like our hearts, like our hopes, like our fears.

I am an artist – I love color and see color everywhere, especially here in South Africa where we have a virtual rainbow of every shade from ivory to ebony, so I'd never say I am color-blind. I understand fully the scientific and genetic reasons for both our skin colors and other adaptations made by where our ancestors lived. And I know it really makes no difference – we are all the same on the inside, fundamentally.

I chose – or found my way back to, however you want to look at it – a tribe with a history of welcoming those who respect and adhere to their culture. The Zulu people, from the time of King Shaka and likely before, have been known as a warrior people – and I've been told repeatedly that I didn't choose the easiest South African tribe to join. Yet there is, when approached with curiosity and reverence and respect, a degree of warmth and inclusion I really can't convey in words. It was explained to me that there is a hospitality, a closeness here between white South African people that is never extended to black people and that I show it to Zulu individuals and groups readily and unfailingly.

There have been those who've been on the receiving end of my somewhat famous flash temper when protecting those I love who would probably disagree, of course, yet it's mostly true. I am a human being and relate to other human beings as just that – seeing someone who has a heart and a soul and the same hopes, fears, plans, and dreams that I do.

For me to be allowed, and not only allowed but mostly welcomed, in the Zulu community is a true privilege. To be seen as someone who has come home is the greatest gift. I hope that the words on these pages convey not only the adventures I've had and the ups and downs of making a huge shift, midlife, but also paint a picture of what could be if many of us allowed ourselves to be who we truly are. What an incredible world that would be.

Three

Cape Cod, a small peninsula on the northeast coast of what we call "America" here in South Africa, is a big tourism destination in the summer, but the winters are very cold and raw. It's beautiful in its simplicity, all scrappy pines growing in sandy soil, windswept and often not quite straight as a result, much as I grew up emotionally scarred and stunted. There are quaint villages still amongst the almost suburban sprawl, huge chestnut, oak, and maple trees lining the streets, little "shoppes" with hand-carved wooden signs and shiny painted shutters. The houses are coated in one of six traditional Colonial colors.

It is where I arrived on this Earth, this time. My mother's family goes all the way back to the Pilgrims who came from England in the early 1600s, with a bit of Wampanoag Indian mixed in, of course – depending on who is telling the story. Personally, I doubt very much that anyone whose ancestors arrived that long ago doesn't have a bit of Native American in them too. My father's ancestors came from Germany and Ireland, so I'm very American in terms of genealogy. On my mother's side, there was family living in Salem during the times of the witch trials, though they moved all of a dozen miles or so out of town. We never spoke much about it, so I don't know their stories. I do like to think my healing gifts have their beginnings there, too, in that insane time when puritanical beliefs and intuitive healers clashed in such strong ways. I know that there was a serious and deeply seated fear of anything outside the Anglo-Saxon Christian realm of belief in the family I was born into.

My parents were not the parents I would hope for, for any child. They had deep wounds of their own, which then intertwined and created a household full of fear and anger and hate with just enough love thrown in to make it utterly confusing. It was a very difficult beginning. There was what can only be called abuse on every level, yet what I think has most deeply affected me is being repeatedly told what a horrible child I was. That no one would ever love me. That I would die alone and broke. To say nothing of "God damn you to hell" being shouted at me on a nearly daily basis.

My mother and father have lived lives that I would imagine have been rather unpleasant and difficult as well. As far as I know, neither one of them really grew into their own creative gifts, as talented as they are. I wish things had been different for them from their own beginnings. Certainly that would have changed everything for me and my siblings. Or maybe we would not be here, who knows. Perhaps they were only mirroring back aspects of my own tortured soul to me, so that I might see and then heal those broken parts. I'm not sure we are meant, as human beings, to understand all of this fully. I've made peace with both what happened and the fact that most of their behavior remains incomprehensible to me.

I am profoundly grateful to them for the lessons they taught me, for all they sacrificed in terms of their own happiness in order to put me through some immensely difficult experiences. I would not have the wisdom, empathy, or compassion I now possess if not for them and a cast of equally disturbed souls I met along the way. All of the pain and shame and mistreatment were, in their own way, gifts.

Still, the long-term effects of feeling so unwanted and so incredibly different from those in your family of origin are deep and insidious. For a long time, anyone who seemed to like me – to say nothing of loving me – was highly suspect. Didn't they know there was Something Wrong With Me? That I was The Worst Person on Earth? That I deserved nothing more than to take care of others then go directly to Hell? It's a form of brainwashing, really, and while I've done so much healing over the decades since our mismatched group of souls lived in that little cedar cottage on the Cape, only very recently have I stopped fighting being loved. Sadly, some never reach this point.

I was, given what was going on at home and perhaps by nature, an extremely shy child. I was sick – a lot. There was pneumonia and surgeries I still don't completely understand and bedwetting and upset stomachs, along with every cold and flu that passed through. I used to keep the whole family up coughing at night and was quarantined up in my room a great deal of the time. There were beatings – with metal spatulas and wooden spoons or "the paddle" and worse, threats for hours of the punishment to come. As the eldest, I felt responsible for the others, especially my youngest sibling, my only brother. I often took the blame and the punishment for what I now see as very minor "crimes." There were strange psychological games too – only being allowed to smell the wrappers in the rare and prized box of Whitman's chocolates, for example, and never allowed the candy itself, as the others were.

This was all my normal, though, and it would be decades before I understood just how unusual my childhood was. The ironic part is that now people constantly remark on how extraordinary my life is today. To me, it's far more "normal" than it's ever been.

⁙ ⁙ ⁙

My earliest memory is associated with the color yellow. I never liked it. Wouldn't wear it – I'd been told, given my pale skin, that it would be a mistake. Wouldn't paint my walls any shade of yellow. And when highlighters came out in other colors, I never touched the fluorescent yellow one again if there was another option.

I never knew why until I was thirty-seven years old and found myself sitting in a group meditation exercise in the intensive care psychiatric unit of a prestigious Chicago-area hospital. At that point, life had become really difficult. The color yellow was only one of many, many everyday things that could trigger me in a heartbeat. It was a simple exercise. The therapist led a few of us through a series of colors, asking us to picture whatever came to mind and focus on that thing while breathing in and out.

All was going well. Most things I saw as we went on were related to nature – unsurprisingly, as the natural world had always been my refuge. Then we got to yellow. Yellow made me uncomfortable. All of a sudden, my body felt awkward in the industrial chair, and my breathing quickened. Instead of a still image, I saw what I'd now identify as one of those GIFs, short videos that show up on social media and play automatically.

I saw a blue, blue sky and a screen door, ajar, and a flash of brilliant yellow. It's funny, as much as I've processed this, I still start breathing rapidly and very shallowly when I bring it to mind. At the time, I felt an urgent need to run, and I cannot remember for the life of me if I did leave the circle or not. My guess is that I dissociated and stayed, as I know for certain that the exercise stopped there for me. I did not want to know more. I didn't want to think about it and so I very likely shut down. As was my usual pattern, I went to my room and fell asleep as soon as I could. Given the medication issues going on, they let me nap some, and I was alone when the image began to expand a little.

Typically, at this stage of my life, images of a "new" memory would come back as single snapshots. A little blurry or unclear, much like the old Polaroids I took as a kid. Then, in just the way I was taught to splice negatives together to make a short film, they would join together into a little movie. Sometimes there were blank frames, sometimes black and white. This one came back in full Kodachrome color with sound and smells. The whole nine yards.

I was little, about two and a half, so everything seemed very big. The walls with their few framed pictures loomed over me, the furniture waiting like mountains to be climbed and explored. Even inside, I could hear the birds outside singing away, their various songs creating a symphony. The windows were open, soft cotton curtains that billowed a bit with each breeze. A beautiful, beautiful day, and I have the sense it was unseasonably warm, a special treat near the end of a long winter.

We had a little canary, bright yellow, who lived in a small, simple cage set on a wooden side table in the living room. I was, of course, forbidden to poke my finger into the cage itself, though the tiny bird seemed very unlikely to actually bite the end of my finger off, as I'd been told it might. The canary was my mother's, an object of great affection for her, and it was definitely off limits. Of course that added to its appeal.

In my very young mind, I thought that it must be lonely, this yellow bird. Did I already feel lonely, at that age? Maybe. In any case, I was sure that this birdie needed some friends. And there were many bird friends waiting to be had, just outside the window. I could hear them – perhaps they were calling to the canary, whose name I've never been able to recall. That's certainly what I believed.

So I went to the front door, reached up on tiptoe, and undid the toggle lock, carefully and quietly opening the heavy door with a mighty little tug. That done, I went over to the cage and opened its tiny door, cooing to the yellow bird just as I'd seen my mother do, inviting it to come out and play. When it did not – the caged bird does apparently hesitate to leave what it knows, after all – I opened the screen door wide to the outside so that it could hear its friends waiting for it to come out and play.

That did the trick. Before I knew it, there was a whoosh, a little breeze over my head, and that flash of yellow meeting the blue sky and the trees beyond. For a moment, I felt so pleased with myself, with that warmth that spreads from the inside out when you know you've done a good thing. Then I heard the scream and turned to see my mother with her hands over her mouth, speechless. And clearly not pleased at all, though I think my very young self felt it more than saw it. She pushed past me. I fell down on my bottom, and she was out the door in a heartbeat, the screen door knocking as it closed after the forceful push to open it.

My body tightened up and I began to cry. I don't know how long she was gone. I'm not sure I had a sense of time at that age, really. She came back and yelled and cried and yelled and yanked me off the floor. She hauled me through more of those high walls and threw me down into the soft place that felt like I knew it, felt safe. Again, more time passed, I imagine. I remember feeling as though I wanted to disappear into my own body, become tiny and retreat, or maybe fly away too.

The next thing I knew, I was being dragged by my arm again, in a room that was likely the kitchen, given the lino-leum tile on the floor. There was a flash of those, a sense of being turned, the ceiling light bright in my eyes, and then being switched around so that her other arm was holding me as she opened an interior door with her right hand. My bottom was sore, pounding with pain, and it hurt to be held against her hip. She took a big breath in – she was still very upset, perhaps crying, though I felt it more as shallow breathing and trembling. As she took my right wrist in her hand, there was a really sharp and deep pain that went through my right shoulder as I flew through the air. I saw the painted cinderblock wall, that same light green I'd see later in schools and hospitals. A brief glimpse of wooden stairs, worn on the edge. And my head hit the wall with a loud dull sound, as more pain poured from the top of my head down into my body, the sickest sound and sensation, one that took my breath away. A pulling upwards, and then nothing for a bit.

When I "woke up," my father was there holding me on his lap and playing with my right arm, gently moving it back and forth. My head was really cold and my face was wet, though I don't think I was crying. My mother was sitting on a bed with my baby sister next to her, moving and gurgling as young babies do. She was crying, too, her face was wet, as well. She said that they had to take me to the hospital, over and over, that something was wrong with me. And my father said that they couldn't. "We just can't, Lin. We can't."

Was it because she'd hurt me? Or they didn't have the money? Was I bruised and broken before this day? I don't know. I do know that this would become a pattern, this breaking me either physically or, more often, emotionally, and then labeling me as broken and casting me aside. Not giving me up in the traditional sense yet giving up on me as a person worthy of life in my own right.

This is the very first fully intact memory I have of my life.

Four

Some stories from my childhood are ones I know deeply in my heart, and yet I've been told they are just not true. And who knows – maybe they're based in fact and maybe they aren't. There are coincidences and plenty of corroborating evidence. There are also denials.

Still, this one is mine, and it's time to tell it. Though we never spoke about it, I believe it was the cause of a huge fracture in the foundation of our family. One that made it impossible for us to really grow together.

It all happened in our little house when I was about five years old, judging by the size of the babies involved. I was in the living room, with my parents, my aunt, and my childhood pastor and his wife – dear friends of my aunt and uncle. In front of us were two infant carriers (this was way before infant car seats). In one was a baby with barely visible blonde hair and in the other a baby with darker brown hair.

I could feel my mother shaking and trembling, almost whimpering, even though there were other bodies between us. Looking up and over, I could see my father's jaw clenched so tightly that I wondered if he was breathing. Even at this young age, I'd developed a very strong awareness of energetic changes in people and surroundings, even the weather. When these signs showed up, I knew that I'd best try to either create a distraction or calm things down as best I could. I knew that they could escalate or explode very easily.

I felt all of this viscerally, and as I write this, my body stiffens and tightens too. I was, I am, so not supposed to talk about this. There is a visceral fear that I'll be in so much trouble for it. For some reason, I feel like I might end up in jail. Even now.

I realize now that it had all started the night before. It was after dinner. My mother had been sick to her stomach, which wasn't all that unusual, and was crying. My dad had his head in his hands and said that he didn't know what to do. They were so sad. It was palpable and suffocating to my young heart, and I said out loud, "Too many babies for Mumma. Just too many."

My father looked up and asked my mother if she'd told me, and she said that she hadn't. They both stared at me for a while. And then they asked which baby they should give away to someone who didn't have any. They asked me. A four-year-old. And I blurted out, "The brown-haired one."

When I remember this, I can see the picture window, the couch behind the group of adults – it feels very, very real. There was some grownup talk about foster care and adoption and final papers. And then the pastor reached down and picked up the baby, the brown-haired one. She appeared to be about six months old, all chubby and snuggly, though she was not smiling. Both babies seemed to know something was up.

As the pastor picked her up, my mother cried out and fell down onto her knees, my aunt there in an instant to support her. She wasn't on the ground for more than a minute, though, before she propped herself up, went over to the couch and sat down, hollow-eyed. I saw a photograph of her many years later, at my brother's wedding, with that same look. The windows were open, so to speak, but no one was home, no lights were on within her. She'd sort of vanished.

I heard the front door open – we hardly ever used that door, so it wasn't a sound I knew well. The pastor took the baby out in the carrier, into the cold and the snow, and handed it to a man who had his sedan running, the exhaust making a pattern of smoke in the freezing air. He opened the rear passenger door, took the infant – my sister, though

I'm not sure how I know it was a girl – and placed her on the bench seat in the back. I watched all of this from the window seat while my other sister, Carrie, then two years old, played with her doll on the floor, nestling her and swaying her back and forth. Somehow at that tender age she was able to model the love for her doll that could not be given to her little baby sister. Though maybe it was, truly, an act of love on the part of my parents to let her go.

As the car drove away, I began to cry. I knew better than to do that, having been told on many occasions that I'd be given something to cry about if I didn't stop by my father, so I wiped away my tears with the soft sleeve of my footie pajamas. When I turned back to the living room, my mother and aunt and the pastor's wife were all huddled on the couch. My father was outside, pacing frantically back and forth across the gravel driveway. Our minister stood by, watching him pace, though neither of them had coats on. There was a lot of moaning and whispering between the women in the living room.

No one seemed to notice us kids for a while. Then my aunt brightly announced that it was nap time and took us upstairs, even though it was early enough in the morning that we were still in pajamas. When I was allowed to come down later, my mother was cleaning the kitchen, scrubbing the counters and the sink. Again.

That's not the end of the story, though, or not all of it.

After several years of estrangement as an adult from my parents and siblings, I was reunited with the twin sister we "kept," Hannah. We had years to catch up on, as we really hadn't spent any time together alone as adults. One evening, as we chatted for hours, she asked if she could ask me a weird question. I agreed, and she blurted it out: "Do you have any memory of me having a twin?"

I'd pretty much buried the whole thing by that point, though stray, photograph-like memories had come up in therapy. It had never really gelled as a cohesive story, but when she asked me about it, it was as if huge, heavy iron gates went up, a whole series of them, vertical and horizontal. I answered, "Yes," and then the gates closed down just as quickly. I was able to say that I'd seen images, flashes of two babies, one with blonde hair and one with brown, but that was about it, I think. And I asked her why she wanted to know.

She told me that when she turned eighteen, she was still living on the Cape, and had recently moved from our parents' house into her own apartment. This was long before cell phones or caller ID, remember, so she had no idea who was calling when her phone rang. A woman on the other end asked for Hannah, and said she was her sister. Hannah questioned the caller, saying my name, and then Carrie's name. When the caller replied "no" to each query, Hannah said she was sorry, that she must have the wrong number, and that those were her sisters' names. Then the line went dead.

Not long after that, maybe a few days later, she went over to my parent's house. As she walked in the door, Hannah heard my mother's voice, high-pitched and very anxious, almost angry. Mum was speaking into the phone, saying that she never wanted to hear from the caller again, that the caller was never supposed to have her name, that the caller didn't exist to her. Hannah said Mum was rattled and sort of manic in a way she hadn't seen her be in a very long time.

And then there was Hannah's own memory of being quite young, maybe four or five, and being all dressed up by my mother and told to be on her best behavior. She thought that I wanted to come along but was told I wasn't allowed to, and she was taken by our father over to the big house – the mansion he was caretaker for, to meet a young girl, just her age. She had dark brown hair. Hannah was told never to speak of the meeting, and she didn't – not until she told me that night in Virginia.

I recently asked an older cousin about this. They didn't live near us at the time the baby/babies were born, and she had never heard a thing. She couldn't imagine it had been kept a secret for so many years. But she did remember her mother frequently coming up to the Cape from New Jersey, where they then lived, to help my mom. She thought that it was entirely possible my aunt was there, staying with us, as I recalled. My aunt has passed away now so it's impossible to ask her. And my uncle, one of the few men I trust from my childhood, swears that it didn't happen. Though he wasn't there, of course.

So there's the story. We did a little looking for this woman and came up with nothing. My sister's birth certificate was issued far later than normal, and there is no baby book for her as there was for the rest of us, something I hadn't realized. She wasn't ready at that point to work with a private investigator, so I dropped the whole thing, feeling it was her prerogative to choose to look or not for her potential twin.

This is part of what happens when you're experienced at disassociation. It's a helpful means of self-protection, but it leaves holes. There's much I'll never know nor understand. There's so much more that I could never ask, that we never were to speak of. And there's solace that I also dropped many family "traditions," that I broke the chain, that I did my best to give my own daughter a very different sort of life, that my life has changed and expanded in myriad ways, once I began to see the truth more clearly. That's all I could do, all I can hang on to and be grateful for.

I can choose to let go of what I can't remember, to remember what I can with some compassion for all of us involved, and to live a very different life. To weave my own story. My younger sister, given away at such a young age, had no choice. I don't know if, at six months old, she felt she belonged or not, but I do know that I never ever felt that, or loved or wanted. I hope that for her, her adoptive family gave her that acceptance, the love and bond that all children need. For me, it would be a very long time and halfway across the world before I'd begin to feel it.

We all deserve that, no matter what our faults. The truth is that I am not perfect. The truth is that I have made many, many mistakes along the path of my life and that I'll likely make many more. The truth is that I am fully human – flawed, fallible, and fairly average. The only difference between me and others is that I'm somehow willing to talk about the things that many will not discuss, and that I believe it's good for us all to speak openly of the things we were taught are unmentionable, not to be spoken of.

I'm not the only one who does this, of course, and yet so many cannot. Those of us who are able to honor those who have gone before us and risked so much: the suffragettes, the refugees, the creatives who have put themselves out there for all to see – to improve their lives and the lives of their descendants. We do so by following their example, by inviting others to join us in breaking those simple but stringent rules of "don't ask, don't tell." By joining together in the knowledge that we are not perfect and reveling in our mistakes rather than adhering to what society teaches is "normal," whatever that is anyway.

We do all this, really, for love – don't we?

Five

When I was five, my father took a job as a caretaker in a very wealthy town not too far from where we were living. It came with a small three-bedroom cottage on about five acres of land, and while it was not on the ocean as the "big house" was, you could often smell the sea air on our side of Main Street. Not unlike that odd little game my parents would play – only allowing me to smell the liner papers in the occasional gift box of Whitman's chocolates – we couldn't actually live with the "rich folks," but we were close enough to know what we were missing.

This, I would realize later, must have had a great deal to do with my parents' general discontent, their sense that everyone thought less of them and only wanted to use them. It was also something that would come up decades later after I landed in South Africa and met a beautiful man who could never quite trust that I was on his side.

I still think of that little cedar-shingled house as my childhood home. There are all sorts of memories stored there, still. This is where, for example, the twin baby was given away. This is where I first learned that I didn't belong – but was not lucky enough to be put up for adoption too. I spent many evenings wishing my "real" parents would come get me, imagining the scenario when they would recognize me as their long-lost child, scooping me up with their faces teary yet grinning. Those nights must have been when I first began to play with my gift of manifesting, though I wouldn't understand that ability for a very long time. They are one of the first times I remember really wishing my skin was different – or, better put, that I had the color of skin I thought I should have.

Mary Maddox was the first – and for quite some time, along with Sam, her husband, the only – black person I spent time with beyond those I'd try to run up and hug in the grocery store. I distinctly recall wanting to touch her skin, her face, in the same way I did with my grandmother. There was something about her, well beyond the fact that she was black, that pulled me in. I imagine it was love, or something like it. Certainly there was a connection between us, and I always felt that she knew the truth just by looking into my eyes. I know I wanted, badly, to go and live with her and Sam, to stay with them, that I felt so strongly that I belonged with them, rather than in that cottage across the way.

My bedroom, shared with my sister Carrie, was at the front of that house and faced the street, so that at night the headlights of passing cars would cast shadows that both scared and enthralled me. There was a big old weeping willow tree in the backyard, hollies scattered about, and a half-height stone wall along the sidewalk lined with gigantic horse chestnut trees that dropped seed pods resembling medieval weaponry each autumn. There was a potting shed in the back, too, and eventually an area for animals and a huge garden. My city-born and bred father must have been in heaven.

The big house was across the street, about a half block down, and had a huge gate and tall stone pillars. There was a long, winding driveway and expansive green lawns and hills we would toboggan down in winter. I remember some outbuildings – my dad had a lot of cold frames there – and there was an old-fashioned metal and glass greenhouse behind the mansion itself. On the ocean side of the structure, there were more hills and immaculate lawns and sweeping views of the bay. It was quite grand and yet felt as though it had been there for the longest time. From my young perspective, it was almost a castle.

It was not the owner's primary residence, of course – they lived in that place called Florida that I longed to visit, largely due to Disney World and Flipper the dolphin, whose TV show I was addicted to. In winter, their upholstered furniture was all covered with sheets, creating a rather spooky scene, especially in the dim late afternoon light. It was eerie for other reasons, too, all those empty rooms and the faint scent of mothballs. You could almost hear the echoes of their grandchildren playing games on a rainy day or the tinkling of glasses and silver at a fancy dinner party held in the enormous dining room, though I'm not sure I was ever allowed to cross the threshold of that space.

Rather than playing games, I sat for hours on end across the street at a folding table set up on the grass between the driveway and the sidewalk under those huge chestnut trees. After weeding the garden and picking veggies and berries, it was my job to man the "stand" as tourists and year-round residents alike stopped to see what we had and whether my mother had made her home-baked banana or cranberry bread that day. There was a little cash box, and I had to write down the prices, add them up, and record how much money was received and the change given. I can still do that sort of math at a lightening pace in my head. I knew if I messed up, there would be hell to pay. And at the end of the summer, we'd pay for our school clothes this way, though I often wore my cousin Lisa's hand-me-downs, still smelling of her in a way that brought some comfort.

I realize now more clearly what being the "help" meant to my parents – how it led to something or perhaps added to an existing practice that I now call "compare and despair." A feeling of not being good enough. Of not being allowed in the fancy spaces or invited to the ball – just like Cinderella. That was something that, even then, I knew grated on them, my mother in particular. It would be a long time before I would understand why. All I knew was that she hated the Disney movie about Cinderella when it came out.

All of it has given me keen insight as to how people generally can feel "other" – the homeless population I would spend time with in Lincoln Park chatting until late into the night, the bedraggled souls who would call in on the domestic violence hotline I manned from two to six a.m. once a week in my single days in Chicago, the HIV-positive patients and their caregivers in the remote communities in KwaZulu-Natal once I moved to South Africa. This inner knowing that I have, this sense that not one of us is better or worse than the other, all came from seeing the debilitating effects of believing that I was less than I should have been, or my parents being sure that they were looked down on constantly which they somehow transferred to me. We were, all of us, the help.

The other permanent "help" were Mary and her husband Sam. They were, I'm guessing, in their forties then and had been there for a long time, or so I was told. Sam was the butler and Mary was the maid, and they took care of everything. I don't remember exactly what Sam wore, but Mary was always dressed in the standard dull grey maid's uniform, with a white starched apron, heavy hose, and those incredibly sturdy white shoes nurses also wore in those days.

They were my friends. And, I thought, my father's friends, though when they weren't around, I heard my parents refer to them in the same way they referred to anyone with dark skin – in terms I won't repeat here and knew even then were wrong. I loved them, and to me, Mary was absolutely beautiful. She had deep, coffee-colored skin and twinkly brown eyes, and put on lipstick with a precision most rocket scientists would envy. She had her hair "done" and wore a net of some sort when she was doing messy work.

Both she and Sam knew who they were and didn't seem to worry a bit about not being as good as anyone else. They both had a sort of sovereignty to them that was not present in other adults I knew. It's the same sovereignty I see here in black South Africans, in the faces and spirits of the women, particularly, in the deep rural areas of KwaZulu-Natal – some sort of strength derived, I feel, from a long and deeply seated sense of where they come from, who they are. It's a trait I admired then and still do.

Mary was a fabulous cook, I thought, though that might have been based on the ranger cookies she made for us pretty regularly, always giving me an extra one in the kitchen. She showed me how to polish silver and, yes, how to apply lipstick. More than anything, she showed me how to get through the tough times. I can only assume that, as a black woman in 1960s America, she knew only too well how to navigate a world that felt unwelcoming, where it was made clear to her that she did not belong. I'd go over to the big house to help my father with things in the greenhouse – one of the few times I had alone with him and something we both loved. When he'd had enough of me, he'd send me up to find Mary, warning me not to bother her.

I don't believe I ever told her about the things that happened to me, but she clearly saw the bruises and the scrapes and the hurt in my eyes. Rather than address them directly, which likely would have seemed impossible at the time, she would gather me up in her sturdy, soft arms and hug me in a very un-New England way, squashing my face against the scratchy apron and into her heart. She would sing to me, sometimes, spirituals that I still love to hear and songs she made up. Her eyes would sparkle and flash, her heart wide open, with me her only and devoted audience. It was magical.

Mary had a lot of sayings – "No use crying over spilt milk," that sort of thing. I wish I could remember them all now. One was that "you can't be nobody but you, sweet girl, and nobody can be you better, either." That's the one I've spent my whole life trying to learn. I'd love to run into Mary's arms and tell her I finally understand what she meant. I bet she'd laugh that big belly laugh and, her eyes twinkling, tell me it was about damn time. She'd be right.

The other saying was the one I've also seen is true in the end. It was part of a song – whether she'd learned it or made it up, I don't know. I can't recall most of the words except the end: "It'll be all better by and by." Back then, during the mid to late sixties, I found this impossible to believe. The turbulence and turmoil of Vietnam was being played out nightly on a screen behind Walter Cronkite. There were demonstrations by and against the hippies. And in my short lifetime, John F. Kennedy, Martin Luther King, Jr., and Robert Kennedy had all been assassinated. I'd already been abused in every way possible, been told by my own mother that I was ruined, and figured out that my whole purpose in life was to take care of her and my siblings, so I hadn't really experienced the "better" part yet. And my dear Mary, with her beautiful dark skin, was seen as other by so many around us. Her children were threatened and her only means of supporting herself depended on her keeping her mouth shut and her opinions to herself. How could she possibly believe things would improve?

It would take me decades to understand that the only way to get through the trials of life was to believe. And in the end, she was absolutely right. The only way I know to thank her is to find that joy every day, and to bring it to the world. Once I turned myself around and reoriented, it all did, indeed, become all better, by and by. Though I still laugh when, these days, I'm seen as this wealthy American woman. Some part of me will always be this little girl who was "just the help."

Six

The day of my sixth birthday party arrived one late June morning in 1967. My mother had been busy all week preparing for the big event. It was the nicest birthday party of my childhood, and one of few. I am pretty sure it was the last one.

It was a joint party, actually, for my sister who was turning four and for me turning six. It was a circus theme – I can see the cake my cousin decorated with carousel animals and bright colors. There were fun games, including trying to open little rolls of Lifesavers with our fingers masking taped together and Pin the Tail on the Donkey, and it was a gorgeous day. We played on the swing set – maybe it was new, for our gift? I'm not sure.

My nose was a little out of joint because I didn't want to share my party, and because it was held on a date between our actual birthdays, so I was not a-c-t-u-a-l-l-y six yet, and it felt like a lie, and we weren't supposed to lie. All of that got mixed in. I remember feeling lonely, even with our friends there. Though I felt like they were mostly my sister's friends, so maybe that's why. I didn't have many friends, and that hollow feeling persisted throughout most of my adulthood, even with all the great folks in my life as the years went by. As a child, there were so many things I was not allowed to talk about, so many secrets, so much shame. It's no wonder I couldn't allow myself to be close to other children, when I had to use so much energy to hold back all the things that we were forbidden to share – in fact, there likely wasn't much left to talk about. All of which taught me to lead with strength in the form of big thick walls around who I truly was, and to do anything and everything in order not to appear vulnerable, though I was suffering on so many levels. It's an extremely lonely way to live.

So maybe out of that loneliness, or maybe because I was told to, after everyone began to leave and the aunts and my mom were cleaning up, I took some pieces of birthday cake to "the hippies." That phrase referred to three guys who helped my dad on the estate that summer – there were always new helpers each year. This particular group all had long shaggy hair (one even had a ponytail, a novelty in our little village) and tie-dyed t-shirts and drove a funky VW van with beds in the back, ragged curtains on the windows, and a huge array of bumper stickers promoting peace and rock bands. I was mesmerized by them, of course, and loved to watch them from afar. When they didn't sleep in their van, they slept in the bomb shelter underneath the potting shed, and that's where I went to look for them after the party was over.

I walked from the back door off the kitchen across the yard to the entrance of the potting shed. I was carrying three pieces of birthday cake, so careful not to drop them. This little building was a favorite spot for me, a place I loved to putter and play on my own. It was surrounded by animals – the chicken coop and yard, the cows fenced off to one side – and usually smelled sweet like hay. I loved that scent.

The door to the potting shed was left open that night, so I entered the dark space, scanning in the dim light for the guys. I saw the fireplace I liked to pretend to cook over, piles of books, and other things. Unusually, there were a few duffle bags on the floor with clothes strewn around them. It was normally pretty neat in there, and they kept most of their belongings in the van, so I wondered what was going on. The air smelled like some sort of smoke I didn't know. The chimney didn't work, so it wasn't that the fireplace had been used. What had been burning?

I heard thin, reedy music – the recorder that one of them often played – coming from downstairs in the bomb shelter that had long ago been carved out in the earth. The stairs were made out of planks, as were the railings, which I didn't like to hold onto because they were splintery. We weren't allowed to venture down into the bomb shelter, but I'd been down there a couple times with my dad, so I figured it was okay to go and find them when they didn't hear me call. As I turned the corner and started down the last part of the stairs, trying hard to balance the pieces of cake on the flimsy paper plate, I tripped or stumbled somehow. I remember seeing two of the helpers sprawled out on the lower bunk just before I fell, hearing one of them call my name as I went down, and scraping my knee pretty badly. The smoke I'd smelled earlier was thick in the dimly lit space as he carried me over to the bunkbed and poured something out of a glass bottle onto the scrape, and the other guy said, "Hey, hey, don't waste the booze…"

And then it all goes black.

This memory came back first as a drawing I did when I was hospitalized after my suicide attempt, part of a flurry of images I drew in the art therapy room at the same hospital where I figured out the mystery of "yellow," most of them ones that revealed preverbal trauma, or especially difficult episodes to recall. While there is still a gap in my recollection to this day, I drew the bunk bed, with a little girl lying across it, her dress rumpled and blood both between and running down her legs. A pair of underwear with little pink roses on the floor, also bloody. A bong, fairly detailed. A dark green glass bottle and a few beer bottles. One of those thick green glass ashtrays with white joints, half burned in it. And a plate with cake crumbs.

The next thing I recall is being outside in the yard, huddled under the big weeping willow tree in the half light of evening. Very scared because I'd lost my underwear and there were tears running down my face onto my knees, which were both bloody and scraped. Afraid to go in because I was messy. Afraid to stay out because I was cold and didn't want to get sick. Paralyzed, uncertain about what to do, sure that I'd be in big, big trouble. Somehow my dad found me and carried me into the house.

Another gap in recall, just blank space, then I was in the clawfoot tub in the upstairs bathroom. He bathed me much more gently than usual. I don't think he said much, if anything, other than "you're alright" over and over like a mantra, his jaw tight and the veins on his arms popping out. The little kids were in bed by then, the house quiet, and after he dried me off, again much more carefully than usual, he carried me in his strong arms and laid me on the big bed in my baby sister's room, where she was asleep in her crib. He told me he'd go get Band-aids and then was gone for a long time. I think I fell asleep.

When I woke up, I couldn't breathe and there was something heavy on my chest, a strange keening sound in the air. I opened my eyes and saw my mother's face, contorted in that way that let me know she was in that wild state that terrified me every time I witnessed it. Tears running down her face, saying, "You're ruined, I have to do this. I'm so sorry. You're ruined. I can't keep you. This is so hard, she's ruined. You'll never get clean from this." Over and over and over, sobbing and screeching and making this animalistic wounded sound. She had a pillow between us, and she'd pick it up and look at me and then put over my face, pushing really hard on me. I couldn't fight her off. I was so tired, and she was so strong. Everything went black again.

The next part came back as if I were on the ceiling, watching it all happen from above in a way that told therapists I'd dissociated, something I'd already become very good at by that age. I heard tires on the gravel driveway and then my father's steps on the stairs, coming down the hallway. His voice, shouting at my mother, as I saw him enter the room, asking her what the hell she was doing. Telling her to stop, stop, stop. He pulled her off of me, and I felt a sudden intake of air in my chest, even from my place up above.

I saw myself roll off the bed as my parents struggled with each other, literally physically fighting. My mother screaming at my dad that he'd ruined it all, that I was better off dead, that she had to let me go. Calling him a son of a bitch, damning him to hell, phrases she used often. She was scratching at his face and neck and he held her arms back tightly, turning deep red and purple as he did when he was angry. All he said was, "No, no, no, Lin. No." Again and again.

And then her hands were around his throat, and I was back on the ground. I'd seen him put down his pistol when he came in, heard it clatter against the enameled metal top of the baby's changing table. I picked up the gun with both hands – it was really heavy to my young body- and as I'd seen on the westerns my dad loved to watch with us, shot it straight up in the air. The weight of the gun must have pulled it down because the bullet shattered the window, just one pane up in one corner. Months later, I would wonder how that hole got there, my father giving me an incredulous look when I asked aloud.

The noise shocked my mom into an entirely different state, the frozen quiet one that always followed the outbursts, the one that scared me far more than the out-and-out crazy. She began to shake and cry in earnest. My little sister Hannah was two years old then – she woke up in her crib and was crying her eyes out, screaming. My dad came and loosened my grip on the gun, putting it up high.

That's all I've got. It's enough, I'm sure, for you and plenty for me. That day began with a circus and ended with an entirely different one. And somehow, we all survived. I never saw the hippies again, and I don't know if my father found them or not. His helper from then on was a very clean-cut local kid who went to the Naval Academy at Annapolis. I don't think I ever went in the bomb shelter again. There were planks nailed across the top of the stairs, so maybe no one did.

I went back to this house for the first time in forty years shortly before I first visited South Africa. I'd been told the original cottage had been torn down, and indeed, a beautifully designed new house had been built further back on the property where the garden once was, and the woods where I once learned to walk quietly and with intention, finding arrowheads along the way, were mostly gone. The stone wall out front was still there, and so were the old horse chestnut trees, more gnarled and twisted than ever. There was a shiny new gate across the driveway and the dogwood trees out front had grown huge. And the shed, which had once been behind the house and easy to avoid, was now the first structure you saw, off to the right. It has a new roof, lovely light fixtures and a pretty little path between it and the main house. It looked as if it might be a studio, a place where good and beauty are created.

Today it looks as if it's been transformed, just as I've been, and now we both stand whole and solid, with light coming in our windows even as we shine outward into the world. You just never know how a circus will end.

Seven

High school holds challenges for all of us. I had some extra ones to navigate, beyond the less violent yet still complicated family issues.

Exploring the new frontiers of dating and sex is never easy, I suppose. And yet, for me, every step of that journey brought back memories I couldn't quite see, nightmares that made no sense, and physical sensations that were confusing as all get out. I'm surprised I made it through – that any of us make it through. Us being the ones whose bodies had been introduced to what might be the wonders of sexuality in the most cruel and brutal ways, so early that we had no words to use for those experiences. (Not that we'd use the words if we had them because, you know, we don't talk about that.)

I wonder if you notice my tendency to talk about we, us, others when I get into tricky territory. I do. And I know it is a protective thing, a way to try to remember that I was not the only one, even though the idea makes me shake with grief sometimes. All those children. All those adults who were those children. And me too. It's sad for all of us. And it reminds me why I tell these stories.

One year when I was in high school, we had four foreign exchange students visiting our school from Sweden: two guys, two girls. I was fascinated by them. They were a few years older than most in my class, I think, and the girls, especially, had a certain sophistication to them that was a welcome addition to the kids I'd known forever. I wasn't in the popular crowd – I didn't think enough of myself to be, though most of them were nice to me. Truth be told, I didn't fit in anywhere, and that's likely why I was drawn to these four visitors.

By some miracle, they actually talked to me, and, after a while, came over to my house to visit one afternoon. They invited me to a party at a nearby military academy that night – one of the girls was dating a cadet, and the whole thing was exciting. I eagerly accepted, and they picked me up on their way over that very evening. I was so pleased to be included, that they perhaps saw who I really was and not the lonely little girl many of my classmates had grown up with after we returned from the aborted move to Ohio. It felt like a new beginning at a time when I was really ready to start over, to expand my world. So off I went. Happy, for once, and feeling seen. Welcome, even.

I wouldn't feel that way again for decades.

It's funny – sometimes the stories of the incidents that had the biggest impact on me are the hardest to tell. Not because I don't want to tell them but because there are such huge gaps, I wonder if it's possible to make them coherent. All I can do is tell you the parts I know.

We arrived at the dorms on the huge military academy campus I'd often heard about and went up to the boyfriend's room, where we each had a bottle of beer and then joined a small group gathered in the hallway. There were some introductions, some joking – inside jokes I didn't get. I felt awkward, but not particularly uncomfortable.

My usual way of dealing with feeling shy in those days was to throw myself into the mix – and this felt a little bit like a shark tank, as we headed outside to where a much larger gathering was going on. There were a couple kegs of beer and a fire in an old oil drum. There was the smell of pot in the air, though I don't think I was offered any. We drank out of the usual big plastic cups, the cloudy clear ones in those days because I don't think the red Solos had been invented yet. Imagine that.

I remember looking around a couple times for my friends, not seeing them, and feeling a little panicky, uncertain of what to do. So I went to get another beer, of course, and had trouble with the keg tap. A really big guy with a southern accent helped me. I was having a little trouble standing – not because of the alcohol, I could hold liquor really well in those days. I wondered if I was sick, maybe. The big guy's friend took my hand and led me away from the fire. I wanted to sit down. I was a little dizzy, and he said there was a nice place – over there. It was dark and as we approached the woods, I stumbled a lot. I wondered what was wrong with me …

And then I woke up. My head hurt. Really badly, shooting pains like someone was plunging a sword in and out through both my temples. I could smell woodsmoke. I was in the woods. I was cold, I was wet. There was laughter. I heard a zipper and realized my jeans were off, and I was really cold. My mouth was dry – no, there was something in my mouth. It was hard to breathe through my nose. I couldn't open my eyes, it was all dark. There was a weight on top of me. It was moving. Another pain, and another, and another, all the way up into my chest, my sternum was burning. I couldn't feel my legs. It all went blank again.

The next time I came to, I could see a little light out of the corner of my eye. It was cold out, and as it was very early spring, there were brown leaves all over the ground and yet, in the tiny area I could see through with my head to the side, there was one red leaf.

As a child, red was my favorite color.

As I felt more and more weights on me, more and more motion, more and more pain in the places I could feel anything, I stayed "awake" more and more. And I knew what was happening. I did what I'd learned to do in these situations – I used my brain. I took an inventory.

There was something on my head, and it was really tight around my forehead. A hat? No. There was a hole in it where I could see that little bit. That red. Maybe it was a ski mask. It smelled really bad, though. And there was a bump under my head, maybe it was knotted? Could it be underwear?

My head really, really hurt. And it was wet, in the back. The smell of woodsmoke.

Was I near the fire? It was so cold, though.

My feet were completely numb. I didn't know where they were. That scared me.

My shoulders hurt. And my hands were under my back. Tied together. That scared me, too. Much more vulnerable that way.

The pain in my sternum was so bad I wasn't sure I could breathe much longer. I couldn't feel anything below that.

And something rough and made of cloth was in my mouth. That didn't help with the breathing. I felt like I might throw up and I knew I couldn't. I would choke.

Given all that, and past experience, everything in me wanted to run. And given all that and past experience, I knew I couldn't. And of course, I had no feeling in my feet. So I decided to play possum. I didn't want them to know I was awake, and I didn't want to know why they were laughing. I focused my one eye, the one closest to the ground, on that red leaf. I studied every vein I could make out, and I sort of floated away. My breathing rate slowed, and I was in a place I'd been before, where there wasn't really any pain and where I was safe.

For a while, that worked. Until it didn't. Until there was a shrill whistle, and shouts from the campus military police: "Break it up. Break it up now. Let's go, let's go." Zippers being zipped. Water thrown on the fire, or maybe beer. Shuffling of feet. Swearing out loud and under their breath. "What do we do with her?" "Shit."

And steps coming closer. As they did, I began to become aware of pain in my body. All over my body. That tight covering being pulled off my head, untied and emptying. "Fuck, she's bleeding!" "Clean her up!" My jeans thrown at me as I was pushed forward, my hands untied. Rough hands trying to pull my jeans on, as if I were a young child. Hissing in my ear – "Get dressed, get dressed now, you bitch."

More steps approaching, in a much faster, serious way. My eyes were swimming, everything was blurry, but I could see the uniforms, the bully stick swinging, hear the radio crackling. "What the fuck is she doing here?" More swearing, some stumbling and mumbling by the guys standing around me. "Did she fall? Get the first aid kit, Murray." Then silence. "No, no, no. Jesus fucking Christ. Get this townie whore out of here, NOW!"

Someone – a big guy, though maybe not the first big guy – picked me up and carried me, once it became clear that I couldn't walk. And I couldn't, not even supported, though it might have been because the very last thing I wanted to do on Earth was put my arms around those guys' necks.

The next thing I remember – so maybe I passed out from the pain – was being in the woods near my house, in the front seat of a sedan, with the same cadet who led me out to the woods before it all happened. I couldn't or wouldn't speak, and just wanted to whimper, though I like to think that I didn't actually do that. I was horrified to wake up to this guy's face, to be alone with him. His jaw was set tightly, much like my father's would be when he was angry.

He fumbled around in the back seat, leaning over the front seat backs in a way that exposed his belly, and grabbed a towel out of his gym bag. He shoved it at me and told me to wipe my face, then got impatient and did it for me, spitting on the towel to moisten it. He told me that nothing happened, that I got so drunk, that it'd be better if I never set foot on the academy grounds again. That I'd made him and his friends look bad in front of the cops, and they couldn't get in trouble again. He asked me if I got it, and I nodded, then looked back out the window as he started up the car again and backed out of the little turnaround there.

He asked me where I lived exactly – we were close to my house by then and I don't know how he knew how to get there, though the next day I realized my wallet had been gone through. When we pulled in the driveway, he told me to put lipstick on and fix my hair. He made me look at him and he adjusted my jacket collar, ran his hands through his own hair, and came out and opened the car door for me. My dad was looking out through the living room cur-tains, and the cadet put my arm around his neck, told me to lean on him and smile like I loved him. We made our way slowly to the front door, and when my dad opened it, he stopped, extended his hand to shake my father's hand and introduced himself, though I do not remember his name to this day. He explained that I'd twisted my ankle on a hike with our friends and he had to carry me out of the woods, that I'd likely need some ice and aspirin.

He called my dad "Sir."

My dad liked him. They talked for a while after I went to bed. And for weeks, my father asked why I didn't go out with that cadet. And suggested that perhaps going into the military would be the best way for me to make something of myself. Again and again. He never noticed the scratches on my face, the blood near my hairline, the mud on my clothes. He never saw a thing.

And my Swedish friends? I never heard from them again. Or perhaps I couldn't look them in the eyes. I can't recall. And I decided, somewhere deep inside, that I could trust no one.

For decades, I didn't.

After that night in the woods, I saw red everywhere. A stray leaf here or there, a string caught in an old bird's nest, a tattered old piece of flag on a high pole, perhaps dropped off there by the wind. Today, I'd see all of those as symbols that I'd never been alone. Then, I had no idea what they meant or why I was suddenly nauseous when I saw what had always been my favorite color. It felt a little like torture, rather than gentle reminders.

Because in those first days and weeks, I could not remember a thing about that night, other than that I had done something bad, that my body hurt, that I was torn up "down there." Eventually I recalled the car in the woods and my brain, trained as it was to both disassociate and cling to the altered, more acceptable story that it created, decided that it had been a date rape in the woods. That explained enough, was bad enough, created enough shame to feel right. I couldn't look at anyone – especially my friends or my dad. That tale felt both wrong and right, and there was a queasy feeling in my stomach every time I thought about it, so mostly I didn't.

I'd decided I was sick that morning after I woke up and looked in the mirror and saw the scrapes on my face, the places where there would soon be ugly bruises on my arms and legs, the hollowness in my eyes. I certainly must have seemed unwell, because my mother didn't question me when I mumbled that I felt awful from somewhere under my covers as she came in and pulled up the window shades with her fake-cheery "Rise and shine!" early that next day.

I waited until everyone was gone before I got up and stood under the shower for so long that the steam filled the hallway outside the bathroom and made the carefully polished wood floor slick. My father worked nights, so I was back under the covers before he got up and readied himself for work, and he left me alone. I slept until the nightmares began, a host of wild animals screeching and howling, baring their teeth at me and scratching me with their sharp claws. They, too, had once been my friends in other dreams on other nights. Before.

Somehow I developed one of my signature hacking coughs – perhaps all that dank and damp in the woods had made me susceptible to the colds going around. Who knows. It bought me a whole week in bed to recover before anyone saw me much. I wore a knit watch cap pulled down over my forehead, and that hid the worst of the abrasions. My scalp itched as it healed, I remember that.

By the time I went back to school, the scrapes and bruises were dulling. My left wrist looked the worst, but it was cold out still, so I wore oversized sweaters and sweatshirts. I hoped no one would notice. When a few did, I just murmured something about tripping in the woods. Mostly, no one said anything. I drew myself inside, in the way I had when I was little, in hopes that I would blend in, or even better, disappear entirely.

I couldn't focus at all on schoolwork, and I slept a lot. My grades suffered. I would be in trouble for that later. Worse, my parents used it as confirmation that I wasn't worth sending to college. The high B average took a hit, though all those semesters of doing well never seemed to count for much, anyway. School and my future were really the least of my worries in the weeks following "the incident" down Cape.

I started spending more time with a guy I'd had a crush on for some time. Adam was an almost-bad boy – went to the Voc/Tech school rather than the excellent local high school I attended, worked at a gas station, was a loner. He was, looking back, a sweetheart of a person, and I felt safest with him. We weren't having sex – I was putting that off because I didn't want him to see what evidence of the rape remained – but we were doing pretty much everything else you could do, mostly clothed. There was some comfort in being with him, the only comfort I found in that month or two. Adam liked being with me and didn't expect anything. He was good company, but it wasn't enough. I was sliding away from everyone I knew, and I was just hiding out with him.

This was the first time I remember being seriously suicidal. I'm sure I had been clinically depressed before, yes, and I knew how to conceal that well. Or maybe no one really cared enough to notice. In any case, I snuck off to the corner of the library and read about ways to kill yourself. I talked to an old friend, pretending to do research for a paper, asking him what he knew, as his dad was a therapist. I became fairly obsessed and had the internet been available, I likely would have done it. As it was, I came close. Until I started to notice that I was queasy all the time. A stomach virus that really just wouldn't go away.

I threw up a lot, which was unusual for me, even when I was sick. It happened at Adam's house, up in his garage apartment, and when our mutual friends asked me about it, all of a sudden it hit me. The two girls who had introduced us were old souls, not people I knew all that well, yet I trusted as much as I was going to trust anyone. And so I told them I might be pregnant. They assumed it was Adam's baby, and I latched onto that story like a dog with a bone. I believed it to be true, even though it could not have actually happened.

I created some long-winded way that it was possible and tried to explain that to him. I still remember the mix of pain and sadness and mostly confusion as he listened to me, not knowing what to do. So I got angry, left, and didn't speak to Adam again until years and years later, when we reconnected on the Classmates website in our mid-forties. He wrote that he needed to apologize, that he'd treated me badly and had regretted it all these years. I wrote back that it was the other way around, that he'd done nothing wrong, that I'd explain it to him someday. Maybe he'll read this and know that he was just a victim of everything that had happened to me to that point. And how sorry I am that he became part of the collateral damage in any way. Maybe it was something he needed to work through too.

My focus shifted and become laser-like, in a zombified way. I got a friend to drive me to a clinic a few towns away, where my mother's cousin wasn't the truant officer as was the case where I lived, where I hoped no one would know me. I was a couple weeks shy of the legal time limit for an abortion – this was the late seventies. I had friends who'd gone through this, and I tried hard to recall what they had said, after they had gone through it. They'd survived, so I could too. I could do this. I worked really, really hard to convince myself of that. I scheduled the procedure for a Thursday, counting my babysitting money to be sure I had enough to cover a taxi both ways. An investment in keeping the secret. There was no one I trusted to go with me – or at least no one I wanted to involve in my mess.

I started to have dreams. Three towheaded boys. One of them, named Matthew, running down a hillside full of daisies and wildflowers in a pastoral setting. No matter how hard I ran, I couldn't catch up with him. The other two running in opposite directions. I'd try to catch up and pick them up in my arms, but I just couldn't. I'd wake up crying,

"I want my boys" on my lips. Every night, for a week or more. The same dream.

And yet, in the daytime, I knew that I could not have this baby. I cut a deal with God, as I'd done for my whole lifetime though I was past imagining the Lily Tomlin/Ernestine switchboard at that point, as I had when I was younger. When things were really bad, I assumed my calls to Him just could not be placed, that the circuits were busy. I told God and anyone up there who was listening that I just couldn't have this baby. That I loved babies, that I wanted them someday, but that I didn't know the daddy and I just couldn't bear a child not knowing who their father was. And as time passed, I was very clear that I could not stay on the Cape. I wasn't capable, really, of asking for what I wanted, so my pleas were focused on this unborn child. Yet, I knew that if I had this baby, I would never leave that sandbar and if I never left, I would die inside, if not literally. I would drink myself to death, in the best-case scenario, and that wouldn't be good for the baby.

It felt as though I was not being heard. Every morning I checked to see if my period had arrived, and I cried as I prayed that it would come soon. I looked at the days on the calendar, staying up really late in an effort to slow down time. I packed a bag to go on a youth ski retreat, of all things, to an old monastery in New Hampshire with my church youth group. The morning came to leave, and I was ready. My mom dropped me off at church, asking if I was feeling well enough to go. I nodded my head and got into the van, knowing that when I came back on Monday, there would be the final countdown of three, two, one days until I had to do the one thing I wasn't sure I could do. And yet had to.

The old monastery where our retreat was held had long been a safe place for me, a true retreat from everything. In retrospect, it was perfect timing. I allowed myself to block out all that was going on, safely ensconced in the sparely furnished bedroom of this beautiful old monastery. I wasn't sick once, and when I thought about it, I hadn't been for the prior week. It felt like grace, like someone had freeze-framed my life, and I tobogganed and sledded and drank copious amounts of Swiss Miss hot chocolate. With those tiny marshmallows. One night, the marshmallows in my cup formed the shape of a heart.

And the next morning, in the old bathroom with the tiny, tiny tiles laid in mesmerizing patterns, my prayers were answered. Not the most convenient of places or times, as there was a great deal of physical pain involved, yet a path to freedom began to open up that day. I lost that baby as alone as I was when it was conceived, yet in a place of love and believing, a sanctuary not unlike what the woods had once been for me, when I was a child myself.

I snuck a lot of the industrial-strength toilet paper and a trash bag into my room, and told my roommate, a good friend who I couldn't possibly sully with all of this, that I was having a really hard period, really bad cramps. She'd come back in and check on me once in a while as I drifted in and out of sleep, tucking me in, smoothing my hair back, dispensing aspirin. I let her care for me without knowing the depths of my need.

Mostly, I cried. Tears of relief, of joy, of seeing my tiny window into the world begin to expand. I began to dream, not of my little boys with their blond hair reflecting the sun, but of new horizons, lands unknown to me, waiting to be explored. A life that I was scared to think might actually come true.

I began, possibly for the first time in my life, to believe in grace, and in the possibility that somehow, someday, all would be well.

Eight

While the natural beauty of Cape Cod sustained me through so much and part of me misses it still, I knew I didn't belong there anymore. Perhaps I never did. So I waited out the rest of my time in high school, moving somewhat robotically through my senior year and dreaming of the day I would get on a plane for the first time and take off, literally and metaphorically. It amazes me now that I did. Only a few of my cousins had moved off Cape permanently and so I didn't have a blueprint for that – yet somehow I knew. At seventeen, I knew, and as soon as I finished my senior year of high school, I flew the coop. I didn't even stay for graduation. A couple for whom I'd been a mother's helper one summer had moved from Boston to Atlanta, and they asked me if I'd come stay for a couple months to babysit their two young sons. The timing was perfect, so off I went.

It was the first time I'd been on a plane, this short flight to Atlanta. I was so excited and quite a bit nervous too – and completely floored by the directive given by the flight attendant. "In case of an emergency," she said, "oxygen masks will drop down from the ceiling. Please put on your own mask before helping those who may need assistance." Here she acted this out with a woman in the seat just opposite me – PUTTING HER OWN MASK ON FIRST before helping her child!

A huge force of outrage welled up in my chest, and I looked around at my fellow passengers, expecting them to be equally appalled. They were not in the least disturbed. They just watched her complete the safety briefing and munched on peanuts as if nothing were wrong. I, on the other hand, had already calculated just how long I could hold my breath, having just completed my lifeguard and first aid training. I'd looked around and identified a hand- ful of kids and an elderly couple who might require help. I was, as usual, ready to assist anyone who needed it (and likely some who didn't) because this was What I Was Born For. A newly minted lifeguard, willing and able to help.

Looking back now, I want to both laugh and cry. That young girl had absolutely no regard for her own self yet would go on to help a lot of people over the years, both in America and here in South Africa. At great cost to herself though, to her health and wellness and potential. She had a great deal to learn about using her gifts, and that learning would begin with this couple in suburban Buckhead. Their fights were legendary, and at the end of the summer, we would all feel that my continued presence was needed in the house in order to maintain some stability for their young boys. What was meant to be just a couple months away would turn out to be a more permanent move, something I'd repeat later in South Africa.

Given that, I didn't see at first that leaving home meant leaving my siblings. Leaving them with my parents. There was no way to protect them from afar, and I had no idea how much my absence would change things for them, particularly for my brother. I still remember the letter he sent me, a month or so after I'd gone for what was, ostensibly, just the summer, though I knew by then that I wouldn't move back. He wrote that everything was different without me there, that it was awful, horrible, really bad. That he missed me. He asked me to please come back as soon as I could.

And I didn't. I couldn't. By then, I was well on the way to enrolling at a state university, determined to go to college even though my parents didn't believe I was worth the investment and refused to fill out my financial aid paperwork. I was trying my best to begin to build a life of my own.

My sisters never sent letters, but when I was home to visit, they made it very clear that they were not happy with me, that they resented me and my freedom and had no interest in talking to me about how wonderful things were in Atlanta. We'd never really been close, yet I'd never felt this deliberate freezing out. It was what my mother did to my father when they fought, all too often, and all I wanted to do was run away and never come back. As years passed, I did stay away, and our only communication became greeting cards at Christmas.

From the time I left for Atlanta, the fracture between me and my family of origin, as I began to think of them, continued to widen. Our contact was only occasional phone calls and letters, updates from time to time. As the years passed, I would see them a few times. I would bring my new fiancé, Charles, to meet the family, and my mother would come to our wedding in 1985 in Atlanta and act quite motherly – one of my very best visits with her. There were those glimmers of hope, as she was much more stable once all of us kids were grown, and I could see how different it might have been had she been able to get help when we were young, but she was so busy acting "normal" that I don't think anyone really understood what was going on. Mental health wasn't really discussed – this was in the 60s and 70s when cancer was referred to as the "C word."

There was a time when she didn't speak to me, when I told her Charles and I were getting divorced, that I wasn't ready to be married and needed more time on my own. But eventually she forgave me, and I took a long weekend trip to Maine with her and my father, which was a completely new experience and one I treasured, hoping to find that kind of connection with them both, long term. It wasn't to be, though, and I can't even remember what caused the next rift.

I would settle in Chicago and marry again, this time to George, but only my sister Carrie attended that wedding. My parents refused to come and do that again. I'd used up my one wedding pass, apparently. I'd grown a lot, had a good job, was volunteering with the homeless and church, but none of that was good enough. It only mattered that I had failed. I learned, once again, that I would never be good enough in their eyes.

I also felt, to be honest, that they weren't good enough for George's family – and so therefore, neither was I. This led to a sort of imbalance that never resolved itself, even over the twenty-six years we were married before I left for South Africa. I thought that his family was a good one and mine was sadly lacking. An early visit to see my parents and attend the wedding of one of my New Jersey cousins, whom I barely knew, was fairly disastrous in my mind. George remarked that he was glad I didn't grow up on that side because he didn't think he'd ever have found me. I'm still not sure exactly what that was supposed to mean, but it confirmed my deepest fears that I was being judged along with them, and so it seemed best just to stay away.

My parents did, of course, visit when our daughter Lina was born. They were both very good with infants and young children until they developed a mind of their own. And we attended my sister Carrie's wedding when Lina was three, my nerves raw from dealing with her illness and my mama bear instincts fully on alert as I knew she and my mothering skills would be critiqued the entire time.

When, at two years of age, my daughter was first given a diagnosis of Asperger's by one doctor and Pervasive Development Delay by another, my mother's only reaction was to ask when we were having another baby. Much the way puppies were replaced in my childhood if their behavior was troublesome, or the young calf who cried too much, missing his recently removed mother, was sent to the slaughterhouse. I see now, in hindsight, that the patterns set in childhood had in no way changed, and certainly had not healed.

When I was thirty-six and realized I could no longer talk to my mother without feeling ill, I told her I needed a break from them all. I told myself that I was protecting my siblings, that my mother would put them between us and make it unpleasant for them. The truth was that I needed space to process, to uncover all these memories and more, to heal. I was committing the ultimate sin in my parent's eyes, and likely in my siblings' as well – I was being selfish. Something in me knew that it was time to put myself, my child, and my husband first, and somehow I did.

But several months after this, I decided my little chosen family would be far better off without me, that I was so bad, so broken, that I couldn't heal. I see now that choosing myself over the family I'd been born into made me feel so guilty that I couldn't stand the pain and felt I had to leave this Earth. That was over twenty years ago, as I write this. It took me a very long time to clear myself of all the effects the madness, fear, and despair had on me. If

I'd waited longer to prioritize my own well-being and get help, I doubt that I'd be where I am today. I would have succeeded in taking my own life. Seventeen years of damage, seventeen years of healing.

Along the way, I've tried to reconnect with two of my siblings. And they've tried, too, yet it seems to be impossible. They've followed different paths, all three of them, and none of our paths intersect. Given that we grew up together, I wish we'd continued to grow together, to collectively weave a new story. That wasn't to be. As sad as it makes me, as painful as it sometimes still is, I chose to save the one life I could: my own.

Nine

I spent the day in my basement.

I wanted to do it. I really did. After so many almost attempts, I was ready.

I was very, very sure. Sure that I was the very worst mother on this planet. Sure that my husband and daughter would be so much better off without me. Sure that the sooner I left, the sooner the world would not be contaminated by the god-awful presence of my body, mind, and soul.

In a way, it was yet another form of serving the world, or so it seemed. I was doing the right thing, I was sure of it, and I needed to do it now.

So what kept me walking around in circles, mumbling to myself, crying uncontrollably, and letting out a high-pitched scream every twenty minutes or so? I didn't want to make a mess. Really. I didn't want to create any further damage, or cause pain to whoever found me, especially to my loved ones. I was trying hard to protect them in the very act of leaving, of making a quick and very final exit. I wanted to allow them to move forward with their lives, unencumbered by the immensely heavy baggage I'd brought to them. The fact that I'd been largely unaware of what had happened to me only made me hate myself more.

I guess I have to thank my mother, ultimately, for the fact that I failed to find a way to kill myself. She was the one who taught me to keep things clean and sanitary, after all. As all her other lessons had, it had stuck. I was so hell-bent on not creating a mess that I became, once again, paralyzed. I could not do what I strongly believed would make things better. I couldn't leave after all.

I also have to thank the doctor we now refer to as the "pinhead psychiatrist" for giving me the drugs he did – ones that were commonly known to be contraindicated for those with PTSD. That's what landed me in that non-metaphorical subterranean space – our suburban basement. I spent hours circling the perimeter and stepping over the brightly colored plastic riding toys my five-year-old daughter had scattered about. All while doing the laundry, of course. Keeping it all clean until the very end. It seems that this drug I'd been given routinely caused patients with trauma backgrounds to become flooded with memories. In many cases, as in mine, there was so much unprocessed trauma that the patient would become completely overwhelmed and rendered incapable of reason. In so much psychic pain that many did not survive.

I didn't know that then, though. All I knew was that my doctor, the one who'd taken that oath to do no harm and had clearly forgotten said oath, was MIA. He'd gone off for a long weekend and had also forgotten, it seemed, to arrange for anyone to cover his calls. I was left leaving messages for him hourly, all alone and quite quickly losing what tiny threads of hope I had.

There was another option I didn't see at first – not for several hours. My therapist, Jennifer, had sort of handed me over to this doctor because (in my disordered think-ing) I'd overwhelmed her and she'd done what the people I believed should be taking care of me always did. She'd given up on me, shuttled me over to someone else. Washed her hands clean of me.

Only she hadn't. That was all in my mind, and some tiny, tiny light within me knew to call her, as a very, very, very last resort. I didn't have much to lose at this point. And, miraculously, she caught me. She did. Something I will always and forever be grateful for, her presence on that day and in the coming years. Over time, she proved me wrong and blew holes in my carefully constructed picture of my inability to be cared for. My complete lack of the right to be loved. My never being enough, being worthy of love, of care. It took a long time for that construct to come tumbling down. Jennifer had been treating me for a year or two at this point, and would continue to walk with me, professionally, for another eight years or so. And as my friend and cheerleader, to this very day.

In that moment in the basement filled with Little Tykes toys and cardboard moving boxes I'd never unpacked, Jennifer answered my call. The first person to do so, all day. And I have no idea what I said, not a word. Or if I even had words. What I do know is that she asked me if I could meet her at her office, and that somehow – on the wings of angels, perhaps – I got myself there, traveling the back roads for the ten-minute drive between us. Somehow I did it, relying on muscle memory to drive, on staying in this world and focused enough to take the first step to what became my own personal resurrection in time.

She took me to the hospital, over thirty minutes away. Did we speak? I don't recall. The next thing I do remember is being in an ER cubicle, the plastic admission bracelet being put around my wrist and Jennifer telling me that as much as I didn't want her to, she needed to call my husband.

He arrived in what seemed like hours, though my sense of time was completely gone by then. The pain in his eyes is something I'll never forget. Whether it was concern for me, a lack of empathy, or concern about what others would think, I don't know. He certainly did not want me staying there. Jennifer must have told him that I really had to be admitted, or perhaps the doctors did.

From there, I just have flashes. Being wheeled in a door underneath the Intensive Care Psychiatric Ward sign. Having to give them my personal possessions and my belt. Nothing that could possibly be used to harm myself was allowed – not even the cross on a long chain I wore, given to me just as I began this descent. I was literally malnourished at this point – eating only brown rice for weeks prior. My pants were falling off, so I had to wear a gown until George brought yoga pants from home.

It's all a blur. The meeting that I've written out elsewhere in this book. The newly admitted patient, a sex offender, who found his way into my room somehow the first morning I woke up there, having finally fallen asleep in the wee hours on the hard, plastic-wrapped mattress. Sitting and laughing at the absurdity of it all with other women, there for electric shock treatment or bulimia and anything in between. Eating bland meals served with blunt utensils and Styrofoam cups.

After I'd been there a couple days and found some sense of normalcy and relief, after they had begun titrating me off the ill-prescribed drugs and onto the ones that would be the beginning of a bridge to change for me, I met the social worker on duty. She'd be able to talk with me about how to manage my family life in light of all that was beginning to bubble up, I was told, and that was something I really wanted help with. I walked in the room with some openness only to find that I already knew her. She was a dear friend of my former business partner – I'd known her when she was in grad school, and here she was, all grown up. A lifeline. Another incredible gift, a synchronistic event, a sign from above and beyond that there was hope for me. That somehow, my past and my future might weave together. I saw that for a split second, but it was enough.

The very next morning, in those early hours when I could sleep, I had a dream. I was sooty and dirty, dressed in rags, with more rags wrapped around my feet. It was cold and damp and the fog moved around me in misty clouds. The path I arrived on was clearly bumpy, full of jagged stones with threadbare plants bordering it on both sides and dark beyond that. I was road weary and bone thin. My eyes were sunken in, visible even though they were cast down, look-ing only at the places on the ground where my next step would fall.

To the right, my field of vision was very different. It was light and airy and smelled fresh and clean. There was a beautiful brick path that wound through hills of green and lavender. There was birdsong and the sound of the breeze in the distant trees. A whole new world.

In between the two places was a huge threshold, an open gate or doorway of sorts many feet higher than me and faced in old stone on the darker side with exquisitely carved granite on the bright one. From my vantage point above it all, I could see both.

Suddenly, I was in my body – the one wrapped in tat-tered clothes, struggling to breathe in that heavy, thick air. It was more uncomfortable than I can possibly tell you. Wretchedly so.

Given the memory of what I'd just witnessed, I made the extraordinary effort it took to raise my head, and in doing so, I saw that there were words carved into the stone, ones I had to struggle to make out. Once I put them together, I recognized the German phrase from the gates of Auschwitz: *Arbeit Macht Frei.* In English, "Work Makes You Free." Pretty much what I'd always been taught – and given that, it was also often pointed out that I was terribly lazy, and that this was the reason there was no hope for me to be free, ever.

It hurt to even look at it for a second, and I could feel my heart sink once more. Feelings of shame and hopelessness flooded my heart, and all of me wanted to just sink to the ground in a heap. As I did, one single beam of light crossed my knees, just where they met the rocks, and travelled up to my face, causing my eyes to open. Something in me remembered, and I pushed myself up, feeling the sharpness of the rock cutting into my hands. I bound them up again, took a breath as deeply as I could, and began to propel myself through that gateway. The energy came from a force far from me, a very powerful one. Before I knew it, I was on the other side.

I collapsed again, this time on the smooth brick with soft green moss in the margins, landing on my back with my knees up and feeling the sun on my face. It was so much easier to breathe there, and so I did only that for a while. When I opened my eyes, they rested on the beautiful granite side of that portal, where a different set of carved words were much easier to read. Tears came as I read the original phrase, the one that is in the Bible and originated long, long ago: "Truth will set you free." Clear as day. So clear that something in me knew, once and for all, that I could stay.

I could stay. I had never felt that before. I woke up at that point in the dream, and that knowing stayed with me. It is still with me, even though I've forgotten it from time to time.

The understanding of this fundamental truth is what led me to decide in that clinical setting, as institutional and cold and scary as it might sound to others, that if I could stay – and some part of me wanted so badly to do just that – well then, everything would need to change.

And it did. I spoke to the doctor who cared for me there about this weird idea I had – that I wanted to change my name. As a way of marking this change in my life, of beginning to quiet the tickertape of horrible old messaging tied to my birth name, Gretchen, and my childhood nick-name given to me by my mother, "Gretch the Wretch." I wanted to birth the me who had always existed deep inside – though I don't think I could verbalize that back then. Hindsight, likely, and yet that's what it really was.

The psychiatrist in charge of the unit assured me that changing one's name was actually therapeutic. It could allow for old messaging to be reprogrammed and a new identity to begin to form. She did suggest, however, that I choose a name that would serve me in the long term. When I questioned what she meant, she said that perhaps I shouldn't go with something like Moonbeam. I smiled and told her that wouldn't work in my small conservative vil-lage. She smiled back and said that she was sure I'd be ok.

Within twelve days, I was home. I had so much work to do, so much excavating before I could create the life I live now. Somehow, miraculously, in just a month or two,

I stood in front of a judge and told her in an unfamiliar yet clear and strong voice that I needed a new name in order to claim my life as my own. There were tears in her eyes as she signed the paperwork and wished me well, wiping her face with the overly long sleeves of her shiny black robes. It seems incredible to me now that I did that on my own, that no one went to the courthouse with me, but that's how things were then. All through serious illnesses of my own and of my daughter's, dealing with grief and mourning miscarriages and trauma, dealing with issues that would destroy many, I was nearly always alone. I really didn't know any other way.

Once my name change was official, I sent out a simple, beautiful announcement card to friends and family, shaking as I imagined their reactions yet propelled by that same mysterious force that allowed me to walk through the gateway in my dream. On the front of that notecard I had printed a Chinese proverb: "The beginning of wisdom is to call things by their right names."

In all the changing, the wisdom became mine. In name and in spirit. The truth has, indeed, set me free.

Ten

Name changed, determined to no longer wear a mask of normality, I set out to recreate my life on a fundamental level. Given that we were living in a small suburb north of Chicago where everyone knew everything about everyone, given that I was still a wife and mother of a young child with special needs with the same day-to-day tasks and responsibilities, this was not so easily done as said. People, including my own family, tiptoed around me, and I napped a lot at first, the drugs and therapy sapping a lot of my strength.

Over the years I would experiment with many forms of healing – everything from hypnosis to Feldenkrais to Reiki to myofascial release. In time, I recovered – or more accurately, rebuilt – in ways the professionals never expected. I was told by a well-meaning intern in a group circle at the hospital that statistically I should be an alcoholic, an addict, a prostitute, or dead. Or all of the above. I remember staring blankly at him, with no idea why he would say such a thing, and asking him, "And how is that helpful?" At the time, I thought it was really negative and judgmental, but over the years I realized it was a useful challenge after all. I spent at least a decade trying hard to make sure that his words didn't come true. Perhaps it's part of why I recovered so well.

Life went on, between therapy appointments and constant testing to figure out what was really going on with my immune system, why I was in so much physical pain. Over the next fifteen years or so, I would be diagnosed with melanoma and, one year, have a deep excision and skin graft only to need a full hysterectomy for another suspected cancer and related issues the very next year. I'd fall on black ice a year or so later and break my neck in two places though that wasn't diagnosed, so I walked around with my neck broken for thirteen months, in ridiculous pain and getting sicker every month. That accident would bring on vertigo, which added a whole new dimension to things. All of this while dealing with long-term Lyme disease, which started just after George and I married in 1989 and wouldn't be diagnosed or treated until after we moved to Virginia in 2008.

There were, in those years, good memories too. We took Lina abroad to London for the first time, celebrating Thanksgiving in a whole new way. I travelled on my own for the first time ever to a holistic healing center, which opened up many doors and started me on my path to the work I do now. George and I attended many performances at all the incredible venues Chicago has to offer. We brought a puppy home, finally, which added a welcome dimension to our little family. I'd wanted more children but after several miscarriages, we gave up on that idea.

It was a good life, looking in from the outside. Certainly a privileged one in many ways, and certainly I did all I could to make sure that Lina had a different childhood than I did. I never laid a hand on her, so concerned that I'd not be able to stop as my parents never seemed to be able to stop hitting me. I read every parenting book I could find, queried parents whose approach I admired. As George worked crazy hours and travelled a lot, most of the day to day was left to me. While I learned how to better deal with my triggers, I still had a flash temper and would give myself time-outs routinely so as to keep that level of anger away from my daughter. And I started painting again after spending those hours in the art therapy room at the hospital, slashing my paintings for the first year or two with a razor, then later finding my way to abstract work, so that no one could tell me I was doing it wrong.

What I couldn't see or know then was that all this illness and dis-ease very likely had to do with the fact that I was trying extremely hard to fit in the boxes society – my parents, church, media – told me would make me happy. From an early age, I read clear through the Bible several times, trying to figure out what I was doing wrong. I knew that no matter what I did or didn't do, I couldn't do it right – thus there must be something very wrong with me. I was bound up in large part by my mother's ongoing prediction that no one would ever love me. Certainly, that couldn't really be true, said a little voice in my head.

So, sure that I wasn't right for my family of origin, I set out to create a family of my own. I married a good, stable, churchgoing man. I did everything I had to do, including giving up my own work and interests, to be the best wife I could possibly be to him, and to give him children. When he decided he didn't want more children, I set about doing all I could to support his success and his career. I kept trying somehow, though I continued to be exhausted and sick, to get better, to do better. I fought hard.

What I didn't realize is that I was fighting myself. I was fighting all that would bring me joy, peace, love, and that feeling of belonging I'd never had. I had drunk the Kool-Aid we are all given and had made my end goal normality vs. embracing my own spirit, my hopes, and my gifts. All that I'd learned in the hospital would take a long time to wear down these old patterns.

In time, I would create that family I wanted so much but in a way and a place that I couldn't really imagine in that house in the woods in suburban Chicago. If you'd told me back then that I'd be in a very different house in a very different forest in a place I'd never heard of, halfway across the world, I would have laughed long and hard, and likely let out a huge sigh. As much as I'd always loved South Africa, at this point in my life, I had no hope I'd ever live here. This would take time and the building of trust in those I would come to call my ancestors, as well as learning to deeply listen.

In 2008, an opportunity came up for a big change. As often happens in the United States, my husband was offered a new position in Washington DC. He'd be working for the client he'd represented for most of his career, but in house, giving him a welcome challenge and a lot of room to grow professionally. Our daughter was starting high school, so the timing made sense, and I welcomed the chance for our little family of three to be on our own, away from extended family. I hoped a new adventure would bring us closer, and that it was a chance for me to create a better life in a new place where no one knew my stories or thought of me as perpetually ill. I'd been working with a very gifted team of various therapists in order to regain my strength physically and restore my spirit. But I had no idea that work had really only just begun.

We found a house just inside the Beltway in Northern Virginia, and I set about slowly making it our own, adding artwork and creating a beautiful garden as well as my first real art studio above the garage. George's job required a great deal of socializing, and we were at black tie affairs every week, getting to know the nation's capital through exclusive events and after-hours viewings at the various museums and important buildings. In juxtaposition to this, I met key individuals – like my meditation teacher, Jonathan Foust – in those first months.

I'd arrived in Falls Church a week or two ahead of my family to get things sorted out, sleeping on a mattress in the midst of sawdust since the builders were still not finished with the house. As I was leaving my beloved team in Chicago, a friend had kindly suggested I contact someone named Jonathan for support in this next stage of life. I'd stopped seeing my therapist regularly sometime before we left, yet with all the adjustments the move would bring and a drive to learn all I could about different spiritual paths, she thought he might be the perfect person to visit with regularly.

She was right. Jonathan, a founder of the Kripalu Center for Yoga and Health and now a leader with the Insight Meditation Community in Washington, is a very tall, very laidback, wise and gentle man. From our first phone conversation, he was – and is – amazingly kind and generous. Upon hearing that I was on my own, he invited me out to his house to discuss the ways we could work together. I was happy to have a break from the construction zone, so I put the address in my rental car GPS, and off I went to his home out in the woods, to be greeted by his huge standard poodles as I took all the natural beauty in. The poodles resembled a pair I'd spent every summer visiting with on the beach, as a child, so much so that it was a bit disorienting. No coincidence, I'm sure.

We chatted in his office, discussing my hopes for this new phase of my life after filling him in on the ups and downs of the previous decades. At some point in the conversation, Jonathan brought up a concept completely foreign to me. He said, in his quiet, resonant voice, "We serve best from a place of overflow." My confusion must have shown because he repeated it again, slowly and carefully, willing it to seep into my consciousness. I shook my head, still not understanding.

He gave me an example. A fountain, he said, like Buckingham Fountain in downtown Chicago, makes the most beautiful display of water shooting up against the sky. And yet if the base container of the fountain isn't filled with water, there will only be spurts of water in fits and starts as the machinery tries to do its job on, basically, fumes. If we human beings don't fill our own well regularly, there's no way we can fully express our potential in the world. We cannot serve if we do not serve ourselves first.

You may recall my utter outrage on that first plane ride I took at seventeen, when we were directed to put on our own oxygen masks before helping others. Not much had changed in twenty-odd years in this arena, so I'll admit it took me a couple years to even take in this concept with the help of Jonathan and other teachers. Once I did internalize it, though? It changed everything. Much as a certain book called *Radical Acceptance* had, when I read it just before we left Chicago. It was written by another Buddhist practitioner, Tara Brach, and I'd read it twice, in quick succession. It began the rewiring of my brain that my work with Jonathan and others would continue – it told me that I could accept myself warts and all, that I didn't need to be something I wasn't, that like the Japanese practice of *kintsugi* where the cracks in broken vessels are filled with gold, the parts where I needed repair could become beautiful and strong.

Imagine my surprise when leaving Jonathan's office that day and starting down the stairs only to run into a tiny woman with wild hair and various cleaning tools in her hands who Jonathan introduced as his wife, Tara Brach. The surge of light and warmth that came up in my body was almost breathtaking. I felt like I'd found people I belonged with, even this early in the move. It was exactly what I'd hoped for, and while much of the next seven years would be spent in situations that were not easy, with people I felt no connection with, there would also be kin. Souls who saw the world much as I did, whose values and interests matched mine. It felt like a huge, huge gift, a very welcome and long-awaited one.

In those years, I would grow into myself in so many ways. I'd learn self compassion, begin to hone my own intuitive gifts in a way that allowed me to bring them to others, train as a life coach rather than becoming a minister or a therapist as I once thought I would. I was finally diagnosed with long-term Lyme disease after more than twenty years of being ill, and while the treatment was extensive and intense, my health finally started to improve. I'd have my mouth rebuilt – seven implants, eight bone grafts – as it turned out I'd killed some nerves in that fall that broke my neck in 2001, and despite going to ENTs and oral surgeons, that had been missed completely. I delved deeper into mindfulness meditation and Buddhist practices, continuing to find a soul home there. I trained in various other practices that had helped me with trauma issues – with horses, expressive arts, writing and photography.

I continued to be the "good wife," regularly attending events related to George's work in Washington as well as abroad. In the midst of it all, I met Desmond Tutu and his declaration that it was time for me to come home rang in my ears off and on as the years passed. But life was busy, and I could never convince my family to travel to South Africa, much as we travelled to many other places. Their interests and mine were very different, the divide growing quickly now, so I did my thing while they were at work and school, carefully hiding away the tarot cards and more "out there" books and other tools of the practices I was coming to depend on for myself and my work with clients.

Slowly but surely, I was becoming more myself. Unfortunately, the person I was becoming was no more welcome by my little family – or the extended one – than I had been welcome as a child in my family of origin.

Eleven

I had wanted to visit South Africa forever, it seemed, from those early childhood evenings spent perusing the old *National Geographic* issues to writing school reports on apartheid, reading for the first time about Archbishop Desmond Tutu and his work. And I had arrived at a point in my life where I was happy to travel on my own, even that far a distance – and at a point where I really needed some time to myself.

My work was becoming more and more aligned with who I was becoming, much to the chagrin of my family, who did not appreciate all my sacred treasures scattered around my home office. I needed both time to reflect and inspiration to navigate that conflict, to move forward intuitively. My daughter was in her junior year of college, my husband was working constantly, and the commitment we'd made to working on our marriage had fizzled out after a couple years of trying here and there.

Lina had no interest in seeing South Africa with me, though I'd thought it would make a great mother/daughter trip, and George never could figure out a time that worked for him, so I began to make plans of my own. Eventually the stars aligned, and in early spring of 2015, I booked my tickets to leave in late October. I'd never been away for more than a week on my own and only once or twice on longer family trips, but given the distance, it made sense to stay a month.

I pored over all the guidebooks I could find, equally mesmerized and confused by all the tribal names for places and gob smacked by the beauty, even in the small photos on those pages. I wanted to see as much of the country as I possibly could, convincing myself – as a way of legitimizing taking this expensive trip just for me – that I was doing reconnaissance for future family adventures. I was equal parts excited out of my mind and paralyzed by the idea that I was doing something this huge for myself, and those emotions danced back and forth for the eight months before I boarded that plane.

Eventually the time came to begin to pack, and given my excited postings on Facebook, I had no shortage of advice on what to bring with me. Never a concise packer, I packed layers – many of them, and way too much generally. I don't remember what exactly I ended up bringing, just that I really overdid it – and came to see that as a symbol of how much I was still carrying with me psychically, even given all the work I'd done on myself to that point.

Departure day finally came. I'd checked all my documents three times, I'd had a tetanus booster and loaded up on homeopathic malaria medicine, I'd squished an unbelievable amount of clothing in an enormous suitcase and had an equally overloaded carryon bag, thinking I'd leave behind some clothing somewhere along the way to make room for souvenirs. I was certain I wanted to remember this trip always. That afternoon, after I'd checked and double checked my lists my favorite driver, Karl, picked me up, raising his eyebrows when he heaved my suitcase in the back of his immaculate Mercedes. I said, for the first time and not for the last, that I was traveling for a month, and he had the good grace not to say another word about it. My diary notes for that day are a mix of spiritual – cleansing the house before leaving – and practical – getting cash in *rands*, bringing compression socks, and of course, talking to my housekeeper about Thanksgiving, since I'd arrive back the day before. Always the homemaker.

I boarded a plane late in the day on the 29th of October and, through the magic of time zones and direct flights, arrived at the SAA terminal at O.R. Tambo airport in Johannesburg late in the day on the 30th. It was an eighteen-hour flight, with only a short stop in Accra, Ghana, for fueling and the requisite bug-spraying of the cabin. I'd never been on that long a flight and even in business class, my body felt it, yet there was a deep, deep sense of peace from the time we boarded at Dulles. Something in me knew I was going home.

For the first time in my life, I had the urge to kiss the ground when we landed. I did not, though, as it was all tarmac and quite modern and I was too busy trying to sort out my baggage and looking for the representative from the tour company andBeyond, who was meeting me. I'd be spending a week toward the end of my trip in KwaZulu-Natal at a private game reserve called Phinda with friends who'd been long-time clients of this company, so I had them book my whole trip. Looking back now, it seems overly luxurious, of course, yet that was what I was accustomed to – George liked very much to stay at first class hotels and to eat at incredible restaurants, and I came to enjoy all of it very much as well, once I got over my feeling of not belonging to that social group. Over the years, he'd achieved significant wealth and liked to take us on beautiful trips – we were at our best when traveling together. I remember looking at the check for our dinner the night before I left, at a beautiful countryside restaurant outside the DC Beltway, and wondering how many *rand* that was, and how much good it could do in rural South Africa. I'd think about that a lot, that first trip, and for years to come.

Eventually I found the guy who'd been sent to meet me. He guided me through to the Amex office to exchange dollars for *rand*, then presented me in the carpark with a lovely leather folder with my whole itinerary and tickets I'd need along the way. I'd chosen to spend most of my time outside the cities, visiting the Western Cape and the Kalahari along with some time at the tip of the continent and visiting a friend in Cape Town before heading to KwaZulu-Natal and Mpumalanga for the last week, so I'd only have two nights in Joburg.

As we drove towards Rosebank, where I'd stay in a beautiful small bed and breakfast on one of the gorgeously blooming jacaranda-lined streets, the sun began to set. It was that classic huge red ball you often see in the movies, and it was stunning, even if it was over the dirty expressway, lined with all manner of people balancing huge loads on their heads or wobbly bicycles. I was tired and badly in need of a shower, but still it lit me up inside, filling me with a sense of well-being.

By the time we got to the hotel, dark had fallen – it was spring in South Africa, and the days were still a bit short, so I wouldn't really see the neighborhood until I went out the next day. I was greeted warmly by the staff and my huge bag hauled upstairs by a brawny young man without comment. The only sign that I was in a "third world" country was that my room keys were attached to a fob with a red button that I was told would set off an alarm, one that I was encouraged to use at any time to summon help. I was also given a stern reminder to be sure that both the room door and the glass slider door overlooking the garden were kept locked at all times.

I don't recall, but I'm guessing I only ate a protein bar for dinner that night, despite the fact that the hotel housed a restaurant I'd been told was very good, and unpacked a bit after showering. I know I slept very, very hard – that is, until the sound of what could only be a pterodactyl woke me in the early hours of the morning, interrupting the gentle birdsong that had me stirring a bit. I pretty much levitated off the bed when I heard that shriek coming from just outside the sliding door. I peeked through the blinds only to be stared back at by a huge bird with rather intense eyes. I'd never seen this one before, not even in zoos, but it had friends and they were all strutting around the green lawn, somehow kept immaculate even in the drought.

I realized how hungry I was and quickly dressed, glad I'd hung up some clothes in the cupboard the night before, and found my way downstairs to the lovely little restaurant. Its glass doors opened up to a garden full of aloes and lilies. Every single thing charmed me that first day and for a long time to come: The alstroemeria, one of my very favorite cut flowers to buy in the US, growing along the path and single blooms of it placed in tiny pitchers on the tables. The deep orange of the eggs on spinach for my breakfast, the smell of rooibos tea made even better by steamed milk and called a red cappuccino, the lilting accent of my waiter as he questioned me about my flight and life in America.

I was feeling a bit woozy, an odd sort of inner ear thing I thought might have been from the flight. But I was excited to meet Deb, an online coaching friend who had recently returned to SA from Canada, along with her husband Jamie and toddler son Zenzo, who I'd brought some books for. I went up to my room and applied sunscreen – I'd be religious about this for some time, then not so much after I moved here – and grabbed my sunglasses.

They were at the door at the appointed time that morning – very not South African but they had been living in the Northern Hemisphere for a while – and I sat in the back seat with Zenzo, who wasn't at all sure about me until I pulled out the books full of cars and trucks and things that go. It probably was a mistake to sit in the back seat since I was feeling so woozy anyway – I had to ask to make a quick stop to be sick as we drove through stately neighborhoods near my little hotel, the streets lined with the beautiful purple blooms of more jacarandas. It felt like I needed to clear, and I did.

We headed downtown to the CBD – central business district – after that little episode, and I was very glad to be with Jamie, a giant of a guy, as we moved through the streets on foot. Zenzo is adopted, a black child, and Jamie and Deb are as pale as me – I noted the curious looks, yet mostly people seemed to beam at us. An early precursor to my life with my own partner and family down the road, perhaps. Looking back, I really appreciate that tour through the "foreign African," or African immigrant, inner city neighborhoods, the windows missing glass in many cases in these low rise brick buildings yet more satellite TV dishes than I could count, the little *spaza* shops selling everything plastic and fresh fruit, the ingeniously but barely held together bicycles everywhere. The taxis – what we'd called minivans in America – had various clever or religious sayings painted over their rear windows, and they navigated through the streets without much regard for rules or safety.

It was a baptism of sorts, made more comfortable by a stop in one of the renovated old factory buildings with a food market full of amazing smells. The staff of a little coffee shop at the entrance were completely decked out in costumes – I had forgotten it was Halloween. It was a weird and unexpected moment of Western culture and not by any means the last. My stomach still queasy, I happily ordered a coconut water at one of the massive poured concrete counters only to be completely surprised – and delighted – when it was served to me as a whole coconut, a rough hole hacked in at the top and a straw stuck in it.

This kind of delight would come to be commonplace. The smallest happenings would make joy bubble up inside me at any given moment. I still feel that way, from time to time, as though someone should pinch me – that utter amazement that I am here, living in South Africa. On that day in Joburg though, and for the next twenty-four days to come, I didn't know that I would come back to stay. I was intent on drinking in as much as I could of South Africa, of this magnificent continent. I took thousands and thousands of photos on my phone, on two cameras, and in my mind, and acquired as many souvenirs and reminders as I could fit in my overstuffed luggage.

The next couple days would take me from the inner city streets of Johannesburg to the airport at Cape Town, then a long drive up the western coast to an extraordinary place called Bushmans Kloof in the Western Cape. There, I stood on a huge flat rock at the shore of a dam. Watching woolly-necked storks play in the water at sunrise, I knew, all at once and very deeply, that this was not just a vacation.

I'd come, basically, to go walkabout. It had been three years since I'd handed George an envelope of divorce papers, telling him that I'd done all I could to help us change things on my own. He'd pleaded with me to stay, said that he'd try anything until I said we must go to therapy together. Anything but that, apparently. We read a book together, we became a bit kinder toward each other, and talked more from time to time, but ultimately nothing had changed, and I knew nothing would. He needed me to contain myself, to be appropriate, to be a standard-issue suburban executive housewife – and much as I'd tried to fit that mold and thought life would be far easier if I could do just that, I knew that, in time, it would kill me. I'd been sick most of our marriage, and I wasn't willing to force my abstractly shaped soul into a conventionally defined identity. Not anymore.

On that rock that morning, I promised myself I would do all I could to listen on this trip, to really see, to reflect on just what it was that my self needed in order to truly thrive. It was a big moment – one of those forks in the road – and like Robert Frost, I chose to take the path less travelled. For sure. At this point and all along the way, really, I had no idea what was to come. I had begun leaping, and I had no idea not only if the net would catch me but if there really was a net at all. In time, I'd see that I could only catch myself, over and over, creating a safe place within, cajoling the parts of me that had learned to live in fear, into taking risks and comforting myself in any way I could along this crazy path. Learning to laugh throughout everything that life brought.

Everywhere I went on this trip – from Bushmans to a beautiful small hotel in Cape Town to Grootbos in the middle of southernmost South Africa to the magnificent reserve called Tswalu in the Kalahari Desert – I would be greeted in my room by two robes, towels for two, even rose petals in the shape of a heart on my bed, along with the inevitable questioning of my husband's whereabouts. It was as if the universe was testing me, showing me that the world saw me as married, assumed and expected that my husband would be with me. I, however, saw how untrue that was, even when we were physically together. It was a huge realization and perhaps more, a reconfiguring of who I was and how I saw myself, that whole month. An unfurling or unwrapping, so that I could see who I could be, without all the trappings of the life I'd so carefully con- structed to keep me safe. Certainly, it was a redefining of all I knew to be true and a time to discover what I really wanted. A reckoning.

All of that was on my mind as I continued to discover South Africa and how incredibly right it felt to me. It's not that it was easy, exactly. This place is not that. It is rough and tumble and has a lot of sharp edges, on every level. It does. And it holds incredible beauty, strength, and grace. The people I met that first month intrigued, delighted, and challenged me. This country has been through so much – its racial issues are, unlike other places in the world, very much out there and known, yet are far more complex than commonly recognized. The habits and effects of colonization still show in every aspect of life. My guess is that it will take several generations for them to dissipate fully. My life would continue to be a study in all of this and more. I just didn't know that yet.

Twelve

The journey really began in earnest a couple days later in a blindingly shiny white van at the airport in Cape Town. The driver had met me inside with the normal placard with my surname written on it – nothing new there. We walked into the parking garage, exchanging pleasantries – a routine I'd become used to over years of traveling with George.

I asked, as I usually do, if I could sit in the front passenger seat, and he was happy to have the company since we had a long drive ahead.

As we drove out of Cape Town, two things caught my attention. The first was hard to miss – the enormity of Table Mountain is startling. The city is built under and around it and the thick fog, as the driver explained, made it look like the Table was wearing a tablecloth. The second observation came a little further out as we weaved through the cloverleafs of the expressways in order to drive north. It wasn't the first time I'd seen shantytowns outside a large city, not at all, yet this went on forever. Against the white fog, the colors of the shipping container parts and odd bits that were stacked next to each other were oddly beautiful, yet imagining life in such a place was sobering.

My driver confirmed that while water and sanitary facilities were scarce, people lived there for their entire lives. He explained that though apartheid had ended twenty-one years prior to my visit, there were still over 400 informal settlements outside Cape Town alone, with hundreds of thousands of occupants. As people had been moved from their longtime homes, they had to leave their ancestors behind, in terms of burial sites and reestablish those cultural practices in the settlements themselves. To leave their literal ancestors – the grandparents who might have raised them – and their spiritual ones again was next to impossible. And though both colored (South Africa's term for biracial people, a term I struggled with using for a long time, given its usage in the US) and black families had the right to live anywhere they liked, both economics and tradition had made those changes excruciatingly slow.

I felt pulled toward these areas, though, and asked naively if we could drive through one. He laughed and said no, that he couldn't take me or the company vehicle in, but there were tours I could go on when I returned to Cape Town. I knew that wasn't the way I wanted to visit – growing up in a tourist spot had made me quite sensitive to the impact of that sort of thing – so I just nodded and set the intention that one day, I might find a better way.

I dozed a bit, very comfy in the luxury vehicle, and when I woke up, we were driving through huge fields – the farming area in the Western Cape provides beautiful produce for the country. We were stopped by my very first roadblock, and I observed carefully, glad not to be in the driver's seat. This was a fairly official roadblock for work being done on the pavement, with a boom gate – though it was manually operated, which made me smile. Further down the road where they'd been laying fresh asphalt, we'd see a much simpler way. There, big rocks were just placed willy-nilly on top, enough of them to keep anyone from driving on it. Simple yet effective.

Since the name of the lodge was on the vehicle, we were waved through quite quickly. Before I knew it, we were in a land unlike anything I'd ever seen before. There were rocks everywhere, sandy to rust in color and ranging in size from pebbles to just plain huge. They looked like sculpture, or like baby giants had been playing blocks – piled high, the top ones often hanging precariously. It was amazing, and I asked that we stop. I thought the wind would blow me away, but I took lots of photos – only to get back in the car and discover even more magnificent pilings just down the road.

The driver took pity on me. We stopped at a great little café across from a beautiful overlook and warmed up with rooibos tea – which, it turns out, is grown only in the *fynbos*, or shrubland, of the Western Cape. I'd been drinking it for years, and here I was! Those kind of little coincidences were everywhere that first trip and continue sporadically today. They make me feel like I'm in the right place, like déjà vu. Godwinks, a friend of mine calls them, and they're something I pay a lot of attention to.

As I stood the next morning at Bushmans Kloof sipping another cup of rooibos, my whole body felt a sort of shudder. I realized then and there that this was no vacation, not at all. That this was, indeed, *ubizo* – a Zulu word I didn't know yet. A calling, and a lifelong one. The reason behind my trip across the world, yes, and more than that. The reason, perhaps, I'd been through so much in my life, the reason I had come to this planet at all. It felt like such a strong knowing, throughout every cell of my being, yet I didn't have a clue what to do with it. Not at all. Not yet. I could hear that still, calm voice telling me to just listen, to observe, to let it all unfold – and so I did.

Over the next few weeks, I would hear and see extraordinary things, beyond what I'd imagined, and have many hours sitting in game vehicles or even airport transport vans on my own, to just process it all. And I'd need it, as the messages were everywhere.

I had read a lot of Rumi, Hafiz, David Whyte, and other poets over the several years I'd felt the stirring of this call. I'd talked with wise friends and elders, trying to find ways to weave wisps of knowing into something solid, something I could stand on and move from. While I was tremendously reassured to know that others had been on similar paths centuries before me, I still hadn't figured it out. It would be a while, informed by this month in South Africa, before I would see that there was nothing to hold onto here. No safety rails, no marked path, certainly no net. I'd just have to leap, over and over, trusting that I was exactly where I was supposed to be. Even if none of it felt familiar, even if I felt I was lost. And even when I felt I'd been here before, long ago.

I spent a few days on the land of the Western Cape at Bushmans Kloof, hiking each morning to a different cave art site. I imagined what it must have been like for the early San people, learned more about their culture, and then spent time with a local youth dance group founded by the chef at the resort. I watched them tell stories through the incredible movement of their young bodies, kicking up the sand as their ancestors would have as they roamed the land, the sun highlighting the beauty of it all.

The visit blended parts of my old life, making several visits to their world class spa, with wholly new experiences – watching ostriches run across the wide plains, being surrounded by dozens of magnificent eland on a late afternoon drive, taking time to explore all the fascinating artifacts in the little museum. To say nothing of eating the most delicious food seemingly all day long. One thing you will never do at a South African lodge is starve, and Bushmans takes that responsibility very seriously. My time there was a beautiful entry, a transition between my old life and what would become my new one, though I didn't know it at the time.

I spent my last afternoon choosing one meticulously handcrafted item after another from the well-stocked gift shop and arranging to have it all shipped back to the house in Virginia, wanting to have as many reminders as possible of my time in South Africa and thinking it would be at least a year or two before I could get back. The next morning, after one more visit to see yet another cave art site and wonder over those who walked this land long ago and used such similar methods of self-expression to those I spent hours in my studio doing, yet another shiny white vehicle picked me up. I was off on the next part of my adventure.

That day was spent on the road between the rocky coast and Gansbaai, a small fishing town on the southern tip of South Africa, where I'd stay at a lovely lodge called Grootbos, in the middle of a quite unique *fynbos* – a fascinating ecosystem of shrubby open land filled with flowers, birds, and butterflies. As we drove, the land changed quickly from the giant baby's playground of stacked rocks to winding roads that quickly gained elevation and then descended rather abruptly. There were baboons galore along the way – the *calderas* (craters) in the low parts were essentially literal fruit bowls and the baboons would wait on rock walls along the sides of the road, drop into the back of one truck and then, filled with peaches, perhaps, exit and wait for another truck holding apples or plums.

The Ceres fruit juice I'd long loved in America is from a town called Ceres along the route we took. We made a stop there for petrol, and I learned about two-*rand* fees for toilet usage and how to manage the turnstiles that made sure you paid. Then I was taught my first clicks under a flowering tree by a Xhosa man relocated to the Western Cape from the Eastern Cape as many do, looking for work. He patiently coached me and my lazy American-English untrained mouth until I managed a couple of the clicks that punctuate some of the tribal languages here in South Africa. Once I returned and really began speaking isiZulu, my face actually hurt after my Zulu lessons. In the Western Hemisphere we don't really use many of the muscles in our mouths, which is why, perhaps, people say my face has changed since I've been here.

After a full day on the road, we arrived at Grootbos, where I was warmly welcomed – again, a luxury resort much more in keeping with the way I had become accustomed to traveling. There were the same questions regarding my husband's whereabouts and a room kitted out with two bathrobes, two pair of slippers, and chocolates on either side of the bed at turndown.

At first, this made me sad. I was very used to traveling with George, and we made good companions in that regard. I missed having someone to share things with. I was in contact with him and my daughter, of course, but their responses to my many photos and stories was less than enthusiastic. For so many years, my entire life had been focused on their needs and keeping a lovely home for all of us. This walkabout trip was a deviation from the norm, though I had started traveling by myself both for work and learning several years before. Not so far, though, and not so long and certainly not so enthusiastically. I think we all realized from the beginning that this trip was entirely different.

I remember spending one cold night in my beautiful suite at Grootbos by the fire, eating dinner by myself and feeling quite surprised that I was so content. I hadn't had this sort of time on my own in decades, and clearly I needed it. The time to reflect felt important, as did the chance to listen to my own heart, reconnecting with the voices that I'd blocked out since my early twenties in my determination to live a "normal" life, a good one. To be a good employee, a good wife, a good mother. At fifty-four years of age, I had only started to figure out what it meant to be myself – good or not. It was high time I did.

The next couple weeks flew by. I did everything from watching whale mothers and babies from a helicopter above the very tip of South Africa to sun-burning my feet as I laughed at penguins frolicking on the rocks along the coast going back to Cape Town. I took a tiny plane north over the Orange River and braved a disconcertingly bumpy landing due to the heat in the Kalahari Desert. I was planning to spend several days at Tswalu, an extraordinary conservation initiative located in the Northern Cape near the Botswana border.

The burnt sand, ochre, and dusty green shades of the Tswalu land are where my first real bush experiences took place. Where I knew, with conviction, that I'd been here before, some way and somehow. That deep yearning I'd been feeling for so long – those voices telling me it was almost time, and then that it was time – was rooted here, in Africa, in this soil. As dry and parched as the land was, it filled me up in some way that remains impossible to convey in words.

It was a thrilling adventure, from the time I arrived at the tiny airstrip structure with its roof full of sociable weaver nests to seeing the imprint a rhino had left in the side of the game vehicle. We took chilly morning drives, hot afternoon ones, and nighttime drives, where we used a red flashlight to see the amazing nocturnal creatures. I saw my first leopard and lion kills, walked the rocks looking for an entirely different kind of primitive art, and spent quiet time watching the sable gather around the watering hole from the little veranda off my room.

I'd happily have stayed another month, truly, yet the next part of my journey called. Before I knew it, I was back on that airstrip early one morning, boarding an even smaller plane and heading to O.R. Tambo airport for what would be the first of many transfer flights – this time, to Durban.

Durban isn't really highlighted in the South African guidebooks, though it's the third largest city and its province of KwaZulu-Natal boasts a number of really excellent game parks and lodges. Mostly, you'll read about bunny chow (not made of rabbit, I promise) and maybe surfing. For South Africans who live in areas with colder winters, Durban is a beach getaway. Over the festive season of Christmas and New Year's, it's full of cars with Gauteng and Free State license plates – much like the Florida coast, albeit more African in feel.

I hadn't originally planned on going there, but one of the friends I'd made during life coach training, Caro Fourie, suggested I meet her at Phinda, a beautiful game reserve I'd heard a lot about, where she and a mutual friend were hosting a retreat. Caro met me at the airport along with her lovely husband Edward, the epitome of a gentleman, and I spent a couple days at their beautiful home on the south coast just above the beach. Their longtime house-keeper, Thuli, was the very first Zulu, first Shembe, first *sangoma* I met, and she welcomed me very openly, taking me to her bedroom and lighting candles, showing me her tools. Looking back, that's what I recall most, though it was likely thirty minutes out of a couple days – it's fitting, I suppose, that she was the first to show me so much that would, in time, become my life.

But I hadn't made that crossover yet, so the still largely Western me climbed in the Fouries' Jaguar to make the three-and-a-half-hour-long road trip up to the Zululand bush – for the first of what would be many times. We drove through Durban, passing the outlying townships of Inanda and KwaMashu – with me wondering once again if I would ever get a chance to explore and document what life was like there – and then onward through the rolling sugar cane fields, catching glimpses of the Indian Ocean as we drove. The huge expanses of high grass looked like oceans, too, the gold at the tips catching the sun.

I was mesmerized. This entire stretch, the hills undulat-ing with little settlements of houses here and there, often with mist sitting in the shallows, feels like a fairy tale set-ting to me, even today. Back then, I was just fascinated with every bit of it – even the practice of flashing hazard lights to thank the drivers passed along the way. It all charmed me, every single aspect of it.

The drought had been going on for a couple years – and would continue for a couple more – so things were generally shades of brown and gold. Precious water was reserved for the sugar cane and the paper tree forests through which we drove next, the rows laid out in various forms of geometry and the trees growing so quickly that they were always thirsty.

Before long the highway narrowed to two lanes, and we passed places like Empangeni, Richards Bay, and Mtubatuba. I tried to pronounce all the Zulu names, corrected by Caro in her rather posh British/South African accent. The topography changed, the land flattening some and acacia trees dotting the fields, more and more traditional homes in clear view, goats and cows wandering about looking for any fresh grass they could find in the now dusty earth. The herds of Nguni cattle were breathtakingly beautiful, their spots and blotches randomly decorating their ashy hides, even though you could see the ribs of many of them given the lack of food and water.

We passed the southern entrance to what I was told was the oldest game park in all of Africa, Hluhluwe-Imfolozi, and then pulled off the N2 to visit an open air market called Zamimpilo, run by a group of mamas from the nearby community of Hlabisa. The names of these places alone fascinated me – and the market itself was heaven. I wandered and picked up item after item, again wanting to take as much of this place back to what I still considered home, limited only by how much *rand* I had in cash. The exchange rates, of course, worked in my favor, and as I'd come so far, I wanted to bring gifts back to share. We bundled everything in the ever-present plastic bags – a shock, coming from the US where they'd already been banned in some states – and put it all in the car along with my already overstuffed luggage, then continued the drive north.

We rode through what was now proper bush, all shades of beige and gold and brown. The wind blew sand in circles in a lazy way with a stunning amount of trash mixed in. My heart was so happy, there were tears in my eyes. I had no idea why, and Edward would comment on it later, since he'd been watching me in the rear view mirror as he drove. There was a deep feeling of both peace and excitement, mixed with something I still can't name, just this knowing that this place was what I'd been searching for. It made no sense, and everything in my American-programmed brain would fight it over the next week as that feeling grew stronger and stronger. By the time we'd stopped in the little town of Hluhluwe and taken the turnoff for Phinda, I couldn't even speak, tears streaming down my cheeks for no reason I understood.

I was completely verklempt, or so I thought, until the animals began to wander into view. In the midst of the dusty plain dotted with dry tufts of grass (the drought had changed the normal thick, high grass coverage), it was easy to see the warthogs wandering, digging up whatever they could find with those huge tusks. One mama was so intent on finding food that her young babies literally scrambled to keep a latch on her teats so they could continue to nurse as she moved around. Even in the afternoon heat, giraffe roamed just outside our car windows, now open to the at-once familiar smell of the bush.

The Fouries spotted game further in the distance, pointing them out to my still untrained eyes, as we drove to the private lodge where we'd spend the week with their son and his fiancé along with a mutual friend, Sarah, a dear soul I was really looking forward to spending more time with. The sand became quite deep along the way, indicating that we were now in the sand forest – Phinda is part of the Maputaland coastal forest and protects this very rare ecosystem.

The Fouries had been guests and supporters of the Phinda reserve for twenty years, and they were welcomed as old friends by a team happy they'd brought a new guest along. In retrospect, it's hard to write these words because this "friendship" would lead to a lot of pain and betrayal, though I will always be grateful to them for introducing me to this area and helping me find my way home. Back then, though, I was mesmerized and charmed by every bit of it. It was a magical week, on so many fronts.

That first day, I met Dingane Yeyeye, an old friend of Caro and Edward's and our guide for this visit. Dingane is from a local community called Ngwenya and began at Phinda as a tracker, training and eventually becoming one of their most requested guides. That first evening, he and I spent hours talking, my ears adjusting to his strong Zulu accent quite quickly. It was a welcome conversation given that I'd been traveling alone and making observations about the different tribes and the ways I saw white, colored, and black people interacting across South Africa.

Dingane confirmed some of my thoughts and filled in many holes in my rapidly growing bank of information. He was fascinated that I'd seen so much so quickly, that my interest and passion lay with the people already. The conversations would continue throughout the week and deepen far beyond the norm. He would be the first person to see me as *sangoma,* or traditional healer, and he created a wonderful opportunity for us to do ceremony in the sand forest toward the end of the week, ending up with tequila accidentally poured in his eye for his troubles!

I wasn't prepared at all for how much I'd love every aspect of this place, how deeply I would feel a connection to the land, the creatures, and the people. The days would unfold beautifully over the week we were there – Caro orchestrating something new every day and all four of the Fouries and Dingane teaching me the tools I'd eventually need for life in the bush. It was wonderful to be in the game viewer early each morning, snuggled under a blanket with my dear friend, Sarah, who is American but lives in the Middle East. We'd spent a week at Kripalu, the yoga center in western Massachusetts, just months before, studying trauma treatment with Bessel Van der Kolk, and to be here together in Africa was almost surreal.

After the morning drives and the inevitably great animal sightings, given Dingane's expertise and dedication which bordered on obsession from time to time, there was always a huge breakfast laid out for us on the veranda – fresh pawpaw and pineapple (it turned out all my favorite fruits are grown in KZN, even litchi), baked goods, meats and cheese, yogurt and muesli – the table was full. And then Sam, the beloved chef who'd been at Phinda forever, would come and make us eggs or pancakes.

In a place where I would learn early that many ate only the local dishes like maize-based *pap* and *phutu* for breakfast, lunch, and dinner, this opulence would soon make me uncomfortable. I can't imagine how it feels to local staff, working long hours for the equivalent of $200 US a month and struggling to provide for their children while guests paid three times that amount per day to stay at the lodge. Yet those guest fees create many jobs along with protecting the animals, providing funds for conservation and community projects, and bringing the land back to its natural state after generations of farmers drove the wildlife out.

It's a real quandary and one reason that I've come to see over my years here that there really is no black or white, no good or bad. Life is what you make of it, and it comes with dips and curves and decisions with no real right or wrong answer. From my now-removed perspective, I see that life in the United States, and perhaps in the Western world in general, is about being comfortable, which means different things to different people, of course, but it is ultimately what drives everything from business to politics. Being uncomfortable – or unsafe – is just not well-tolerated.

For example: more than once, when showing someone from abroad around, I've been asked if I couldn't just get "them" to pick up their trash, to recycle. The piles of glass bottles and cans, the old plastic blowing around in the dusty wind, can make those from suburbs of manicured lawns and garage doors mandated to be closed by a certain hour extremely uncomfortable. Yet without knowing the history and the sociology of this place, judgment is more than a bit unfair. The priorities of other societies and cultures have no real place here in Africa, despite generations of impact in the form of colonization and, more recently, the media.

This first visit planted a seed deep inside me. The paleo-anthropological site that many call the cradle of humankind lies just outside Johannesburg, and yet the very people who have inhabited this place the longest are still seen by many as somewhat less than, even savage. Even in my first days in South Africa, my heart was drawn to the tribal people, as it had been throughout my life. Visiting places like the District Six museum in Cape Town, where I sat on a bench labeled "White" (actually, *Blanke,* which happened to be my maiden surname), inspired what I'm sure will be a lifelong quest to understand how one group of people can simply decide that they are infinitely better than another. To say nothing of believing they have a right to treat that group of people in such inhumane ways, to use them to further their own end goals of profit and comfort. How had this come to be?

As Audrey Smedley wrote at the end of the 20th century, "All anthropologists should understand that 'race' has no intrinsic relationship to human biological diversity, that such diversity is a natural product of primarily evolutionary forces while 'race' is a social invention." (Origin of the idea of race, *Anthropology Newsletter,* November 1997)

Still, between the 1600s and 1800s, common belief became that there was a concept such as "race," a social hierarchy in which white people of European descent rose to the top and black people of African blood were pushed to the bottom. The first white settlers arrived in Jamestown, Virginia, on the east coast of what would become the United States in 1607. The first African slaves were brought to Virginia in 1619. A year later, the Pilgrims, my biological ancestors, arrived in Plymouth, Massachusetts – just miles from where I would grow up – making the first African "immigrants" among the very first "settlers," since the slave ships arrived a year earlier.

The Dutch arrived in Cape Town, South Africa, only thirty-two years later, bringing colonialism to a land previously ruled by myriad African tribes. The enslavement of human beings wasn't a new concept, of course, yet what we think of as slavery today was born, and many South Africans are descended from those brought to the Cape Colony from 1653 through the early 1800s, just as many Americans today are descended from the occupants of those early slave ships brought to the coast of the American colonies.

Generations later, in the 1830s, a man named Samuel Morton, a physician in Philadelphia and the originator of the "American School" of ethnography that claimed that the difference between humans was one of species rather than just variety, decided that he could define the intellectual ability of a race by skull capacity. He filled the skulls he collected with pepper seeds to determine volume and claimed that those with larger brains – defined by skull capacity – had higher intellectual capacity and a smaller brain had less intellectual potential. I'll leave it to you to guess which skulls had European roots and which were

African. He rooted his work in the Bible, of course, though he rejected the creation story of Adam and Eve, deciding there was ample biblical evidence to support that each race was created separately, and further supported his own theory by studying three mummies from ancient Egypt and pronouncing that races had been separate from the beginning. In doing so, he legitimized, in the minds of many, generations of the inhumane use of one group of human beings to enable another group to flourish in ways that may never be made right. And try as many might, those beliefs are proving almost impossible to change.

I don't get it. I never have. I'd never say that I am colorblind – as an artist, that would be ridiculous – yet it's beyond my comprehension that the color of one's skin or the width of your nose can make you better than someone else. I sleep next to a man with far darker skin than my own, and I can tell you that he is just that – a man. One of the best I've ever known. I constantly remind my granddaughters, as indoctrinated as many young girls are to love the flowing yellow locks of Disney princesses and Barbie, that their brown skin is beautiful in its own right, yes, but also that they are brilliant, good, and kind, and that one kind of skin or hair is no better than another.

This effort is met with mixed results, as they somehow believe that I look like Barbie and therefore that makes blond hair even better, but I'm happy to make this a long-term project. As a family, we are doing our best to raise them to be strong Zulu women who will both respect tradition and be well-equipped to bring their own gifts to the world as it changes, and to see the beauty of their own crowns.

Back at Phinda in 2015, though, I was still observing. I saw the differences between white and black staff at the lodges – not only in positions and pay but in the way they were treated by management. That's not a criticism of Phinda or any of the lodges I visited – they all are run as well or better than any you'll find in the country. It's just the way things are, as I was told by everyone I questioned, most of them surprised that I'd even ask. There's a resignation that is pervasive here now, twenty-seven years post-apartheid.

I've been told that when apartheid ended, black adults everywhere in South Africa thought that things would change far more rapidly than was probably realistic. Babies born in 1994 were believed to be lucky – they would never experience the limitations their elders had, they would be educated in the same way as whites, they would have far more opportunities. The sad fact is that it just hasn't happened. There's significant trauma, of course, country wide, and it will take generations to heal, I imagine.

I find it interesting that there's a deeply ingrained fear amongst the white residents, both English and Afrikaans in origin, of the tribal people having far more freedom and perhaps "doing God knows what" to them in retribution. This is certainly not helped by conspiracy theories around the murder of white South African farmers – something outside my personal experience so I hesitate to comment on it. What I do know is that, sadly, farmers of all skin colors are being killed.

The black African people I speak with seem to want to forget the past and move forward. Their focus is on things being done differently, their desire to be afforded new opportunities denied to them and their ancestors for so long, and on their ancestral land being restored to them, which is a very tricky matter indeed.

The bottom line is that both sides – and the colored and the Indian and Malay populations as well, which are only on the periphery of my understanding – did horrifying things to each other. That's what the Truth and Reconciliation Commission and its meetings were intended to do: let people openly air what had happened and understand the impact of all the actions on everyone. Archbishop Tutu and Fr. Michael Lapsley, who spearheaded the Commission, would go on to found the Institute for the Healing of Memories to continue that work, something I continue to applaud and hope to be more involved with. Yet there is still a great burden of grief, anger, hatred, and fear. I hope that time will heal all, perhaps in ways we cannot yet comprehend.

When I tell people I've been betrayed more than once here in South Africa and lost a lot of trust as well as a lot of money, people on both sides of the globe assume those betrayals have been by black people. Sometimes it has been – the six years since I came to SA permanently have been an extraordinary training ground. Yet my greatest loss here, financially and perhaps psychologically, has been due to the very family with whom I spent this first week in Zululand. This makes a horrible kind of sense to me. The people who've hurt me the most have always been those who were to be my family, historically, and seeing this has helped me to change this pattern over time.

I felt more at ease being on holiday with the Fouries than I ever had with my husband or my family of origin. I felt connected, especially to their son, Brad – a muscular, talented thirty-odd-year-old who had recently become engaged to the beautiful Jacqueline. I knew of them from online posts – they both modeled for fitness magazine cover stories and were very much "beautiful people" so I honestly didn't expect to have much in common with them.

But in those hours of game drives and sitting around the pool hoping the elephants would come and join us, we formed a solid connection. I had all sorts of intuitive insights about some past life ties or something that tugged at me. I had no idea what was to come, of course, yet we all felt that somehow, we would be part of each other's lives. We fit so much into that week – covered so much land, saw the effects of the drought in ways that were both disturbing and inspiring, met the team that has healed the reserve in so many ways, did ceremony in the sand forest, drummed and danced with Dingane's friends, ate and ate and ate some more. I had never felt so much like I belonged to a place I'd never been before, in less than a week. It was awesome and unsettling, too, in that I had no idea what to do about this pull I felt to be right there in the midst of the dust and dirt, listening to the stories Sam, Dingane, and others told each night. On the last day, we visited the gift shop at the southern end of the reserve where I continued to shop like a fiend, asking them to ship everything back to the US for me. Old habits die hard and it was the only way I knew to be sure I had plenty of South Africa with me, once I returned to the house in Virginia.

We were leaving the next morning so I needed to pack, which I did while managing to pretty much stay in denial about the departure. I didn't sleep much that night – my dreams seemed to be downloading memories of ceremonies and places I'd yet to see. Finally, I got up around 4:30 and made my way out to the watering hole behind the house as the sun began to light up the sky. I heard rustling noises on the veranda – we'd have one last morning game drive so the staff was getting tea and coffee and rusks ready for us, as usual – yet my focus was on a pair of woolly-necked storks at the edge of the water, watching for bugs or maybe fish, standing stock still.

Tears poured down my face, my heart so deeply sad about leaving that it literally hurt and my mind very con-fused as to what to make of all this. I sensed someone behind me and turned, wiping my eyes on the not very absorptive sleeve of my sunscreen-impregnated safari shirt. It was Dingane, bless him, holding a china teacup and sau-cer in his rough hands and letting out a strong *"Haibo"* (an expression of shock or surprise) over seeing me in tears for the first time. I'm sure it wasn't a pretty picture but brave man that he is, he told me to stop crying – further research has shown that no Zulu man can stand to see a woman cry – and that we'd make a plan, which is a very typical South African response to any and all problems.

We talked until the others came out, about my fear that I'd never be able to come back and my resistance to leaving at all. Dingane reassured me that I'd be back, brushing aside my wails that I couldn't return until at least June of 2016, saying he knew it would be much sooner than that. And, he added, while many guests promised to return, few did. Some, he said, made noises about moving to SA, or at least spending much of their time there – but that rarely actually happened. "You, though, you belong here," he told me. "You have a black heart, a Zulu heart, and you love the people. You can do it, you can come home, and stay."

I listened and nodded, trying to take in his words so that I could pull them back up when I needed to, when winter arrived in Virginia and I'd wish I had the warm African sun shining on my back and warming my soul.

We made our last drive, my tears leaking out only intermittently and Dingane looking back to check on me off and on, and then returned to the homestead for one more gigantic breakfast. Sam piled our plates even higher than usual. Sarah, who would accompany me on the last few days of this trip, and I said our goodbyes to the Fouries. Caro assured me that South Africa was in my blood now and that I would return. Then the whole team came from the house to sing us on our way, causing the tears to run wild again. Dingane hugged me one last time, telling me he'd see me soon, and Sam handed over enough snacks to keep us from starving on our short flight to Mpumalanga. The driver kindly ignored my tears.

Sarah and I settled into companionable silence as we watched the bush fade into the distance. The paper tree forests flew by and the cows still foraged patiently as we drove back to Durban for our flight to the Mpumalanga airport. The enormity of all I'd experienced that week — and on the entire trip thus far – hit me, and I sat in a sort of stunned state until we got to King Shaka airport. We made good use of the *biltong* and dried mango Sam had packed for us, and before we knew it, we'd arrived at a smaller thatch-roofed building housing the airport many used to visit the many lodges around Kruger National Park in Mpumalanga.

We weren't there for a safari, though – that would wait for another time. We planned to spend a couple days visiting with Kate Groch, one of the most amazing people I've met to date, and her daughter, Maya, at The Good Work Foundation, the digital learning center she founded. Kate and Martha Beck, with whom I studied to be a life coach and from whom I'd heard so much about South Africa over the years, are dear friends so this connection was yet another gift of that circle.

I had purchased art supplies to lead an expressive arts day with the kids at the GWF. As usual, I had no idea how it would actually work, but it did. Sarah and another Sara – a fellow Martha Beck-trained coach in Pretoria I'd gotten to know online – and this second Sara's son worked with me, and we ended up creating with over 100 children in one day.

What I remember most about the visit, though, was being incredibly inspired by Kate. She is a decade or so younger than me, South African of British descent, and as much a product of being raised in apartheid South Africa as any I would come to know. Yet she had a black daughter, one of the brightest, most creative young lights I've ever met, and she interacted with her almost entirely black team in a way that I'd not seen in the whole month I'd been in the country. She helped me to see what was possible, that humanity could win over social constructs, and that investing oneself in the young of the tribal communities could look a whole lot different than the traditional hand-out or the come-in-and-take-over model I'd seen so much of. Kate had gathered a group of really wonderful souls, and their input was reflected in the shiny eyes of the count-less children and youth.

As full as I was from the week at Phinda, I could barely take it all in, yet it has stuck with me over time. Kate's grace, strength, and wisdom – as well as her expansive sense of humor – have informed all I do. I can only hope, once I finish my stumbling first steps in trying to do some good here, that my work comes anywhere close to what she's accomplished.

The time there passed quite quickly. The second Sara had volunteered to drive me back to O.R. Tambo for my flight back to Washington. And so that huge bag got packed up one more time and stuffed in yet another boot, and then we were off. In some sort of divine stroke of luck, we had to make one last stop at a place called Kaapsehoop, which sits high up on rock fields and is known now for its beautiful small village, bed and breakfasts, and the wild horses that roam the lovely fields and forests.

Sara was scouting locations for an upcoming Martha Beck coach gathering in February, and while I was happy to help, I was sad to think I wouldn't be there when it took place. We visited a gorgeous small farmstead, had a delicious lunch, and played with the horses. It was the per-fect place to ground and settle myself before the long flight back to the States, and I added it to my growing list of places to visit whenever I could return.

We climbed back into the car and before I knew it, we were outside the international terminal at Tambo. I said my goodbyes and thank-yous to Sara and her son, Jacobus, got my luggage checked in, then headed to the business class lounge to wait until it was time to board.

There, it hit me, hard, that I really did not want to go. So hard that I could only pray. For insight, for guidance, for knowing that somehow I'd find my way back. And for peace in my heart, as I really, really didn't understand any of what was happening inside me. All I could do was continue to surrender and allow things to unfold over time.

I'd fallen in love with other places before. I'd felt more at home in Ireland, Scotland, and Spain than I ever had in the US. Yet this, I knew, was something different. I was excited and anxious and scared – so many emotions – and there was nothing to be done about it. I boarded the plane, whispering goodbye to South Africa, put on my headphones, and listened to music the whole way back, trying to calm myself before arriving back to what I knew was no longer where I belonged.

Thirteen

I was born in July, a typical Cancerian, and have always preferred to be in my own nest. Usually, after traveling, I couldn't wait to go home. Not this time. I found I was dreading walking into my house in Virginia. I had shifted gears somehow and this new, expanded version of me wasn't going to fit back into the old packaging.

I was a seasoned traveler and had never thought about stowing away on a plane to return to wherever I'd come from. This time I did – repeatedly over the course of the twenty-four-hour flight back to Washington, DC. I wondered if that were possible, or if I could just buy a return ticket and go right back. I spent a considerable amount of the long flight thinking about any other options. Eventually I gave up. I realized I didn't have a choice. But I made careful note never to put myself in the situation of having to do something I clearly knew was wrong for me ever again.

Wheels down at Dulles, I felt sick to my stomach when the flight attendant started doing the welcome spiel in her oh-so-American accent. Unlike the other South African Air announcements, there were no phrases in isiZulu or Xhosa, just flat out "here's the deal, let's get you off the plane" in American-English.

I went into autopilot, shepherded by the other passengers onto the bus and then through US Customs, where I assured the officers that sadly, no, I had no biltong (dried meat). I watched all the other families reunite (no one had made the twenty-minute trip to come and greet me) before finding my driver and chatting with him about the trip while answering his many questions. Before I knew it, I was in front of my beautiful, broad wooden door. I was home, and yet I really, really wasn't.

It was the day before Thanksgiving. My in-laws were already there, and Lina was home from school along with a friend. We all chatted for a bit and talked about preparations for Thanksgiving dinner the next day. There weren't a lot of questions. George and Lina seemed happy enough to have me home, but there was a definite emotional separation that had happened, a slight chill in the air. I had done something far outside the norm, going on this trip, and it felt that they saw it as some sort of betrayal. Given the way I'd grown up, with not only love but basic things like food being taken away if I did something my mother didn't approve of, I still – at that point – tended to expect the same, so how much of that feeling was simply within me, I don't know.

Over the next several days, all I could do was talk about South Africa. Those at home didn't seem to want to hear it, but fortunately there were friends who did, so I was able to unpack it a bit. In between going on and on about this place I'd fallen in love with, I cried. A lot. The grief I felt over leaving SA was deep, and yet the confusion about what all this meant was even greater. How could I have been more at ease with people I'd just met than I was in my own "home" with my family? How could I know that I was tied to places I'd never been before in ways that felt more true and more real than I'd ever felt in my life? How could I miss a place and a people this intensely, when I'd spent mere days there?

I'd let myself wallow in it all a bit, call a wise friend and vent for a while, then sort through my thousands of South African photos on my big screen, letting the animals and the trees and the skies envelop me on some soul level. It wasn't the same as being back there, though.

Even George seemed to see and feel my distress – he came in my office one morning sure he'd brought the cure:

a pale yellow Post-it note with the dates for two weeks in July scrawled on it. Seven months away. He cheerfully explained he'd figured out that he could take time off then, that we could go back to South Africa together.

I burst into tears. Again. I couldn't help it. Poor guy – he quickly added that I could stay longer and see my friends, but that made me sob even harder. I realized that I'd never last until July, that it was far too short a visit, and that, most significantly, I didn't want to go with him. I kept that last part to myself, of course, to be examined when I was on my own.

It surprised me, how strongly I felt about it. Part of it was the way George travelled, the privilege and the way he would treat people I loved. He's not a bad man, not at all – and yet his position had changed him. I didn't often see the man I married anymore, the one I'd felt was one of the truest Christians I'd ever met. And I didn't really know the man he'd become, or like him much on many days. Our values were no longer the same, and I knew that in visiting South Africa, they would clash in extreme ways.

I was dreaming of an entirely different life each night, seeing ceremony and wildness, then trying to be the wife and mother I'd been before I left during the days. My inner world scared him – I had to hide my tarot cards and other tools I used in my work, something I tried to ignore yet was obviously just not right. It wasn't working, our marriage, no matter how hard I tried.

After the avalanche of tears over the Post-it Note, even George could see that I needed to go back much sooner than July, so with his hesitant agreement, I began making plans to return early in the new year. Facebook, in its creepy/wise way, began to show me all sorts of SA-based posts. There was a lodge for sale near Phinda, which I filed under "maybe someday," and two organizations that caught my eye: the previously mentioned Institute for the Healing of Memories (IHOM) and African Impact (AI), a paid volunteerism project with locations all over Africa.

I discovered that IHOM had a training coming up for facilitators in early April and that AI had volunteer programs beginning in January. I got busy filling out forms and collecting all the required documentation. Obviously, a trip back to SA to work with either or both of these organizations would be a very different experience than my five-star tour, and that was just fine with me – something I'd remind myself of over Rice Krispie and boxed milk breakfasts to come.

We agreed, George and I, that I'd return to South Africa and try to assess this calling I was feeling so strongly for three months – the maximum period a holiday visa allows. Lina was less than pleased. While she asked me a lot of questions, so many that I felt I was in a film noir being grilled under bright lights by a detective, she wouldn't say anything straight out. How could I expect her to understand, given that I didn't really understand it myself?

In early December, my Aunt Laney, my mother's sister and my godmother, who had been in the grips of Alzheimer's disease for a decade or so, died. When I'd separated from my parents, I hadn't wanted the other parts of my mother's family to get caught up in the whole mess, so I'd removed myself from their orbit, as I had with my siblings, something I'd come to regret. But that past September, when I was on that retreat on the Cape, I'd begun to mend those fences and had been warmly welcomed.

Given all that, I was able to be there to say goodbye to the woman who'd been like another mother to me, who I loved and was loved by, even when we clashed. George left after the funeral, but I stayed on the Cape with my childhood best friend, happy to have more time with her and wanting to talk with my uncle and only surviving aunt, both quite elderly now, and with my cousins, getting to know them better as adults. I'm so glad now that I did, as I'm not sure when I'll next see them all.

The timing couldn't have been better, and I imagine Aunt Laney, up there somewhere, pulling strings to make it happen. In talking with my cousin Jack, who is about fifteen years older than me, I discovered something I hadn't known before, at least not consciously. When I told him I'd return to South Africa early in the new year, he assumed automatically that I was going to stay this time. This surprised me – somewhere deep inside I wondered, too, yet I hadn't uttered those words to anyone. I couldn't even fathom the concept myself, to be honest. All I knew at this point was that I couldn't go back to my old life and I had no idea what a new one – wherever that might be – would look like.

Jack then told me this story, a bit surprised I didn't remember. When I was four-and-a-half years old, I asked my parents to take me to see him at college. For some reason they did, before or after one of my hospital visits. Once there, I asked him to take me to the university "liberry"

– he assumed so that I could show him I'd learned to read. Once we trudged through the snow to get there, he asked me what book I wanted to look for. I told him that it wasn't for me, it was for him. He said that was fine and asked what the name of the book was – and I told him that he needed, please, to find the book to teach me Zulu, since I could only read in English so far.

Something in me knew. Even at four years old – and a half. And somehow the timing of my aunt's death, Jack's mother, brought us both home to his sister's wooden kitchen table at the very same time, so I could hear this and know it again for myself. Life is funny, isn't it? I hadn't seen Jack for decades before this visit.

Back in DC, my plans for volunteering through African Impact firmed up. I needed to do all the things – doctor appointments, prescriptions, winding up with coaching clients, seeing friends – before we left for our long planned trip to Zurich, Switzerland for our family Christmas on the 22nd. I managed somehow to do all that and pack for both Switzerland and South Africa, though packing had always been a crazy-making ordeal for me, and this time it was for three months. I was out of my comfort zone in more ways than one.

The plan was to spend the holiday with George and Lina in Zurich, then fly to Heathrow with them, where they would return to Washington and I'd go on to Joburg. As things worked out, I'd fly through New Year's Eve and arrive first thing on the first day of 2016, which seemed a fitting way to begin a new phase of life.

I did all the practical things to make this happen as George and Lina dealt with any feelings they had without really talking much about it. We thought that I'd stay through the end of March and see how it went, then maybe return over the summer. One option was that I would split my time that way – three months in SA, three in the US – and see how it went, but wanted to see how this trip went first. George talked about supporting whatever charitable work I'd do there, both of us trying to create something that worked, something that would allow us to stay married, albeit in a different way.

The conversation with Jack played in my head. I certainly had an awareness that this might be a permanent thing but my brain couldn't begin to believe it. Things between the three of us had been different since I came back, and I was hoping that some time away together might give us the opportunity to talk it all out, to come to some understanding.

Unfortunately, as our departure got closer, things unraveled further still. George and I had been sleeping in separate rooms, mostly, for a couple years now, and he booked separate hotel rooms for the first time ever – putting himself in a luxury suite, Lina in a lovely guest room, and me in a tiny quarters at the back of this incredibly deluxe hotel. The level of passive-aggressive behavior, always a thing between us, was rising, and it made me feel more than ever that I just didn't belong with him. And that I didn't really matter to either of them very much - just my role, my abilities to care for their needs.

I couldn't blame Lina. I had shown her, perhaps unwittingly but still, that I would put her, George, and everyone else before my own needs. Even when it made me sick, both physically and emotionally. She was twenty-two years old by this point – several years older than I'd been when I left home – and she'd watched me struggle since my suicide attempt when she was only five years old. I can only imagine what that brought up in her, and what internal struggles she's had to contend with since my leaving.

She would spend hours, late into the night in that tiny hotel room in Zurich, querying me about all sorts of things that mostly had nothing to do with anything, being careful not to say a word about her own feelings. I'm still not sure what answers she was looking for, to be honest. As I said again and again to her then, I didn't really know what would happen, how life would look. I just knew I needed more time in South Africa to sort through it all.

The days were full, that week in Zurich. We were traveling, as we sometimes did, with one of George's law partners from Chicago, a gentle soul and outstanding human being named Jon. I'm sure he picked up on the strain between us, but ever the gentleman he truly is, he never said a word. I tried to hide the fact that I used a different lift to access my hotel room, though by the end of the trip even that pretense had dropped.

We ate incredible meals, including at my favorite restaurant right next to FIFA – a foreshadowing, perhaps, of living in a soccer-obsessed country. We walked in the northern European woods and visited the picturesque zoo along with a charming Swiss village high in the mountains.

And, in between, I watched the balding, paunchy yet very wealthy Russian men with their much younger, perfectly formed women carrying pricey designer bags that would, if sold, feed a village in the rural areas I'd be returning to soon.

While I wasn't up to that standard, I had been living a lifestyle that had never brought me the comfort or belonging I'd been taught to believe it would. I'd certainly enjoyed the rewards of George's work and had done all I could to help him be successful, yet that role, along with all the trappings of the American dream, had never felt like it truly fit me. I'd buried myself, my values, and my truth so deeply that it had taken decades to begin to unearth my real identity – something I expect I'll be doing for the rest of my life. I remain grateful for all the opportunities to travel, see the world, and expand my horizons on so many levels, yet these days I am content to be right where I am and bring whatever good I can to this place that speaks to me so strongly, this ground that feels so fundamental, so human.

Before I knew it, the last day of the year arrived. I packed once again, putting all my "good" clothes in one suitcase to send back to the Virginia house with my family, folding them neatly and realizing, on some level, that I wouldn't need them again, that I was saying goodbye to a lifestyle as well as to my husband and daughter. For how long, I didn't know. My bags for South Africa stood ready to go, full of summer clothing as I'd be switching seasons, too, as I headed into the heat of January in Limpopo, where I would do my first volunteer stint.

One of the hotel's impressively uniformed staff came and took my bags to the lobby, where I met George and

Lina and said goodbye to our friend, Jon, who would stay on through New Year's. Then we three got into the shiny SUV for the trip to the airport. I don't remember what we said to each other on that leg of the trip, or in the Zurich airport. I do recall trying hard to stay in the moment – needing every bit of Buddhist training I'd done to even begin to achieve that. I looked at Lina and George, feeling so much love and sadness all swirled together, and also something that felt like defeat. I'd tried, I really had, but I had no idea what they were thinking or feeling. I lived with this man for twenty-six years of my life, and I still had absolutely no idea what went on in his head, in his heart. Lina, certainly, was shutting down emotionally – maybe we all were. Despite our late-night grilling sessions, I didn't feel she had any idea why I was leaving, or even that I had the right to pursue dreams of my own beyond being her mother. Again, I'd never really shown her that I did. I know she believed that there must be another man – all those romantic comedies, perhaps, we'd watched over the years while George was away working. Maybe that was easier for her to believe than that I'd leave of my own volition.

While, at this point, I assumed that we would be in touch daily – as long as the Wi-Fi and network held out anyway – I'd soon learn that there wasn't much interest on her part in staying in touch. There was this feeling of resentment already brewing, and while I was only sure I'd be gone a few months, there was an air of finality that I didn't really understand on that day. I had a very uneasy feeling, and my heart felt stretched in two directions. All I could do was try to trust that the path I was taking, would, in the end, serve all of us well, and that one day we could talk about it together.

Still, when I left my family at Heathrow Airport on the morning of 31 December 2015, it was incredibly painful. And, in an odd way, exhilarating. Three years earlier, when I'd told George I couldn't do it anymore, that I wanted a divorce, he'd asked what I really wanted. And my answer had been "freedom."

I guess that's what I started to feel in the vast hall at Heathrow, lined by all the top international design stores. Those shops had been a big part of my life, and no longer would be in any way a part of my new life, going forward.

That day, I didn't know. I didn't know if I would stay married, if I'd return to the home I'd so carefully created for us in Falls Church, if I'd piece together a bi-continental lifestyle. I didn't know anything, really. It was one of the biggest leaps I would make, that separating in the terminal and boarding different aircraft – leaving the man who had been my husband for so long and the adult daughter I'd always wanted to be so much closer to. It hurt, on so many levels. It was the end, but it was also the beginning of something wholly new.

Fourteen

The invitation Archbishop Tutu had made to me in the White House five years before still resounded in my memory as I made my way to my volunteer gig with African Impact. I puzzled over it, then let it go, convincing myself that he must say that to everyone. He didn't really know me – surely he'd confused me with someone else. And what the heck did he mean by "it's time to come home" anyway? If I hadn't had the photo of us, I'd have been convinced that I dreamt the whole thing.

I had the training for Tutu's Institute for the Healing of Memories in mind, but that was over three months away – and I didn't yet know if I'd be staying that long, not for certain. In addition to the paid volunteer work I'd be doing with AI, spending a few weeks on a wild-life conservation project up north, and then more time on community/healthcare work around St. Lucia, KZN, I promised myself a splurge on a week or so of tracking on foot with my favorite trackers and guides at the Phinda game reserve. Then I'd decided I'd fit in a quick trip to Madrid to see expat friends before they returned to the States, which would also fulfil my obligation to renew my holiday visa if I decided to return to South Africa and do the IHOM training in Cape Town.

I arrived at O.R. Tambo airport in Johannesburg early on the first day of the new year and spent most of that first night in the airport hotel, wondering and dreaming where all this would lead me. Being back on South African soil was scary and exciting and everything in between, and I was anxious to begin what felt like the rest of my life.

The next morning, I wandered over to the international terminal to meet up with the other AI volunteers arriving that day and the driver who would take us to the small guest lodge where we'd spend the night before heading to Dumela Lodge in Limpopo. I soon found myself in a van with six people from all over the world, many of whom were younger than my daughter. We began to bond as a group that first night in that rundown place with the grumpy driver, all of us wondering a bit if we'd made a mistake as no one had welcomed us in any way and none of us understood what the plan was going forward. It was all a far cry, of course, from the upscale places I'd stayed on my first trip to SA.

The next day, though, we drove through the awe-inspiring Drakensberg mountains, and our moods improved dramatically. Our arrival at Dumela Lodge just over the Limpopo province border proved we had indeed found our way to a place we'd all come to love. There, I spent my first few weeks in a very basic rondavel, single occupancy, along with myriad geckos, skinks, and some pretty spectacular spiders for company. Rondavels are everywhere in South Africa – traditional round thatch-roofed houses, typically four to six meters in diameter, with one open room. Usually there's an outside toilet, but this one, like many, had been updated for white people with an internal full bathroom.

South Africa was two years into a four-year drought, and the bush was very sparse, which made our job of photographing and creating identification kits for the individual rhinos and elephants easier at the reserves we were assisting through African Impact. As at most game reserves then, they were doing supplemental feeding given that the normal grasses weren't growing due to lack of water, and that changed some of the animals' natural behaviors. Yet it also let us get to know individual creatures, since they would come back to feed on the lucerne (a South African variant of alfalfa) each day.

There was a tiny female rhino born the day before we arrived, and she danced around her mother like a satellite circling a planet. She was very social and imprinted on the buffalo as they fed together. She acted a bit like a ballerina and a bit like a buffalo, and was quite something to watch. At one point, they couldn't find her or her mother on the reserve. They'd called out helicopters and then called us at the volunteer project to search for them from the game vehicles. Thanks to all I'd been taught my first visit at Phinda, I was able to find them, which made me feel as if I'd really begun to be at home in the bush.

Sadly, when that little rhino was five months old and I was getting settled in my life in the Zululand bush, I opened my Facebook app to see a video of her erratically, frantically dancing around the body of her mother, who'd been brutally attacked and killed for her horn by poachers. That was a big lesson for me in how life is here – for the animals as well as the people.

I've come to learn that Africa has a markedly different attitude about the fragility – and the fleetingness – of life. Being fragile doesn't work here. Everyone knows that a long life isn't guaranteed, so they believe it's best to enjoy the time you have and really live your days. Where in America, there's a lot of calendaring and life planning, here anything can happen and usually does. Plans often go out the window, and you have to learn to adapt quickly.

It suits me. It feels more honest. That's why I've tried to live my life differently here than I did in the States. I've learned that life is to be enjoyed, every single minute. There is evil, of course, everywhere. And there is so much good. I've seen this throughout my life, and yet never more clearly than I've seen it here in South Africa, in the time I've spent in the bush. In those early months, tracking quickly became a big part of my new life. I returned to Phinda several times in those first months, in between volunteer gigs, and I learned more about it from the best. I am never happier than out in the bush, on foot, with good company and my senses wide open.

I discovered tracking has a vocabulary, both spoken and wordless, that's all its own. My favorite directive became "loop around," a phrase I've come to love both literally and metaphorically. I first heard it while sitting in the game vehicle assigned to me at Tswalu, a beautiful reserve in the Kalahari Desert not too far from Namibia, during my first visit to South Africa. The vehicle itself proudly wore a huge dent on its right side, but Andrew, the guide who drove it, was disturbed by it. He made his apologies when he first picked me up at the tiny little airport with the thatched roof. It seemed a rhino had made a bit of a strong show of his territorial rights a couple days before and had punched the metal in with his horn. Andrew hadn't had time to get it fixed before my arrival, and he and the tracker, Josiah, were worried it would scare me off. Far from it. It only made me grin widely and ask when our first game drive was.

That trip, I'd only had to wait a few hours, going through the pleasantries of signing in, enjoying a welcome drink to settle my stomach after the very bumpy business of landing in a small plane in extreme heat, and settling into my room. I'd have been quite happy to spend that first afternoon on my little veranda, watching the incredibly beautiful sable, a very large buck, kneeling in the way only they do at the watering hole only meters away, but soon it was time for my first drive in wild territory. I'd loved the game reserve drives and excursions at Bushmans Kloof – especially when we found ourselves surrounded by dozens of magnificent eland, to this day my favorite antelope – but this, I knew, would be far more exciting.

Game viewers are open-roofed, four-wheel-drive vehicles adapted for off-road use, and they're tall. Andrew and Josiah climbed in nimbly, and I followed suit, more awkwardly. It would take time to learn to quickly get in and out of the game viewers, though I've mastered it now. I would learn later that my guides had heard on the radio system from colleagues that there was something special, a rare sighting, roaming about that afternoon, so they were eager to investigate, and off we went at rather high speed.

As we bumped along, sand flying left and right, the winter sun was already lowering in the sky. Andrew, who was driving, made attempts at narrating our route, but it was just too hard to talk. I was happy to simply drink in my new surroundings – all terra cotta and gold with only isolated bits of sage green here and there, given the drought. There were jagged rocks and low mountains in the background. Andrew would slow here and there so Josiah, tracking, could scan the ground, occasionally dismounting from his seat off the front of the jeep to check things out. At the time, I had no idea what he was looking for, but now I know he was checking for footprints and scat, any telltale signs of animal activity.

Josiah pointed out a few sets of lion prints – lion prints! He said they were old, though, so I shouldn't get too excited. We carried on, and at our fourth or fifth stop, I could sense a shift in the energy of both the guides. They had me lean down off the vehicle but asked that I didn't get out – something I'd come to see as a good sign later. Could I, they wanted to know, identify the track next to our rear tire?

I knew it had to be a cat, but that it wasn't the same as the lion prints we'd seen earlier. I made a wild guess: a leopard? Their jaws dropped; I was right. These were fresh prints, so off we went, more slowly this time, weaving a bit on the sandy road as Josiah followed the tracks ... until they disappeared. I sat back, sure that was the end of the adventure. I was still smiling. I'd very much enjoyed the chase, the moving air cooling me down a bit, and I was happy to be in such beautiful surroundings.

And then I heard those words for the first time: "No worries, we'll just loop around and find him." Loop around. I had no idea what that meant and wouldn't understand for a while that though it sounds like a wild goose chase – and can certainly feel that way sometimes – it means to follow the roads in a circle or square to see if the animal has crossed any of them and narrow in on a plan to locate it.

We took the next right on what could hardly be called a road but did have worn tire tracks. It was less sandy, grassier, so I don't know how Josiah saw anything, but he was very focused. We took the next right and continued at low speed on the sand road.

At what I could loosely call the next intersection, he got out (another good sign), walked around in circles for a bit, then grabbed his radio and went further, silently motioning for us to stay. Guides are typically trained in gun safety and carry a rifle. Trackers, though, are usually not armed, except sometimes with a *panga,* or machete. I can't remember if Josiah carried a *panga* or not. Off he went, though, this gentle giant of a guy who walked as silently as anyone I've ever known in his size 13 boots, looking for a leopard. This blew my mind at the time, and still brings up a lot of respect – there aren't many left who can do this with such confidence and dedication. It's an art and a skill that I fervently hope will be kept alive.

Josiah came back, flashed a huge grin, and used hand signals to show Andrew where to head. The sun was beginning to set to our right, and I was distracted by the vast sky, painted in shades from gold to peach to crimson against an ever-darkening blue.

We took a couple wide turns at fairly high speed, bringing my attention back, and stopped rather suddenly. In front of us, the setting sun, dead center, had nearly disappeared over a big, grassy berm. Dust was swirling around us, and animals I'd never seen were running around and kicking up the sand, with odd little squeaking noises and yips floating in the now-cool air. There they were: wild dogs to my left and right, just outside the vehicle, so close I could almost touch them. A whole pack, at least a dozen puppies playing on the hill. The markings of wild dogs are both exquisitely beautiful and bizarre, every one of them a different pattern. They are expert hunters, and they exuded a kind of raw energy even at rest. My guides were breathless, too, pausing only to be sure I knew what we were seeing and how lucky we were to see it. A rare, rare sighting.

I could see three of the dogs circling at the base of a tree a bit behind us on our right side, almost as if they wanted to climb it, whining and moaning a bit. I tapped Andrew's shoulder and gestured, but he just smiled and pointed back at the wonderful sight in front of us. I kept my eye on both, quite curious about what was going on in the tree.

Then I noticed what appeared to be a tail hanging from a big branch. When Josiah looked back to see if I was taking in all the puppy play, I motioned to the tree and, staying silent, mimicked the tail hanging with hand signals. He finally looked through his binoculars, and that big grin returned. He gave the binos to Andrew, who I think had been a bit annoyed with me for pulling his attention away from the sighting he'd so beautifully found. Now, Andrew quickly put the jeep in reverse without turning on the engine to bring us quietly closer to the tree.

In the dimming light, we could see a pale belly hanging between branches, the hanging tail clear now. It was the leopard we'd been tracking. With a very full belly, sleeping soundly. Below him were the three adult wild dogs – it had become too dark to discern whether they were male or female. Their full attention was on the leopard sprawled out high above them, and they circled and circled, stopping now and then to stare up, willing the cat to drop down. He didn't, of course.

In the vehicle, we spoke in hushed tones. Andrew shone the light from the torch with a red lens, giving the scene an eerie glow. (Sidenote here: I was really excited when I first heard the term "torch," thinking of flaming branches or even the tiki torches you buy in the States, but no, it's just the local lingo for flashlight.) The wild dogs were clearly unhappy and disturbed, and neither of the professionals in the vehicle could be sure why. Was the leopard the hunter or the hunted? We'd never know for certain.

This is one of the greatest lessons the bush has taught me, or tried to teach me: how to be comfortable with not knowing. Was that big belly full of a wild dog pup or two, or some other prey whose remains were out of our sight in the darkness of the upper branches? Were the dogs curious or hungry or bent on revenge? We could – as we can about everything in life – create a story and be rock solid sure that was the truth. Many human beings move through life that way, absolutely certain that their truth (or religion or way of raising their children) is the only truth. I wonder how the world would change if we could all open our minds to more possibilities than what we've been taught is "right."

So began the lessons of tracking – all of them, to me, incredibly strong metaphors for life. Don't know what to do about being unhappy or depressed? Loop around and go back to when you were last happy and light. What was different, what's missing in the present that lit you up before? What would make things better, instantly, in a bit and long-term? Focusing on finding those clues alone can take you out of a very dark place, at least in my experience. Tracking requires that you keep your eyes open – not only forward and side to side but also behind you, using all your senses at once to bring awareness of the world outside your mind.

On my return visit, I was back at Phinda in between volunteer assignments. I learned much of what I know of the wild there and spent many happy hours tracking with a devoted and excellent guide, Ian, and a spectacular tracker named Sipho who had worked exclusively with rhino for several years prior to our time together. We would get up and out on a vehicle quite early in the morning, even before the standard guest game drives, and stay out all day, with Ian radioing our location so that someone would magically arrive with a beautiful lunch in the middle of what seemed like nowhere. We'd often stay out until late afternoon.

We had quite a few adventures together, the three of us. One morning, we hadn't had much luck tracking on foot, and I could sense that the guys were frustrated. The best guides will do anything and everything to be sure each trip out into the bush is magical in some way, and that day was no exception. We made the usual stop for lunch under a cathedral made up of a huge, old fig tree overlooking a circle of spectacular, almost neon-yellow-green trees. Ian told me the story of a wedding one of his colleagues had held there. Fever trees – *umhlosinga* in isiZulu – got their name from the early Boer settlers who often camped under them near rivers as they expanded their territory and built new farms. Unfortunately, they often got fevers, something they attributed to the trees but that in reality was malaria from all the mosquitoes near the water.

The trees themselves are not deeply rooted, so they don't last forever. But they form beautifully gnarled sculptures as they die off and make great lookout posts for birds of prey and housing for who knows what in their trunks. The coolest part, though, is the fluorescent dust that coats their trunks, making them light up where the sun hits them. If you rub your hands on them, your hands will glow in the dark. Another metaphor for seeing the light in the shadow.

After we all had full bellies and had told our usual collection of stories – Sipho in particular always wanted to hear tales of what America was really like – we wet our hats and bandanas with the melted ice water in the cooler box to ward off the afternoon heat. I stretched out on the last seat of the game viewer to nap, but just as I began to doze off, I heard the radio crackling and Ian's footsteps coming to check. I opened one eye and saw that same grin begin to form on his face and sat up.

I heard the word *inja* (dog) and knew we would be taking off as soon as we could get packed up. Sipho was already folding up our table, and I hurried to help. On those solo days, I felt far less a guest than a teammate, and I didn't want to miss this one! We all climbed back in and off we went, Ian filling me in on the way. A big pack of wild dogs had been seen not too far away, and as it was the middle of the day and between game drives, most guests were relaxing back at the lodge. We seemed to be the only vehicle out and looking, which meant that if/when we found the dogs, we'd have time to observe them all on our own before others caught up.

What ensued was a wild goose chase for a long time, or wild dog chase, as the case may be. But after doing a whole lot of looping around, we did find them – napping. A whole cadre of patchy piles of fur piled next to each other, under the shade of a few splendid old trees. We watched for a little bit, seeing them stretch here and there, not knowing if we were on the front end of their siesta or if they were getting ready to go hunt. There were a few false starts, but overall, they were pretty conked out.

At this point, I was becoming more aware and fairly bush-savvy, and I carried this experience back to African Impact. I had learned to see things from a much wider lens. I'd learned to keep my senses open, taking in information from everything around me in every way possible. This helped a lot with the conservation work I was doing – I could quickly identify individual elephants, for example, by the scars on their ear or the odd tip of one tusk. I practiced this awareness on many wildlife adventures, from the daily curiosity of sitting out on the veranda under hundreds of epauleted bats roosting in the thatch ceiling to making up names for the myriad creepy crawlies in my rondavel to overnight camping trips.

One evening, our group leader went through the rules of the AI tented camp we were spending the night at, as the light faded quickly. She told us that we mustn't walk in between the closely placed sleeping tents, especially at night, because animals often came sniffing around. We listened carefully. Sleeping in tents in the middle of Big Five territory (lion, leopard, rhinoceros, elephant, and buffalo) was a first for most of the group.

We all then climbed into a game vehicle for a night drive – a grand adventure as the open-topped jeep rumbled down the beaten dirt road. I enjoyed every minute of it. When we returned, the same leader unthinkingly stepped in between the tents – and, sure enough, bumped straight into a hyena! We all joined her in screaming, then burst out laughing. Lesson learned.

Animal tracking and sightings were thrilling, but my last week with AI was all about the people. I sat in on my first tribal council meeting in a nearby settlement. I was with Lorna and Trico, staff members who'd made some really good inroads with this local governing body. I watched every move they made, listened to every word I could understand, and offered my hesitant greetings in Shangaan, the local language Trico had been trying his best to teach us in the evenings at the lodge.

The elderly men were dressed in mismatched Western clothing, some of them in suit jackets, with their beaded and skin bracelets and *umqhele*, the traditional fur headbands. They had a quiet dignity as they sat and listened, their heads nodding in agreement. African Impact was there to discuss the most important of topics, water, so there was a great deal of interest in what could be provided, and a great deal of concern about where the new tanks would be placed. Every *induna*, or local representative, had his own interests at heart, and as I've since learned, this can slow down the process of decision-making considerably.

I watched the local women through the window, open to allow in any breezes in the extreme heat. They were outdoors preparing lunch for the tribal council on an open fire, the smell of curry and corn meal was already wafting in. I took it all in, having no idea how much all of this would become my world in short order. As much as I loved the land and the beautiful creatures that roamed the bush, it would become clear to me over time that I had come home to be with the people.

Fifteen

I finished the conservation project, sad to leave the Dumela Lodge team who'd taught me so much and the group of volunteers with whom I'd bonded, and made a quick visit to Phinda to rest and restore and track. While there, grateful to be taken care of, eat well again, and sleep in a big, comfy bed, I decided to go take a look at the small lodge for sale – the one I'd seen on Facebook while I was back in the States.

The estate agent, Gerry, picked me up at Phinda, and we drove the district road into Hluhluwe and past turn-offs to a few other larger reserve lodges. It's easy, when you first visit South Africa, to only see what you'd see in the movies, to go from the international airport to the smaller one to an airstrip in the middle of a reserve. Then your whole experience becomes that particular piece of Earth for a few days – the guides and trackers creating your experience of what South Africa or perhaps that province is. Then you might fly in a prop jet to another reserve in a different province, and have a slightly different view – flora, fauna, and even the ground itself vary quite a bit, as I'd seen on my first visit.

When you begin to drive the land, though, the highways and district roads, you see a glimpse of the real South Africa. The dismaying amount of plastic blowing about after payday at the end of the month. The tires set on fire amidst broken glass in the road – a signal of some sort of strike. The children, seeing a rare *umlungu* (white person), holding out their hands for sweeties. The beauty of a martial eagle roosting in a dried-out tree just above a dump full of debris. The jagged mountains in silhouette against the setting sun, with the glowing embers of a fire in the sugar cane fields at their base.

What takes longer to see is the in-between: the realities of life here, the community so dependent on each other, the incredible kindness and, yes, sometimes the unfathomable cruelty amongst neighbors of vastly different economic statuses and cultures.

My first glimpse into what it might be like to actually live in the bush came that day as Gerry pointed out a couple local restaurants and the shops in town. The dust blew around us in the far-too-hot wind. I'd always struggled with heat, and I wondered – as I would again and again – what I was thinking, considering planting myself in this place where the daily high temperatures often are in the high thirties and low forties (mid-nineties to well over 100 degrees Fahrenheit). The practical part of me could see that moving to the middle of the drought-ridden bush was utterly ridiculous. The American in me, trained to seek comfort above all else, would do things like put a dishwasher in my first home here and buy a brand new Toyota Prado, only to scratch it up on acacia branches within days.

My heart, though, was so happy, delighted and charmed by every detail, from the remains of an old house on the road, its paint faded into pale turquoise by the sun, to driving right next to the rusty freight train while crossing the railroad bridge, and those gorgeous Nguni cattle staring at me with doe eyes as they reluctantly moved their huge bodies from the middle of the road. I sat next to Gerry and took it all in as I listened to his take on the much-debated Toyota vs. Land Rover issue. People, I've found, fall into one of two camps – at least those who live in the bush. I've chosen both, of course, over time.

Eventually we found our way to the small gate of the private reserve where the lodge I'd seen advertised was located. It was mostly grassland, with zebra and impala roaming about and the houses spaced far apart yet still visible. It was the sort of place that white South Africans would see as marginally safe for a woman living on her own: well-secured, neighbors within earshot, close to town. My heart sank a bit. I was in love with the open spaces, the wildness of this place, but while this was far from a suburban cul-de-sac, it felt a bit too safe.

In South Africa, a lodge can be anything from a bush home to a large complex hosting many guests. This one was beautiful from a distance and featured a main lodge with several guest cabins. Close up, however, it was easy to see that the wood siding had not been maintained, and I wondered what problems lay underneath. Several years of managing construction back in the States had shown me that solid structure is key, no matter how pretty the outside is. A metaphor for so much, I know, and as I was just starting to see that I'd need to build a new life from scratch here, one that seemed really important. It was wonderful, this place, but not really what I wanted.

I would have to do this over and over – I still do – this not allowing myself to settle for what would be okay. I'd been doing that my whole life, and I hadn't come all the way across the planet to settle for just alright. Those days were over.

Gerry said he'd think about other properties on the market, and we agreed to meet the next time I was at Phinda. When I got back to the reserve late that day, I had tea with a few of the guides and trackers I'd gotten to know. They were eager to hear what I'd thought of Hluhluwe and this lodge, news having spread quickly that I'd been out with an estate agent. I shared my concerns and my sense that living "in town" wasn't going to be right for me. Honestly, I was trying to catch up a bit with myself. How was I looking at property, this soon? I told myself that it wouldn't be a bad idea to have a home base here, that I'd certainly be going back and forth. It was as if I'd gotten on a treadmill going at a much higher speed than I would normally walk.

The men listened closely to my meandering thoughts about all of it, far more sure than I was that buying a place locally was absolutely the right thing to do. One of them mentioned that since I loved the mountains on the southern part of Phinda so much, maybe I should look at another small private reserve called Kube Yini, where I could walk on my own. This was a rare thing; most reserves required shareholders to have an armed guide with them at all times when walking away from the footprint around their homes. The whole group nodded in agreement, so I tucked that name away and went back to my room to pack.

The next morning, I moved on to my next volunteer stint with African Impact. This one was in the small beach town of St. Lucia, a very deeply Zulu area. St. Lucia is beloved by tourists and locals alike for its central business strip of shops and restaurants, beautiful sand beaches where local artists make gigantic sand sculptures, and the wide estuary full of hippos and crocs – both of which roam the streets at night. I signed up to do health care work – nothing professional, mostly home visits to check in on progress and see what residents needed along with helping out in local clinics. I'd taken a number of first aid courses, been a lifeguard, and done some emergency medical technician training when I was young, and it all stood me in good stead here.

This seems as good a time as any to mention that I'd never graduated from college in the States. After I left home at seventeen, I studied, trained, and worked in broadcasting, special education, marketing, retail, construction management, master gardening, mindfulness meditation, reiki and other healing work, life coaching, and likely a few things I'm forgetting beyond my creative practices. I love learning and am still ridiculously curious, but my lack of a formal degree was a great source of shame especially when I was surrounded by multiply degreed people from Ivy League schools back in the States. A jill-of-all-trades, master of none, all that sort of thing. No framed diploma and no college reunions in a world that seemed to respect only official learning and to look down on life experience.

But then I moved to rural South Africa, where I use everything I've ever learned, often and well. That's been healing. Here, it pays to be able to wear many hats, to know what to do in all sorts of situations, to be able to help someone who then helps you with all the things you never learned. It's a great system, one I'm much more comfortable with. And it helps me to address the bottomless pit of shame many Zulu youth feel, caught in a substandard rural education system entirely focused on passing matric exams above all else. There's so much innate creative talent in the people I work with, and nothing would make me happier than to continue to create venues and ways to help them use those gifts to support themselves, their families, and their communities. This is important to me

– given the lack of encouragement and feeling unseen in my own childhood – and I believe creativity is one of the ways South Africa can begin to heal as a country and create new ways of living.

One day a week in St. Lucia, our small group of volunteers led by Zulu staff member Sisanda Qwabe, made the rounds of the homes of the elderly. The *gogos* and *mkhulus* (grandmothers and grandfathers) are addressed as such by everyone, the terms serving as honorifics to show respect to elders. They had traditionally lived in community with their families, but now, the adult children were often away working. So African Impact created this weekly program to help them with any household chores that needed doing, check on them, and, perhaps most importantly, keep them company.

On one of these days, Sisanda dropped me off with Annie, a blonde, blue-eyed woman from the States who looked a decade younger than her twenty-seven years. We entered a dimly lit block house. The only light came from a couple tiny windows and barely illuminated the rather round *gogo* sitting in the middle of her bed and surrounded by heaps of clothes, perhaps waiting to be folded by us. Sisanda made the introductions in isiZulu, translated Gogo's requests to us in English, and then, to my surprise, left us alone for the rest of the very hot afternoon.

Annie and I carried easily a week's worth of dishes, pots, and pans out to the yard, where Annie sat on a mat and washed them with sand, soap, and a bit of water for ages – the debris on them had dried to a hard finish. I took the inside and folded the clothes, the *gogo* showing me just how to do it until she figured out that I was able to do it well enough on my own. I was also to clean the floor, but since the floor was more an arrangement of layers of linoleum pieces and the odd animal skin placed like a scatter rug on top of dirt, I didn't have a clue how to do that – the only equipment available was a rather spare straw broom.

Carefully and respectfully, I took each of the animal skins and shook them outside as hard as I could. Then, hoping a little light would help things along, I laid them on rocks in the sun. Next I removed the oddly shaped sheets of floor linoleum, trying to remember what went where so I could piece them back together like a jigsaw puzzle, and took them outside to sweep off the insects and gecko droppings and wiping them with a soapy cloth I borrowed from Annie. After that, I attempted to sweep anything not part of the normal dirt floor outside, which took a long time. I was wearing surgical gloves a size or two too small and sweating bullets – so hard the sweat ran down my arms in rivulets, mixing with the red-brown dust and creating interesting patterns where it didn't turn into a light coating of mud.

As I went, the grandmother babbled at me in isiZulu, to which I said over and over, in my baby Zulu, *ngiyaxolisa, angizwa*, sorry, that I could not hear her. I didn't know how to say that I didn't understand. She seemed content to fill me in on all the news of the community anyway, and, listening, I figured it would take me at least a decade to even begin to speak the language. At best. Meanwhile, I imagined what my exceedingly well-paid housekeeper in the US would think of all this. While I'd cleaned houses as a teenager to make money for college, it had been several years since I'd given my own highly polished Brazilian cherry wood floors a good clean. I figured she'd be rolling on that floor laughing.

I moved on to cleaning the bathroom. I assume it was installed just for Gogo. She was barely mobile, and the only toilets I'd seen in this or other nearby communities were of the long-drop, outhouse variety. This one was basically a simple arrangement of buckets and, given that water was extremely precious due to drought, looked like it might not have been recently used.

I followed the same floor-cleaning process I had in the living area and bedroom, since Gogo had nodded somewhat approvingly at me and hadn't clicked or clucked in disapproval. I would later learn that a lot of those sounds were actually swearing – thankfully, I was unaware of that then. I took the buckets outside to be swished out with the leftover dishwashing water – recycling took on a whole new meaning in those days. The buckets sat to dry, floor materials wiped and drying alongside them, in mere minutes under the beating sun. Then I stacked them to be ready for the next week's visit.

I'd just plopped down in the sun next to Annie, hoping maybe we'd dry off a bit, too, when Sisanda showed up and grinned at our fatigue. Or maybe it was the mud on us. We got ourselves up and followed her inside to say goodbye to the *gogo*. We found them both grinning and laughing. Sisanda translated that the grandmother was so surprised that this *umlungu* woman actually knew how to clean a house that she'd taken a nap, knowing she didn't need to supervise me. That I'd make a great *makoti* (daughter-in-law), that I should come live next door. She'd begun making a list of potential husbands for me already, starting with her son.

Here I thought I didn't know what I was doing! I don't know that I've ever felt more pleased with myself, or more highly praised. It was the very beginning of my understanding that perhaps I'd be more at home in the communities than I'd ever expected. I smiled the whole way back.

My time in the St. Lucia area was split between three rather different communities. We primarily made home visits – there was a very full notebook in which Sisanda tracked all the residents in need of health care, often for chronic conditions like diabetes or HIV, many of them elderly. African Impact was able to provide limited supplies through donations but could monitor and be sure that those in need got to the clinic.

I felt a part of things in only a few weeks to my surprise, which is a testimony to the African Impact organization and the relationships they've built in those communities and also, as I would learn, the receptivity of the Zulu people. In the nearly six years I've been here, that's remained true. While I've run into plenty of people who've resented my presence for one reason or another or who, at the very least, were extremely skeptical of my motives, I've mostly enjoyed a warm reception – along with a great deal of curiosity, of course. Perhaps it's my ancestors or my devotion to the traditional ways, or something else – there's no way to know. I find the Zulu culture, despite all the warrior history, to be a rather openminded and curious one, and I've enjoyed many hours interviewing elders and community leaders in hopes of one day compiling a book of portraits and local history, to preserve a bit of a culture which is fast disappearing.

The work was really rewarding and great experience for what was to come in my life. The volunteer accommodation, though, didn't work for me at all. I found an alternative arrangement on the other end of St. Lucia's main street in a collection of high-quality tents. It was odd to find that in the middle of downtown, but it worked well for me. I'd spent enough time in tents now that I found the canvas flapping in the wind a comfort, and the one I rented was quite luxurious, with its own full en suite bathroom.

As tired as I was from the heat and our full days, my evenings were often spent texting with my daughter back in America, or talking with her on Skype. These conversations were difficult and, like those in Zurich, consisted of her questioning me without saying much herself. George and I talked too, trying to sort things out without knowing how the future would look. I had no idea what lay ahead, and they really needed to know what my plan was. I was content to spend my days helping out in whatever way I could in KZN and thought I might continue to volunteer for the foreseeable future.

As best I could tell, this was all incomprehensible to my husband and daughter. George decided we needed to separate our finances – I assume to protect himself – and began to draw up the paperwork. This would quickly escalate into a divorce agreement over the next few months – the promises of supporting my work in South Africa, of doing something together, disappeared. I would hear from friends, much later, that Lina had gone through my computer and my emails and found "evidence" that I was having an affair with someone in SA. I'm not sure how, since it wasn't true, but perhaps that was what made things change. It's always easier to blame a third party in these situations rather than look at what is really wrong. In any case, we began to talk less frequently. I couldn't explain my behavior in a way that made sense to them. I was acting in a way that was the polar opposite of what they were used to, and no one wanted to talk about the reasons I would make this kind of a change.

As my American family unraveled, my life in South Africa started to build. I'd leave my little tent late in February to go back to that magical place called Kaapsehoop in Mpumalanga province, spending a few days meeting with fellow Martha Beck-trained coaches and taking in the beauty of the land and the wild horses roaming about in the mist. I'd meet Mindy Middleton, an American living in Dubai who yearned to follow my example and move to South Africa, and reconnect with a few lovely friends I'd made on my first trip.

I'd take a quick flight back to Durban, where I'd meet the consultant who would help me file my application for permanent residency in SA, and then, to fulfill my visa requirement of leaving the country, visit my DC friends in Madrid. It would be a bittersweet visit as they were much a part of my life with George and Lina, and yet a really good touchstone too.

By mid-March, I was back at Phinda, spending as much time as I could walking the land and trying to work out in my head what was happening to me. I just kept walking forward despite an utter lack of confidence that I knew what I was doing – and more and more phone calls and emails from friends back in the States, questioning my sanity. Did I know what I stood to lose? they'd ask. And I'd reply that yes, I did, and I was quite sure that I had much to gain. I understood their concern and curiosity, yet I was feeling so clearly called to be just where I was, without knowing where this particular path would lead.

I'd walk through the bush, learning about tracking with a local guy, Bongani, who was a friend of Dingane's, and getting to know more about him, his family, his hopes and dreams. I'd go on all-day adventures with Ian and Sipho, the guide/tracker team with whom, on foot, I'd later run into four black rhinos. Those days brought me a lot of peace. This visit also brought me the finalization of something that felt huge: the purchase of my first home in South Africa.

Sixteen

The guides on my previous visit to Phinda had been right. I did love Kube Yini, the small private game reserve up in the Lebombo mountains. It bordered Phinda and the larger Munyawana Conservancy, a sprawling area where old farms had been reclaimed and brought back to their natural state, then repopulated with a wide variety of wild animals to form a wonderful Big Five reserve in the middle of several bordering Zulu communities. I loved it so much that I purchased a home there in early 2016.

Kube Yini is a beautiful and private small reserve with a great staff, so when I first found my place there, I thought I'd found a home base from which I could go back to the US as needed, then return for any future community work I'd do. On this particular visit back to Zululand, I met with a local contractor, highly recommended by the folks at Kube, and we began drawing up plans to turn what had been a family weekend and holiday retreat for over twenty years into what would be a "proper" permanent home for me, with a lovely main building with main bedroom, office, a huge veranda and lookout spot above, and a comfy guesthouse. I knew I'd have visitors from abroad and wanted them to feel at home.

It's comical now, looking back at what I thought I needed – a dishwasher, for example – but after many months and many glitches, I had a truly beautiful home that has housed not only me and my loved ones but also many visitors over the past few years. I ordered the brand spanking new Toyota Prado, too, the exchange rates making all this seem a bargain, and a worthwhile investment given the amount of time I'd spend driving alone in the bush. That car and its many airbags would save my life one day, so a good decision, really.

Once I got all that sorted, I traveled a bit – to Joburg for a girlfriend catch-up, to see my friends at Bushmans Kloof, and to Cape Town to see my friend Lilith, a wildly creative healer woman several years older than me. She'd become like an older sister to me – complete with telling me in no uncertain terms that I must write this book for years now.

We spent some time catching up and exploring more of Cape Town. The artist in me was tempted to create my home there – and it would have been far more practical as I had several friends living in the area – but it just wasn't where I was called. It wasn't home.

I have been accused, more than once in my life, of making things more difficult than they need to be. I wondered if I was doing just that in those early days here in South Africa. While many people knew me well enough to realize that life in Washington DC was just not my thing, there wasn't a single person in that part of the world who didn't think I had lost my marbles. In South Africa, there were a few who could see what was beginning to unfold for me– like Lilith and Dingane – yet in the aftermath of apartheid, it remained very difficult for South Africans of any race to encourage me to live in the rural bush on my own. Sadly, everyone is still rather afraid of anyone who does not look like them, and I think it will be a long time before neighbors see each other in ways other than by skin color.

I am so grateful to have such strong ancestors and such a well-paved connection to God. All my practices, everything I'd learned since that day I was so sure I needed to leave this Earth but stayed, has allowed me to move forward without (too much) hesitation, to leap without knowing if the net was there or even if a net existed. My net, truthfully, is a beautiful tapestry woven together by a diverse group of ancestors who have learned over time – and out of dire need – to pull together in the same direction. I wouldn't be here without it and in gratitude, I will always help others find their own unique way to connecting with those who came before them. Being human, though, I did struggle a bit and waffled – couldn't I just live in Cape Town and spend time a few hours north near Bushmans, studying and making art? Wouldn't that be enough?

All of this was going on in my mind as I took an Uber to the Institute for Healing of Memories office in order to begin my facilitator training with them. I arrived a bit early and so sat at a table with the staff as they finished last-minute preparations. I listened to the very different Cape accents, the mix of Afrikaans and English and who knows what else, and took in the beauty of people with very mixed racial histories.

Cape Town, the original port occupied by the Dutch for trading, is where the colonization of South Africa began in 1652, and there's a unique mix of Khoi Khoi, San, Dutch, English, Malaysian, Xhosa, and now various tribes from all over the continent. It is, in many ways, an entirely different society than that of KwaZulu-Natal, and while I find it very intriguing and beautiful, I was already a bit homesick, having been gone for a week. Even I couldn't really fathom how I much could miss a place I'd just discovered, yet I did.

We packed up and found our way into taxis – white minivans found everywhere here and best avoided when driving. The early autumn sun streamed in as we waited for the taxi to fill up and it was quite warm, making me grateful to not rely on this mode of transport in the summer. And then we were back on the road, headed about an hour west to Franschhoek, where we would stay in a small monastery set in the middle of vineyards, a gorgeous backdrop for the intense work we'd come to do.

Our group was even more diverse than the population of Cape Town – there were several from the city, yes, and others from Africa, a few from around the world, all of us with different professional backgrounds yet all with a dedication to create healing in the world one way or another. I could easily write a whole book about those twelve days. I heard the personal stories of colored women from Cape Town and how apartheid had changed the very fabric of the city. I talked to black African pastors of Western churches in Zimbabwe dealing with both typical church issues and those of a more cultural nature. I listened to a former military officer who had walked through horrors in the Congo. It was a heart- and mind-opening week, as well as a huge opportunity to learn skills I felt would stand me in good stead in this new life I was creating. We joked that it was a bit like boot camp, that we'd always be buddies, and I am, in fact, still in touch with several people from the training, all incredibly good souls.

There were about thirty-six of us plus several staff, and I was one of maybe five white people in the group and one of two Americans. We spent the first few days learning about the Institute for Healing of Memories and their mission, philosophy, and approach, as well as getting to know each other as we walked around the monastery's beautiful property. The big trees with their changing leaves reminded me far more of New England in the autumn than South Africa in what I still thought of as spring, but the *hadedas* (the South African ibis) and their screeching calls early each morning reminded me of exactly where I was – as they had my very first morning in Joburg.

On day four, we began a mock workshop. We'd come together as a large group for program activities, and break into smaller groups, chosen to be as diverse as possible, for more vulnerable sharing work. I was placed in a working circle with two women whose heavy Afrikaans accents belied their dark skin and who had been community workers with the Institute for some time. There were also three black men: Jeremiah, a pastor in an Episcopal church in Zimbabwe's capital city of Harare; a large, extremely dark-skinned man from the DRC who'd served in that country's military through very intense times, and a Ugandan gentleman who now worked in Cape Town with "foreign Africans" – those who entered South Africa illegally and hope to earn money to support their families suffering at home. The information we shared in this heart-opening process was, of course, completely confidential.

Our task on that first day was to draw a picture of a powerful time in our personal history. We had some time on our own to do this, and then came together in our small groups to witness each other telling the stories illustrated by our drawings.

I did mine in a simple cartoon depicting the gang rape in high school, the subsequent pregnancy, and how I used both events to fuel my move to Atlanta at such a young age, making the choice not to stay where I knew I wasn't wanted and would only go down a negative path. As I told this tale, there was a lot of nodding from the other women, and a lot of shifting in their seats by the men. African cultures generally don't mix men and women when talking about intimate things, and while all of us had been trained in more western vocations, my raw story was uncomfortable.

I picked up on the men's discomfort and wondered if perhaps this hadn't been the right story to begin with, that first meeting. Yet the IHOM gatherings we would hopefully be facilitating would certainly bring up this sort of thing, so I relaxed and walked the group through what had occurred. I didn't expect what happened after a number of glances had been exchanged.

Jeremiah spoke up. He said that they needed to apologize, that over the several days we'd been together each of them had assumed that I, as a wealthy white woman from America, had never been through real trauma. He joked that they thought maybe my dog had died or something, but they'd never imagined I could have been through anything like this and come out intact – strong, well-spoken, confident. I think he was speaking mostly for the men, but the women, too, nodded vigorously as he spoke. His eyes got teary as he said how I'd just opened his mind to thinking that maybe all people share the same struggles no matter what they look like, no matter where they are from.

I couldn't have been more surprised. I think many of us with a trauma background believe what's happened to us shows in some way, that surely people must know that we are scarred beyond words, internally or externally, even if those scars are not truly visible. It was the first time I realized that I will, seemingly forever and always, be seen as a wealthy white American woman, with all the automatic presumptions made here in Africa. I suspect that black strangers will always call me Madam, that white ones will presume my black husband is my gardener, that I'll be expected to tip well because of my lingering American accent – and that everyone will always assume I will one day go back to the US.

It's hurtful, sometimes, and other times mildly annoying, but I've accepted that my outside is seen far more clearly than my inside. I do my best to maintain my own sense of self throughout it all. If there's one thing I've accomplished in this life, and am so grateful for, it's that I know myself and have worked hard to live from that inner knowing of my own soul and that of my ancestors.

I left this training with skills, yes, yet more importantly with boot camp-level friendships. We opened our hearts to each other over those twelve days and shared our vastly different experiences, developing a deep respect and awe for the courage and compassion each of us wander through life with.

I left, too, with a new charge from Archbishop Desmond Tutu.

In the middle of the training, we all boarded taxis and headed out of the beautiful vineyard area where we were staying to attend a small Friday morning service at St. George's Cathedral in the central business district of nearby Cape Town. The church is imposing, a gothic style stone building on a tree lined street, and we gathered together with Father Lapsley that chilly morning on the steps outside before entering as a group. Archbishop Tutu had been recovering at home since his hospitalization during my initial visit to SA the previous November. He presided over this short service, offering communion for the first time in several months, and I was struck by how much smaller he seemed, how much lower his energy and yet how strong his voice was. It reverberated in the small chapel where some sixty attendees sat in wooden pews surrounding the communion table.

Tutu welcomed us all warmly, his eyes twinkling a bit. He was clearly happy to be back in his robes, in his church home. He moved through the liturgy with an elegance and familiarity that nearly inspired me to consider, not for the first time, becoming a pastor. To watch someone embody their gifts and their life purpose, living in accordance with their soul, is a truly awesome thing. He spoke about his dear friend and colleague, Father Michael Lapsley, and how beautifully he had continued the work they'd done together during the apartheid era and the Truth and Reconciliation Commission with this Institute for Healing of Memories. He asked all of us who were in the IHOM training to stand, and I was incredibly proud to be in the company of both Fr. Lapsley and my fellow attendees. The service was brief and beautiful, and afterward we had time to explore St. George's a bit. We all took photos, in pairs, with the Arch (as the IHOM staff call him) seated in a large, rather regal chair and us crouched down next to him on either side.

After most of the group had posed, I had my turn. Tutu, clearly tired from this first day back in the "office," looked down at me from his perch on his throne-like chair with a puzzled expression. Finally he said, "I know you," and I reminded him of where we'd met. His face lit up with delight that I'd actually come all the way to South Africa and found him again, and after our photo was taken, he stood up and talked with me and my friend Babalwa, with whom we'd posed for the camera, for a few minutes. He apologized for not remembering my name and said he was decrepit now, that he had started to forget things.

I immediately replied that he was not at all decrepit, that he'd lived a good and full life and served the world so well. He waved my response off: "Yes, yes, but I won't be with you much longer." He pointed at me and Babalwa and said that it was our turn now, that we must carry it forward. No pressure, eh? Just a charge from one of the most devoted human beings to carry forward the work that he and other thought leaders and peace makers have been dedicated to for so long. That's quite a message to receive. Truth be told, I'm still sorting out just what it means.

After a lovely farewell lunch and tour of a cooperative vineyard owned in part by its workers, I headed back to spend a couple days with my artist friend in Cape Town before returning to Kube Yini. She was hosting a show of both her art and kizomba dance, and while I was exhausted from the IHOM training, I let her recruit me somehow to do my very first body painting that night.

People danced and swirled around me while I painted the body of an exquisite dancer, all curves and sinew, and watched Lilith translate all the energy of the room onto a canvas in her own amazing, seemingly effortless, painting. I struggled a bit to take it all in. Not just this night, but everything that had come to pass in the previous six months. How could I have literally turned my life upside down in a way that felt so huge yet so right, all at once? My confusion turned to gratitude, and I prayed my thanks as I fell asleep with the party still in full swing, exhausted from it all. And so happy, imagining the life that would unfold before me when I returned to Zululand the next day.

I'd been traveling around South Africa for months now and was more than ready to go home to Kube Yini. The house I'd purchased earlier in the year was still being renovated, so I'd rented the house next door sight unseen – not the best decision I'd ever made. Still, even with doors that didn't close and a whole lot of amphibian friends to keep me company, it was good to unpack knowing I was staying for longer than a week.

The Toyota salesman kindly drove my new Prado up, and before I knew it, I was driving myself around the bush after months of being a passenger. My ex-husband had always said I'd never be able to drive on the "wrong" side of the road and had therefore done all the driving when we were abroad. But for months, I'd been very carefully observing how to do just that, from the passenger seat. And it worked. I'd learned, too, from observing the guides and trackers on the reserves how to drive amongst wild animals, which came in very handy. Still does, to this day.

I often took myself out on drives around Kube Yini and to town, always with a radio. Some wise soul had told me the best way to learn my way around would be to just let myself get lost – great advice, as long as I had the radio, given the unreliable network signal. It was a great metaphor, too, for my life. I thought, at first, that I might live up in the bush alone forever. I was far more tired than I'd realized from the last couple decades and had a whole lot of discerning and dreaming to do. It would turn out that Kube would be my full-time home for a couple years. It was just the medicine I needed to begin following the calling that had brought me halfway across the world.

Seventeen

When I first started writing this book, this is what came out: *Igama lami ngingu Nomadlozi Gumede. Nalu udaba lwami.* In English, my name is Nomadlozi Gumede, and this is the story of how I became myself.

Years ago, when I started the immigration process to South Africa, George and I agreed that once it was complete, I would change my surname in order to reflect my leaving his family. Six years later, I'm still tying up the final paperwork I need to change my name, and while I use my English name legally, it doesn't really feel right anymore. Over time, I've become Nomadlozi, the name – and, in many ways, the identity – my Zulu father gave me years ago now.

I was introduced to Baba Gumede by a new friend, Siyanda, a local guide who often brought tourists wanting to learn about *sangoma* traditions to the Gumede family compound. Baba, as I came to call him, was a powerful *sangoma* and *inyanga* – a healer in the traditional Zulu ways and a teacher of those ways, too. He was also a devoted husband and father of three sons and two daughters. When he was a young man, his grandfather told him that one day he would have an *umlungu,* or white, daughter. He assumed that his grandfather had meant a very light-skinned child. Like most families, his had a white ancestor or two thrown in the mix, and genetics being what they are, skin colors within families can vary wildly. I think by 2016, when Baba and I met, he'd given up. His youngest child was twenty, and he was enjoying being an *umkhulu,* or grandfather. Perhaps he thought his grandfather had been mistaken, I'm not sure. My youngest sister is, after all, very light in complexion, so maybe he believed she fulfilled the prophecy. We'll never know now.

Baba and I immediately connected in a very strong way. The first visit was a typical one, I think – he explained what his tools were, the difference between *sangoma* and *inyanga,* that sort of thing. On our second visit, just a couple weeks later – I'd have gone back the next day if I could have – he told me that, as best he could tell from our consultation, I had no white ancestors, that he basically had to treat me as if I were Zulu. And said that this meant he must only give me Zulu *muthi,* or medicine, not the simpler cures he would typically give an *umlungu.*

As Siyanda translated, I nodded my agreement and tried a few of the isiZulu words I knew – *"Yebo, Baba"* or "Yes, sir." I would come to find those two words to be among the most useful ones, generally, as Zulu men appreciate nothing more than respect, especially from a white woman. As I'd found elsewhere in the world, respect for local customs will smooth your path and create a sort of comradery very quickly. This has been so true in my life here that now I find myself somewhat offended if someone rushes into a conversation without the customary greetings. Those little rituals and the way they naturally slow things down have made my life a far deeper, richer experience – though I still occasionally default to a more American, rushed way of dealing with things. Old programming dies hard, truly, and it's been a wonderful journey to slow down and learn to adjust my expectations of just how much can be accomplished in one day.

Baba Gumede wanted to ease my transition to living in South Africa. He believed from our first visit that I had come home to stay. He recommended a cleansing to allow me to release the parts of my life that were no longer serving me, that no longer fit. I agreed with thanks in one of the few other isiZulu phrases I knew back then: *Ngiyabonga kakhulu. Yebo Baba, ngiyacela.* Thank you very much and yes, sir, please.

He asked me if I knew what treating me in the Zulu way would mean, and I nodded, saying – out of who knows where – "Chicken, goat, cow." And making little cutting motions at my wrists. I'll be honest here – this sort of thing happens to me a lot, and in the beginning it felt sort of freaky. I just know things. Things about this culture and especially the old ways. I cannot explain it and will leave it to your interpretation, yet this wasn't the first or last time I had this inner knowing.

It didn't surprise Baba, at all, he just said, "Light" – he never did learn to pronounce the letter "r," which isn't present in the isiZulu language. When he was in agreement with someone or something, he would always say, "Light," which delighted me every single time. He stared off into space for a bit, something I'd come to learn meant he was listening to the ancestors, and then gave Siyanda a short list of things we'd need to bring. A chicken – I presumed this was an offering of food, which was close but not exactly right. A razor blade and a cloth. And he said I should wear a *doek* (head covering) and a skirt, something I would always do when visiting him from that day forward. He had no trouble with tourists and visitors coming in Western clothing yet he had different expectations for me, which I now see as an early sign of being accepted as family. We set a time for the following week.

I questioned Siyanda the whole way home about what exactly would happen, only to learn that he'd grown up quite Christian and had only a vague idea of what was done in these ceremonies. He did mention that he'd find the chicken, though, and I realized that it would be a live one, not from the shop in town. I fell asleep that night and dreamt those dreams I'd had in America again, of fireside chats and singing and drums, dancing in a way I'd never seen, under the incredible array of stars I now recognized as the Milky Way. Something in me knew that this would be the beginning of something good, something I'd been missing my whole life.

Several days later we were back on the road, Siyanda and I, this time with a very calm chicken wrapped unceremoniously in a plastic grocery bag with only its head sticking out. It had big eyes and looked directly at me from its spot between my feet on the floor of the Prado. I found myself talking to this chicken, saying, "Sorry, sorry chicken" – which has become a favorite Gumede story and a tradition I have to keep up any time there's a ceremony involving a chicken – and telling it that it could come back and be anything it wanted to be, that this was a noble way to go. As a long-time conservation supporter, this part made me uneasy. Yet there is another part of me that sees it as totally normal, too – something else I can't quite comprehend but have made peace with. I have no idea where my words to the chicken came from, but they seemed to make us both more comfortable.

Once we arrived at the family compound, easily recognizable because all the various buildings going up the hill were painted an unusual shade of light aqua blue, and several were marked with Zulu clan names and symbols, we went directly to Baba's rondavel, his "office." It was full of tools of the trade: bottles and jars and calabash gourds full of dried herbs, feathers and porcupine quills, brightly colored beaded items I'd later learn that Baba and his wife had made themselves. There were a lot of ceremonial clothes, too, with shells and beads on them and baskets and tools hanging in between, along with a few animal skins. In short, for me, it was *amaZulu* – heaven. This place was what I dreamed of as a young girl, playing with making medicine in that backyard potting shed, right down to the way it smelled – which probably helps explain my comfort level.

Mama Gumede joined us that day. A large woman, about my size and very regal even in her worn clothes, with the largest breasts I had even seen, she was quite quiet and perhaps even a little skeptical that day. She came and went, supervising preparations for all we'd need to do. Baba explained everything at length through Siyanda, who would take five minutes of Baba talking and summarize it in a couple sentences. While it's true that isiZulu is far wordier than English and even in those early days, I could tell that Baba Gumede was fond of repeating himself for emphasis, it was extremely frustrating not to be able to communicate with him directly, more so as time went on. Over time, we developed the ability to communicate without spoken word, much as I had with my grandmother, and one of the gifts of his passing away is that we can now hear each other well. Yet I would trade that any day for being able to sit in his physical presence again, to hear his laugh, to hear, "Light, Nomadlozi, light" again.

On that day, I found myself in a sort of fenced enclosure with a shy young woman I would later come to call my youngest sister, Ntombi Gumede, supervising a steaming ritual. This was definitely old school, I thought, as I stripped down and made a mental note to choose clothes that were easier to take on and off next time, and maybe to do things in summer as the cold mountain air hit my naked body.

Soon I was squatting and leaning over a huge cauldron of steaming water dotted with herbs I didn't recognize. I began to pray in a way that I had never been taught but somehow knew, speaking all my gratitude – and, in pretty equal measure, all my concerns – to my ancestors. This ritual, like the ones to come later that morning, were new to me, and my Western-trained mind was on high alert and wondering if I'd gone completely insane. The older, wiser part of me knew better, and the relief in finally falling back into these practices I must have known in a different time and similar place was palpable. I was almost giddy, to Mama Gumede's surprise, once I'd wriggled, pink and sweaty from the steam, into my clothes again, my feet muddy from the water and dirt mixing as I fumbled into my flip flops – or slops, as they are called here.

I recall being relieved that the chicken hadn't put in an appearance. Maybe it was more a gift or something. I was turning to the left to go back to Baba when Mama motioned for me to follow her to the right, babbling at me in isiZulu as we walked out of the compound and down the hill. She carried a bucket full of water and more herbs, and my slippery feet hit the occasional paper thorn, a local seasonal menace that grows low on the ground, its origami-like appearance masking its painfully sharp corners.

We walked quite a long way, the acacia thorns on the dry straggly trees snagging my skirt now and then. The sun was quite bright though the air was still chilly. Finally we arrived in a little clearing where Mama and her helpers had pushed away the dry grass and dug a small hole, maybe two feet wide and less deep. The chicken was still there in its plastic grocery bag alive and kicking, though before I knew it Mama had it up in the air and quietly cut the throat with a razor blade, turning the chicken upside down and adding the blood to the bucket of *muthi* and water. I thought to myself that at least it was a peaceful end, murmuring a couple last "sorry, sorry, chickens" under my breath. For the first time and not the last, thankfully, I saw Mama smile her huge full smile, her normally rather stern face melting into stunning beauty and her eyes twinkling. She quickly composed herself and motioned to me to strip my clothes off – *manje*. Now.

I'm not a prude by any means, yet we were not too far from the small road and, given the drought and the season, there was next to no leaf cover. She had chosen a spot in a circle of small acacia trees so there was also the thorn issue. I took a deep breath and followed her mimed instructions, quite sure that my white body would stand out and be seen yet resigned already to being a regular topic for the local gossip mill. We finished the ritual, me bracing for cold water and saying a grateful *ngiyabonga* when it became clear that Mama had been kind enough to use heated water. Water of any temperature was a luxury in those days, so I felt honored to be bathing in it, even if I was doing it standing in my bare feet on that blessed chicken, still warm, heart literally in its throat. I spoke out loud to my ancestors, as instructed, thinking of all the times my own heart had been in my throat as I found my way to this place, scared yet willing, and felt even more peace as I dressed again and followed Mama back up the hill.

We slipped off our shoes and reentered the rondavel, where Mama chatted in rather exclamatory tones to Baba. Siyanda translated and told me that she couldn't believe I didn't protest or get shy and that Baba was right, I must be Zulu. She was so proud of me and still loves to tell this story, smiling in that same beautiful way. Baba said, "Light," of course, and stared off a bit as Mama mixed some powders that Baba gave her on a stone and then put on rubber gloves. Siyanda showed me that I must sit, legs out in the traditional way, on the newspapers Mama had laid out, facing the open door and the view of the mountains.

Mama asked Siyanda to leave and, with Baba instructing her, had me remove my shirt. I was glad at this point to have worn a proper bra, though I'd soon fall into the Zulu ways – breasts are not traditionally covered and aren't seen as particularly sexual. (The back of the legs, though, from the knees up, are an entirely different matter, which is why longer skirts are required traditionally as a sign of respect). Using the second razor blade we'd brought, she proceeded to make small cuts in certain places, all over my body.

As I learned later when a trainee did this for me, Mama is one of the best at this and can do it without causing any pain at all – at least, until she rubs in the *muthi* mixture.

This ritual is a form of high protection, and I'm not sure who was more relieved when it was finished, me or Baba. We all sat for a few minutes, the two of them talking away in isiZulu, clearly discussing me and all we'd done that morning. I wanted nothing more than to curl up on the mat and take a nap, but soon Siyanda came in and translated Baba's instructions for the next few days to me, saying he'd see me again soon, that I should relax and know that the ancestors had welcomed me home beautifully, that I was safe now. I was home.

Baba began to call me his daughter within a few months of these regular meetings and chats. As time passed, he told me of the prophecy his grandfather had made when he was a young man, not yet married, and that he wasn't at all surprised that I'd found him. I'd really had to come a long way, he said – no wonder it took so much time! So he named me Nomadlozi – meaning "with the ancestors" – because, he believed, they'd brought me home. As he pointed out, laughing, how could I ever have found this place, a tiny settlement high up in the Lebombo mountains near Swaziland, if I hadn't been here before?

Home. That's exactly how it feels to me in every way, and so calling myself by the name that fits best seems wise, doesn't it? To use the Gumede surname is an honor and a privilege and makes perfect sense as I have become in every way the eldest child, down to coordinating Baba's funeral and directing his burial.

I'd hoped to have many more years with him. Yet his death a few years ago, suddenly and unexpectedly, brought me much closer to Mama, my newfound siblings, and to the extended family as well. They have, knowing the prediction and all the similarities we shared as well as the gifts Baba saw in me, welcomed me fully and enfolded me into this incredibly strong and beautiful familial circle. All except for Baba's aged auntie, who sits and stares at me through cataract-covered eyes while drinking from one-liter brown glass bottles of beer all day beginning with breakfast. But then she seems pretty suspicious of everyone, so I don't take it personally.

I'd only been in Ngwenya for a few months when Siyanda told me that there was a funeral coming up, one I should attend. It was for a young man of twenty or so who had gone to Joburg to find work after he and his girlfriend had a baby. I can only imagine what the city was like for him, having grown up at the top of the mountain ridge with family, animals, and open sky all around him. It had to be a real challenge, that transition to living in one room with several other young men in a crowded downtown, but like many before him, he did it to give his son a better chance at life and to avoid being a burden to his family by leaving his parents to raise his boy. He was one of twelve children, and his boy was the eleventh grandchild. His own father, a natural farmer, struggled to find work of his own. Every *rand* sent home made such a difference.

One night in the big city, his friend went out to a bar, while our young man wisely stayed at home. After several hours, he came back, followed by a group of young guys from the bar who were harassing him. When they began to beat him, our friend from Ngwenya went to help his friend, and they beat him to death. One of the most promising young men in the community, loved by many, a new father, gone. Just like that.

A couple of days before the funeral, I went to his family's compound to sit with the women, as is the custom. I sat in a hut on mats with the women of the family, a dozen women of varying ages, all of them wrapped in blankets and keening – weeping and wailing at irregular intervals. The mama kept her face covered and was quiet, but shuddered and shook a bit from time to time. There was interest in me being there – at that point, most had not met me though they knew who I was. At that point, I was only able to exchange greetings in isiZulu, and didn't understand the little conversation going on around me. I did know grieving, though, and we sat mostly in what felt like companionable silence.

There was a pile of blankets on the floor, and after an hour or more, the pile began to move. I heard a little mewling noise and used my eyebrows to question. Someone said "baby" in English, making me smile. They uncovered the three-month-old, peeling back so many layers I wondered if he was really in there, and handed him to me. This beautiful child with ancient eyes took one look into my own eyes, winning my heart immediately. For at least a couple hours, he kept making that connection, allowing me to feed him, hold him, rock him. I was more than a little in love by the time Siyanda stood at the door to retrieve me, something my now nearly paralyzed tail bone really appreciated. It would take a long time for me to learn to sit in the standard Zulu way, legs straight out and ankles crossed. I'm pretty sure my fidgeting was remarked on far and wide.

Two days later, we arrived for the funeral. The family homestead was full of people both under the big white tent rented for the occasion and spilling out of it. As is the custom, we split up, Siyanda staying with the men and me pulled forward from the back. They wanted me to sit at the very front with the pastors and elders in the ubiquitous white plastic chairs, facing the hundreds of mourners gathered. I refused, for the first time, choosing to join the mamas and the *gogos*, sitting on the grass mats. For a white girl from America where personal space is highly valued, and for someone who has never liked to sit with strangers touching her, this represented a huge change. Even today, few things make me happier than sitting butt to butt, leg to leg, smushed together like puppies, leaning on or being leaned on. I've never felt more part of a sisterhood than with these women. That day, though, I think I was a distraction, as my very white feet seemed to be quite the object of curiosity.

We sat and rocked, listening to the various ministers speak, watching as the boy's friends danced their hearts out in a tribute to him, singing hymns and "It's a Wonderful Day," my favorite part of any official gathering. At some point, the youngest minister came and beckoned me, which I refused at first, thinking it was about moving to those damned white chairs. He persisted, weaving his way amongst all the bodies to get close enough to whisper to me that they wanted me to view the body. Ah. What could I do but comply?

He led me forward, through the maze of wrapped heads and bright fabrics, my white feet finding a path through all the brown. I stood alone at one side of the surprisingly ornate casket, highly polished in juxtaposition to the dirt floor studded with sharp rocks beneath it, and met the pastor's eyes as he questioned my readiness. I'd seen dead bodies before and wasn't afraid, yet once he lifted the lid, I understood his hesitancy.

This poor kid, this beautiful boy. He had been cut up six ways to Sunday. His skin was held together with rough, uneven Xs of stitches. His throat had been slit, his head bashed, his eyes swollen. He hadn't stood a chance.

And yet, he felt so at peace. I breathed deeply, aware that I was being observed by hundreds of family members and friends, that I needed to be strong. I swayed a bit, the impact of the way he'd died felt deeply in my bones. And then I heard his voice. Telling me, asking me, beseeching me to look after his son, his boy. To help him grow into a good man. To be a friend to his family, to support them, that his parents would miss him. That he was so sorry he had to go, that I could stay. Would I stay, *ngiyacela* (please)? Would I look after them?

That voice, quite sweet and clear and strong, stays with me to this day. Clear and resonant, nothing I could ever forget. I have no idea how long I stood there, but I looked up at the pastor and I said yes, out loud. *Yebo*. I will. And nodded, allowing the lid of the casket to be closed. Went back to my place on the mat, the ladies clearing a path for me, nodding and clasping their hands in the prayer position that conveys so much, so simply, letting me come home to my spot among them. It was the very first time I felt I belonged among them, the first time I knew why I'd come.

Eighteen

While I technically lived on the small private reserve of Kube Yini, most of my time those first couple years was spent in the adjacent Zulu community of KwaNgwenya, where the Gumedes lived. It was only several kilometers from Kube as the crow flies but it takes about thirty minutes to get there, depending on how many herds of wild animals or cows there are in the road.

The word *ngwenya* means "crocodile," and the community is well named. The ridge that runs the length of it does, indeed, resemble the ridge along the back of a croc, and the prevailing attitude is also similar to that of the sluggish, yet quick to attack reptile. It is, like many indigenous communities in South Africa, extremely challenged both in financial and social services and in natural resources like water and wildlife. Understandably, the people see and feel the lack rather than the natural beauty, especially those who have never lived "away." I often tell people from Ngwenya that if the land they live on were in Northern California, it would be worth billions of dollars. They just look at me – not for the first time – as if I were mad.

Finding your way to the community isn't all that hard. You follow the N2, the two-lane paved highway that runs like a spine along the east coast of the country. You hang a right at the local bar/grill/road motel and a left once you go past the taxidermist and over the railroad tracks. If you time it just right as you come to the river, or more likely the dry riverbed, you end up going over the rickety old metal span bridge at the same time as the freight train alongside, racing it across. Dust clouds rise as you drive through the huge groves of enormous fever trees – the place I call "church" because when the sunlight filters through the fluorescence of them at just the right angle it is truly holy. Take your next right, careful of the cows who like to hang out there as well as a little further down when you run into a roadblock of them. Take in the beauty of the Nguni cattle – each of them carrying its own color and pattern. Maybe you'll spot my favorite, Qaphela, who looks like she's wearing carefully applied eyeliner. She'll stare you down for ages before begrudgingly moving out of your way.

After a bit, you'll begin to pass a few homes scattered here and there, traditional structures built of stone, wire, and wood with corrugated steel roofs, or thatch, often patched with a blue plastic sheet and held down with more stones. Once you turn left at the T-junction where the first of many small tuck (food) shops stand, the houses are closer together for a while. Go ahead and stop at the tuck shop for something to drink, but chances are the Coke will be warm – most of the community has no power.

And that pump you see on the left, where all the laundry is spread out to dry on the low quarry bushes? Powered only by cycling it with strong arms – there is no running water, only the occasional bore hole like this one. Most of Ngwenya is reliant on the municipality to bring water in via truck to fill all those big green JoJo tanks, the ones used to store water in non-drought times, which you find dotting the landscape. Something that is supposed to happen far more often than the sporadic deliveries that bring everyone out at once, carrying ninety liters balanced on their heads or larger vessels wheelbarrowed over the rocks and craggy paths.

Take in, too, the mountains as they unfold to your left. The big sort of bump of a summit is Ghost Mountain, and it holds very old Zulu burial sites – bones and skulls and all manner of battle gear, from what I hear. Imagine all that went on here, hundreds of years ago, and you can almost hear the drums. My Zulu father, Baba Gumede, walked the whole of it on a regular basis.

Head up the mountain – I know, the road gets pretty rocky but trust me, it's a whole lot better than it was when I first arrived. This is the "short road," and the easiest to access "up top." Watch out for the goats – the babies, especially, like to come barreling down the mountain side! Beware, too, the possibility that an enormous truck might be stuck or come toward you a bit faster than you'd like – it's harder to control on the descent, since the pitch is fairly steep. Give it a little extra gas to get up that last part, and all of a sudden, it's like you are at the top of the world. You and, often, another group of cows, of course.

While you'll see nicely constructed wooden *kraals,* or enclosures, at some of the homesteads, the cows mostly roam freely either on their own or with a herder who tries to keep them more or less off the highway. Given the four-year drought, they've been left to find whatever food they can. The concept of bringing them in at night is lost on the locals, even though there's huge concern over the losses and injuries from hyena and leopard attacks. The push and pull of conservation over perceived safety of the people and livestock is a subject for another day with no easy resolution in sight. Today, you might also see a few donkeys here and there too – I have yet to figure out their purpose, to be honest. They mostly graze and give very direct stares as you drive past.

To your left, you'll see the old tribal center, which is now yet another tuck shop rented out to an outside family, unfortunately, rather than someone from Ngwenya. Hopefully, these situations will one day be seen as opportunities for local entrepreneurs. Schools are scattered here and there, with varying resources and structures. There's a new high school we passed down low on our way up – it was requested by the local *induna* (councilor) and his committee because the female students were being raped in the woods as they walked the great distance to the closest school available. And beyond the tuck shop, further to the left, is the one clinic for all of KwaNgwenya. I cannot tell you how many times I have seen mothers both young and old, their one-week-old babies in their arms, walking up that crazy steep road we've just driven on their way to the clinic for the baby's first check-up. Imagine: one week postpartum, going mountain climbing. Yet that's the only medical care available, and so they do what they need to do.

At the top of the road, take a right and head up another steep hill past more traditional homesteads, and then your first left. The Silindokuhle Preschool sits high on the hill on your right, the original standard building erected by the municipality, then added onto by us in the form of a kitchen so that we could feed the children well, and an outdoor cooking area for community gatherings.

Yes, "us." I'll never forget the day one of the local *gogos* took me and Siyanda to see it. It had been closed up because the local parents couldn't afford to pay the teacher 35 *rand* per month per student, which is the equivalent of $2.75 in US dollars. Gogo said that the school name – Silindokuhle – meant "we wait for the good," and that I was the good they were waiting for. This, of course, plugged right into my belief that I was here to take care of other people.

Just a couple months later, we reopened the school with a full class of three-, four-, and five-year-olds. Sadly, three years later we would also have to close, given the lack of support for me working in the community. While the *inkosi*, or king, had always welcomed my work and support, the *indunas* – sort of local governors of different areas of the community – were jealous of my focus on one or two particular areas, and this caused issues that made it impossible for me to continue. But that's yet another story.

You can see the surrounding open land where we hoped to build soccer fields to promote inter-community activity and training for the children and youth. Maybe someday. There are great memories in this place, and the children have done so well as they move through to primary school with a good foundation. While the school educated through play, a concept that didn't make much sense to the locals, what was valued most was that we gave them breakfast and lunch – in a place where kids often eat mostly maize meal dishes and sometimes only once a day, especially during the drought when livestock were really stressed and suffering.

I spent many nights pondering this situation and others in the wee hours. What quickly became clear to me was that I could never help everyone. There was far too much need. And apartheid and the long-term effects of colonization meant there was an expectation that help would come from outside, likely from white hands. I came to the conclusion, fairly early on, that the best I could do was help people recognize their own gifts and abilities. After all, better to teach people how to fish rather than try to deliver fish to them daily, to paraphrase the well-used saying.

I'd seen that there was little choice for the young adults in Ngwenya but to leave and go to Durban or Joburg in order to find work, so I was very motivated to find projects that might give them the option to stay home and build their lives. For the lucky ones who did well in the education system and tested easily so they could pass matric exams, there was the prospect of going to varsity, or university, which meant leaving, too – at least temporarily. There were so many creative kids, though. Music is a huge part of the Zulu culture, still, and so is dance. Performing and storytelling through drama, writing, and the visual arts are a beautiful thread running through life here.

I began to look around for ways to provide and/or support projects using that creativity. I hoped this would instill a sense of pride and help individuals, as well as the community as a whole, regain their sovereignty more fully. I wanted them to see that the world could learn from them, from South Africa and the entire continent too. Rather than be seen as those poor Africans who needed to be saved – from what, I still could not tell – they could lead in ways that would make the world sit up and listen.

To help this happen, I joined forces with Thalente Madonsela, a Durban-based television actor who had become very popular on a couple series and had then started a production company to create the kind of opportunities for the youth I'd also had in mind. It seemed a good match. I funded this particular project through the Lehmkuhler Foundation, with Siyanda and I helping with every aspect as we held tryouts, trainings, and rehearsals for the making of a film based in a rural setting, which Thalente wrote.

The daily videos I viewed took my breath away. Ngwenya filmed very nicely, and the local students, along with a few elders in key parts, proved immensely talented and eager to learn. Thalente was less and less available toward the end of the project, but delays here are inevitable and while it was frustrating, I didn't see it as much of a problem. Until the day we screened the film for the community, the tribal center packed with our participants and their friends and neighbors.

It became clear that the movie would still require a great deal of editing, which Thalente promised to do. He also restated his commitment to entering the film in a couple competitions and providing internship opportunities for some of our youth, who were very excited at the prospect of working in Durban on set. But over the next few weeks, it became clear that Thalente wasn't interested in completing the project. This was incredibly disappointing to me and Siyanda, and even more devastating to the program participants who'd had such high hopes. I paid out extra funds to try to get the film finished by the freelance editors he'd also left hanging, and yet there was really no point. I didn't have the connections to further the work without him.

I still don't understand what happened. Unfortunately, many in the community blamed me. This wasn't ideal; I was still building trust. I hoped to do better with a music-focused project. And so I began planning how that might come to be.

Nineteen

Life continued to move quickly, though there was plenty of time to just stare off into the bush and try to work out how I'd gotten here, why I'd come, and what I'd left behind. I thought a lot about how exactly to best assist this community, these people I'd already come to love so much.

I went down to Durban from time to time to visit the Fouries. I had invested in a yoga/café business they'd started, though things had been quite odd at their son Brad's wedding earlier that year, and Caro had treated me in a more passive-aggressive way than normal. Still, I continued to put money into their dreams, telling myself it was a solid business investment.

George had always handled our finances and kept me in the dark, much as I asked to learn about them. I didn't have much financial experience, but was trying to grow my wealth so that I could build up the NPO I'd recently started in order to focus on the many projects I hoped would support the community of KwaNgwenya for years to come. I'd named my charitable organization the Silethokuhle Foundation after my conversation about the preschool with the *gogo*.

Silethokuhle roughly translates to "we bring the good," which was certainly my hope, to bring some light to this very rural community far off the map for most. The need even within KwaNgwenya was so great that I began by focusing on the youngest of the community, through the preschool, with plans to expand with offerings for the youth. Youth here means fifteen to thirty-five-year-olds, unlike in the States. The opportunities for young adults are very limited in rural KZN, so creating outlets and trainings especially for the creative ones was high on my list, even after my less-than-stellar experience with Thalente.

One summer day in February, my "brother" Siyanda, as I'd begun to call him, called and told me he'd met someone

I really needed to meet. Someone he thought I'd work with. Someone I'd been looking for.

I was, of course, very curious. He told me this guy, Jabu Ndlovu, was a gospel singer, a very well-known one people in the area were crazy about. That I'd certainly heard his music if only in ring tone form.

He said he'd had a chance to speak with him at length in Mkuze that day after he performed and that Jabu wanted to form a youth choir here in Ngwenya, to do exactly what I'd been wanting to do to showcase the latent local talent. To give the kids a chance to learn and grow their gifts. Jabu, he told me, had endured a childhood like mine, full of trauma and extreme challenges, and that Jabu talked about it openly and in terms of the gifts it had given him, much as I did. Siyanda was – as only he can be – quite determined that we should meet, and so I agreed.

We set up a time the next day, after this wonderous person was to return from Durban. I did a bit of Googling while I waited. The video of him with his former partner singing in what can only be termed "upscale traditional" clothing only intrigued me more. Ndlovu's voice was exquisite – strong, nuanced, full of depth – and he had an impressive presence on stage.

What I didn't expect is the call that evening when Siyanda said, "*He* is here." And I asked who – he answered, "UJabu" as if the king himself had arrived. The letter "u" in front of one's name or honorific adds respect in isiZulu, but this went beyond that. Clearly Siyanda was in awe of this man.

That should have been a warning, I guess. That kind of awed reverence was certainly the prevailing attitude of many people I'd encounter over the next few years. I would come to know the man – the vulnerable, wounded, sweet, funny, twisted, unbalanced human – and come to see how he was viewed by many as high on a pedestal, a man of God, a charming motivator of many and weaver of words.

They arrived at my doorstep just after dark that evening – Siyanda in his typical t-shirt, jeans, and *tekkies* (running shoes), and Jabu head to toe in white. Perfectly laundered and pressed white shirt, form-fitting white jeans, and spotless high tops. I took one look at him and thought, uh oh. I'd been on my own for some time now and hadn't dated in decades. I assumed, though, that he was nearly twenty years younger than me, and so told myself to focus on business. I hadn't dressed for the meeting at all and was in jeans and a tank top, with bare feet and freshly washed hair. Perfect for keeping things lowkey and work-minded.

What really got to me, though, was his voice. His speaking voice alone reached something deep inside of me in a way that told me this Jabu would become someone important in my life. I opened up to talking with him in a way I generally wouldn't have. While Siyanda did who knows what on his phone for hours, we got to know each other. Other than the one time he touched my bare arm and an electric shock went up and down my spine, we kept it all about the community, the youth, the healing power of music. For about four hours, which went by in the blink of an eye. Siyanda began to yawn – it was already past his 9:30 bedtime, and they had the drive back to his guest house down the mountain where Jabu would spend the night still ahead of them.

I decided before moving forward – and he was very ready to dive in – that I wanted to see if he could walk his talk. Our conversation had been full of synchronicities, so much so that I'd asked Siyanda if he'd told him everything about me and my plans for working with the youth, with an emphasis on creativity. He said that he hadn't, so I was curious about whether this Jabu Ndlovu, this talented, big-city celebrity, was really ready to dive in and try to make a joint project work in this deeply rural area, far from his base in Durban. I'd just had to spend weeks and a lot of additional funding to wrap up a film project featuring area youth. Thalente, also from the city, had left the project hanging at ninety percent completion, and I wasn't at all sure I wanted to try something similar again – certainly not right away. I was funding all of this myself, and while I hoped to get outside funding for the long term, I knew I needed to start being more conservative with my commitments to projects.

We agreed to meet in the morning at the guesthouse. I'd take him on a tour of the community so he could see more of Ngwenya, and we could talk more too. They left, and I climbed into bed with a smile on my face, knowing I'd just met someone who would play a big role in my life. I had no idea what was to come.

He didn't lie, not yet, not that day. When I picked him up at the guesthouse in the morning, he greeted me with a one-shoulder hug, Zulu style, and climbed in the Prado. As we headed down the dusty road, he asked me to stop the car. I did, wondering if he'd forgotten something. Instead, he asked me a question: "What's the most important thing, to you?"

I answered honestly: freedom. The very same answer I'd given George that day in our Virginia living room when I told him I wanted a divorce. The one thing I knew for certain that I wanted. I'd worked hard to free myself from a life that was never true to me, to come to South Africa finally, to find this place I called home.

That wasn't the answer Jabu was looking for, though, and it took me a couple tries before I got it. Love. That reply got a big high five and the smile that I would come to know meant he'd gotten what he wanted. "Yesssss! That's the most important thing, that we do everything we do with love, and from love."

Twenty

After a bit of gazing into each other's eyes and wondering what the heck this was all about – at least on my part – we continued the drive past the lathe gate, along the tree aloe-lined, rutted road, and past the cows drifting aimlessly in the heat. We followed the road as it wound past the local *'imoto'* graveyard full of pieces of abandoned vehicles, and waved at the mamas and young kids wheelbarrowing laundry to the borehole pump, watching them bicycle their arms furiously to bring up barely a trickle of water.

I drove the Prado up the mountain, hugging the side and bumping over the rocky outcroppings, before pulling onto the sandy road that runs along the top of the ridge. It always feels like arriving at the top of the world, and Jabu felt it too – both of us started grinning like young kids. We had arrived in the heart of Ngwenya.

On the way up, he mentioned how much the area reminded him of the rural community where he grew up with his maternal grandparents, closer to Durban. Once we were up top, the comparisons ended. He saw how deeply Zulu this place was, how old and how worn and how spectacularly beautiful. I've never tired of it, and as far as I know, neither has he.

While our first stop was the preschool, I pulled over and showed him a couple of my favorite viewpoints along the way, happy that he saw the same exquisiteness in them that I did. So far, so good – the dry, dusty, and dirty aspects didn't seem to faze the city kid. I was proud to drive up to the school, painted the ubiquitous orangey color that's so popular in these outlying areas. Jabu knew his way around things well enough to open the rusty wire that served as a jury-rigged lock for the equally rusty fence gate.

The kids were all inside, and only Fakile, the rather dour lady who helped with cooking the meals and cleaning saw us park and walk up the path past the barely thriving garden boxes to the door. The look on her face told me that she knew exactly who Jabu was and that in no time at all, via the mobile grapevine, all of Ngwenya would know he was here. He flashed his signature grin at her, charming as always and we made our way through the piles of tiny muddy shoes to sneak into the classroom.

I hadn't told the teachers we were coming, so it was merely coincidence that the children were singing when we arrived. But it sure did impress Mr. Ndlovu! I introduced my new friend to the children, and once the teachers' jaws had returned to their normal position, one of them quickly started a rousing chorus of "It's a Wonderful Day." Jabu joined in, and before I knew it, thirty tiny voices were singing one of his songs: *Ngiyadeserva*. I deserve.

I would hear this song a million times over the next few years, but in that moment it felt like a message. I deserve this. A beautiful man, an amazingly talented, creative, engaged partner in all I'd been trying to do. Someone, perhaps, to spend the rest of my life with, doing what I loved in the place I'd found my way home to. I began to think that maybe this might just be a gift from my ancestors, a way to know that this was the tall man in my dreams, the ones I'd been having for a year or two now. I'd seen myself in various scenarios – home, cars, places I didn't know – with a tall, lean man who aged beautifully in these dreams, ending with a snapshot of us on some sort of veranda, surrounded by a crazy big multigenerational family in our older years and beaming at each other.

I had so many of these dreams that I'd ordered an extra-long king bed and made sure all the doorways were higher than usual as I renovated my new home. But I didn't have time to dwell on those feelings that day. The thing about children is that they keep you in the here and now, and that day was no exception. Once the singing stopped, my attention was demanded, in no uncertain terms. I was all theirs, and they knew it.

The preschool children and I had a ritual of sorts. I'd come in the door and end up with five kids holding onto the fingers of each hand in no time at all. That would quickly make it very difficult to move, so we'd stumble our way out the front door like a twenty-two-legged octopus, nearly falling down in giggles and smiles. I'd take a seat on the front stoop with them falling all over me.

In the beginning, they'd rub my skin very briskly – trying to see if the white would come off. I asked Siyanda in the first week if it was because I was the first *umlungu* they'd touched, and his reply not only shocked me but made me feel the responsibility of being the very first white person they'd ever seen. In those days, the roads were so bad that most children didn't even go down to town until they were five or six years old, so I would be their first and only experience of an *umlungu* for years. As if I didn't already feel such a strong need to make their young lives as full and enriched as possible.

I'd brought several visitors to Silindokuhle Preschool before the day Jabu arrived, and never once had they grasped a visitor's fingers in the same way they did mine. No one else had had the privilege of wearing preschoolers on their laps, shoulders, legs, and heads. But that day? The minute he stopped singing, they descended upon both of us. It still makes me smile to think of the mashup mountain of legs and arms and enormous smiles, all of them clamoring to get close to the two of us. He'd passed that test, with flying colors.

Eventually we untangled ourselves, got back in the car, and drove further along the ridge road, dodging the goats and cows out for a walk that created silhouettes against the blue, blue sky. Ngwenya is always a startlingly beautiful place, and that day was exceptional, as if she were showing off just for the occasion. I'd decided at the last minute to take Jabu to the Mnguni homestead, where my infant godson lived with his grandparents, a seriously traditional couple who had raised twelve children before losing their son, the baby's father, the year before – the one whose funeral I'd attended. My godson was their twelfth grandchild, and several of his cousins attended the preschool.

Mama Mnguni, using the traditional honorific for a middle aged woman as is the norm here, showing respect, is one of the most beautiful women I've ever seen and a foundation of calm and kindness for everyone there and in the community as well. Baba Mnguni is old school Zulu, a strong and opinionated man who loves his family and has managed to support, with Mama's help, all those kids with no education – just his innate ability to raise livestock and farm. He'd eventually decide I should be his second wife without consulting me, but in those days I saw him as a brother and his wife as a sister. Their beautiful farm was one of my very favorite places to be – a safe haven when things in the community got challenging. A place of peace.

Taking Jabu there was another test of sorts. Once again, he blended in perfectly, with ease and grace and a humbleness I found very attractive on many levels. He had business in Joburg the next day, so I headed back down the short road to drop him off at Siyanda's guesthouse even as he suggested he come back and stay in my little guesthouse that weekend, so that we could get to know each other better and begin to plan our choir project.

While I'd had that *ngiyadeserva* insight into what could be earlier, I didn't believe he was interested in me in that way – that is, until he asked me to stop on one of the rocky outcroppings on the way down the mountain. He informed me, in no uncertain terms, that this was not just about business. In typical Zulu male fashion, he announced that he was going to kiss me now and leaned over the huge center console of the Prado to do just that. I didn't mind, not one bit.

He was, it turned out, in his mid-forties to my mid-fifties. He was also a self-proclaimed "gospel powerhouse" to my rather introverted creative and a very attractive Zulu man to what I considered my gently aging but still very pale average looks. I couldn't imagine that he'd actually stay interested in me. I assumed it would be a passing thing, and that he'd come to his senses soon enough so we could go back to being business associates.

I took the flirty WhatsApp messages he sent while traveling in stride. I was more surprised when, after he returned to Kube and I gave him the daylight tour – carefully pointing out his guest room – he quietly placed his luggage in my bedroom. He explained that we'd have more time to talk and be close this way, to say nothing of the wild animals he'd rather not be alone with, but I was quite sure exactly where that would lead.

In fact, we did chat for some time before sleeping that night, this beautiful man holding my hand quite chastely. Then around two a.m., he woke me up, having heard noises. I listened and recognized that the local leopards were very close by, huffing away. He asked what that was, and I replied, "Leopard," in hushed whispers. He nodded and seemed to drift back to sleep. A few minutes or maybe longer later, the noises had changed and he queried again – asking how many there were. When I answered, "Two," he wanted to know what they were doing. So I said that they were making more leopards, as it was quite clear to me that they were getting hot and heavy. In the dark, I heard, "That's a good idea," and before I knew it, he was on top of me – presumably attempting to make more gospel singers.

Mostly, I was just amused. Until Jabu confessed the next day that while he'd never been married, he'd been engaged to be married for the past five or six years to the mother of one of his youngest children. Unfortunately, this news came a bit late in the game. It went against every-thing I stood for, though informal research told me that in the Zulu tradition, if they were going to actually marry, it would have happened long ago. This, along with his expla-nation that things were not going well and he didn't expect he and his child's mother would be together much longer, somehow led me to say that I'd give him a few months to decide what he wanted.

I have no idea why, but I did. I had, of course, been faithfully married for twenty-odd years, and now found myself trying to enter the dating scene in a completely dif-ferent culture all the way across the world. I was, despite

my age and experience, both clueless and getting accustomed to leaping without any idea whether I'd land on my
feet. If I'd known what was to come, I'm not sure I'd make
the same decisions now, yet all of it has led me to exactly
where I belong. Perhaps there truly are no mistakes.

Twenty-One

I was learning so much on so many levels and expanding my old beliefs – sometimes it seemed more like exploding them. Life on a small game reserve was challenging, especially in a prolonged drought. I'd taken so much for granted in the US – not just the white privilege sorts of things that many are examining lately, but basics like clean drinking water (often processed with very fancy filters), organic foods, and lightning-fast fiber internet.

None of my newly acquired skills had been needed in Washington DC, from peeing in the bush and in long drop toilets to tracking wild animals. Learning how to drive on the "wrong" side of the road was one thing, figuring out how to drive the "wrong" direction to pass huge trucks at high speeds was quite another. Driving, especially in rural South Africa, resembles nothing so much as a video game version of Chicken. My time on the game reserves those first months had prepared me well for commuting through the local Big Five areas – I knew how to pass a journey of giraffes, staying more than one of those long leg's lengths away, and to not try to outdrive a rhino. To say nothing of what to do when, while visiting an elephant camp with Dutch friends, we got between a total of fifteen female elephants and their babies and their destination of the watering hole, and I had to back up on a narrow, deep sand road for a kilometer or more while my guests prayed aloud.

Even the ordinary day to day was wholly different. Over the months and years, I would learn to do what South Africans always do – make a plan, the ultimate answer to any problem – but in those early days, the abundance of spiders, insects, geckos, and just plain dirt was a bit of an adjustment. While once upon a time I'd hiked and camped off the grid frequently, I'd become accustomed to five-star hotels and three-ply cushy toilet paper, or loo roll, as it's politely known here. I was taught how to bathe with very little water and to use the leftover bathwater to flush with, letting nothing go to waste. I learned, in time, how to buy groceries – an hour and a half drive each way making it important to choose so that they lasted at least a couple weeks. I learned the night sounds, including those leopards. and to discern warning cries from those of various animals making babies.

I learned enough isiZulu to be polite and also, sometimes, to get in trouble. I began to see how oriented to the Northern Hemisphere our entire world is, and that in the US, at least, how the goal is mostly to always be comfortable. Life is not generally comfortable at all here in South Africa – there is always danger present, and the entire country is a walking case of PTSD. Yet there is immense beauty and nature is, of course, bountiful. It all quickly became my new normal.

Half my week, in the fall of 2017, was similar to the way it had been that first year or so – I'd rise early a few days a week and make my way down, stopping for a herd of impala, perhaps spotting an elephant on the other side of the wire fence, as I drove off the reserve to spend time in Ngwenya with Siyanda or at the preschool, finding my way around on my own more and more now though I'd made strict promises to him and Jabu not to pick anyone up on the road – difficult when there were old *gogos* struggling with the rocky incline.

One day, I did stop to pick up a couple elderly women I thought I recognized, and then a *mkhulu* (grandfather) they knew who turned out to be more inebriated than I'd noticed. I thought to myself that it was a good thing Siyanda wasn't around, only to see his *bakkie* (pickup truck) in my

rearview mirror, following me up the hill. I'd been caught –
though after he lectured me, he admitted that he was more
and more comfortable with me being on my own. Baba
Gumede had begun doing protective work with me, and I
wasn't at all afraid. I really never had been. I knew some in
the community resented my presence, but most had been
very welcoming and supportive from day one – and I had
the *inkosi,* or king, of the community behind me too.

I'd started teaching English at the local primary school,
the one where our preschool would send our kids as they
got older. As a child, I'd loved playing school, and I'd
majored in special education in college, so it made perfect
sense. The first and second graders were a bit shy yet very
enthusiastic and this was another way I could easily help
the community.

I was more hesitant about using the different healing
modalities I knew. Less confident that they'd be accepted,
that I'd be accepted in that way, despite the fact that on my
first visit, I was immediately seen as a *sangoma* by several
local people. Coming from the US, I was acutely aware
of concepts like racial/cultural appropriation as well as the
South African way of white people treating Bantu people
as children, which then leads to an expectation of hand-
outs and being taken care of, which in turn promotes white
saviorism. I've seen for a long time how disempowering all
of these effects of colonialism are for people of color everywhere, and it's deeply true here.

I see my black brothers and sisters as profoundly and
deeply sovereign, powerful, and wise – which means I'd
never want to further take away their innate strengths.

These days, I've found my feet on this front, but back then? It felt like tightrope walking, especially for a kid made a serious perfectionist in her early years, walking a minefield of emotional triggers at home which could send the adults who were supposed to be parenting her into a world of hurt and chaos, requiring her to parent them.

On the other hand, I had experiences from that very first month of really being able to change people's lives for the better, from a health and wellbeing perspective. For example, there are three women who I visited in different areas, bedridden for a couple years each, who are now walking with only a cane for assistance. In visiting them, all I did was listen and observe – their entire demeanors showing me just how strong they were underneath all the dire predictions that they'd be spending the rest of their lives in bed, useless and a burden to their families. As I'd once been told similar things, I knew how devastating that could be, how difficult it made it to even try. In talking with each of them, with a great deal of respect and insights from their ancestors, I could see the true essence within them. On each visit, while doing reiki and teaching them stretches and exercises, I also took the time to begin to deprogram all that negative messaging. And within a few visits – and a walker I brought in one case – each of them resumed a fairly normal life, feeling useful and respected within their families again.

Still, I continued to struggle with doing healing work in the Zulu communities as I had a lot of old programming from the US around things like liability. And at this point, I was battling to get my permanent residency in

South Africa. I certainly didn't want to do anything to jeopardize that, though I wasn't doing anything wrong and very likely helping in more ways than I knew. The calling was there, yes, but I had all kinds of barriers build up to prevent me from following the path of healing work. Wasn't it enough, after all, to have made this huge leap to come to such a rural area in KZN? I wasn't in Kansas anymore, that's for sure.

So I worked with a local guy, Siyanda's brother Dingane, who had established an NGO to provide support in rural homes for HIV/AIDS patients and their caregivers, namely family members. We'd take my four-wheel-drive vehicle as far as we could up into the craggy mountain roads and then get out and walk from there, the drought-dried grass and pervasive, demonic paper thorn groundcover poking our feet as we navigated our way along cow paths to each home. So many homes, given that KwaZulu-Natal has the highest rates of HIV cases in South Africa, still.

As a young adult, I'd watched as this disease decimated the gay population in Atlanta. Decades later, the scenario wasn't so different here – the shame, the resignation, the lack of hope. And here, it had created a staggering number of orphans and neglected children. All of this took a toll on the *gogos*, the grandmothers, in particular. Once *izindl-ovukazi,* the queens who reigned over their families, telling stories and teaching the traditional ways, now they were dealing with both the daily needs of their adult children who had come home so sick they required adult nappies and their grandchildren, who constantly needed their time, love, and resources.

Dingane led the way one morning along a particularly precarious path, the two women from our staff filling me in on this family's story as we picked our way around the prickliest of the thorns. It was still early in the day, yet the sun was beating down, my head sweating under the cloth *doek* I had wrapped as we got out of the vehicle and sunscreen dripping too close to my eyes. The eldest son, once the family's pride and joy, had come home from his job in the mines – the sole source of income for this family, which had already lost all but two of its children to "being sick" – so weak and ill that he had collapsed into bed and hadn't gotten out in a couple months. We'd brought diapers for him, as those were always needed. The clinics were to disperse them, but typically only gave a couple packs of twelve every few months, far less than were needed to save a great deal of work in a time when doing laundry was a challenge, given the drought.

I entered the typical RDP (or Reconstruction and Development Program) block house, one of many built by the South African government, my eyes adjusting to the dim light from the bright sunny day outside. There was that familiar, universal scent of the sickroom mixed with the smells of a rural home – goats and curry and the spicy bush, along with pure earth. The patient's sister, his only remaining sibling of the original eight, led me to him. His very emaciated body was so like those I'd seen in Atlanta, lying on its side under a few of the ubiquitous fleece blankets despite the day's heat.

She spoke to him, shaking his shoulder and telling him Dingane had arrived with an *umlungu* from America, that he should get up, which seemed a bit ambitious given his state. He rolled over with a great deal of effort, summoning a smile as his eyes battled to focus. He recognized Dingane and thanked him for coming, then fixed his eyes on me and, as often happened, apologized for his lack of proper clothing, for not coming out to greet us properly.

I assured him that I understood and, as he spoke English fairly well, we chatted for a bit. He was badly dehydrated, so I gave him some water with rehydrating solution. Mostly we talked about his feelings of guilt around not being able to support the family. After just twenty minutes or so, he'd downed the water and was clearly needing rest so I left him in peace and went out to the first room where his mother, aunties, and a handful of children were sitting on mats, fanning themselves in an attempt to keep the flies away.

Dingane introduced everyone and we exchanged greetings, a couple children braver than the rest coming to sit next to me and eventually gathering the courage to touch my arm. We all chatted, Dingane translating as needed. Gogo told me her story, and the stories of how she'd lost her children, how she missed when times were better and they all made music together in that very room. I saw a couple drums in the corner and asked if I could try to play them, amusing everyone with my not so awful attempt at traditional rhythm. Before I knew it, they were all singing the most beautiful praise songs, and the drums were in more experienced hands than mine. I made hand gestures to ask if I could take video with my *ifoni,* and was answered by broad smiles as usual – I'm often asked (more like demanded) to "shoot, shoot" – and was able to capture all of it.

Shadow and light, this contrast in life. As the eldest son lay all but helpless, and his life energy waning in the next room, the family sang and glorified God and their ancestors, even in their deep helplessness and sadness. It's all true, every bit of it, and it's all lived. Daily.

They thanked us for coming, and for the little help we'd brought, the staff members giving instructions for the coming weeks since they only were able to visit every month or two given the many households in need. I realized yet again what great relief and hope just a bit of time, attention, and materials can bring. There's no end to need here, and likely never will be, yet that doesn't mean that it's not worth doing whatever we can. For me, it's all been a lesson in realizing it's always better to do something, even if it feels entirely inadequate and imperfect.

Over these couple of years, I spent time often at the Gumede home with Baba and Mama and gradually getting to know the rest of the family, though at first I thought they really didn't like me or perhaps resented my barging in at this point in our lives. It turned out they were just shy and unsure of their English, though most of them speak it quite fluently. I spent more time with my siblings and especially my sisters' baby boys, born after I'd arrived, until they reached the point that all rural Zulu babies seem to encounter around nine months of age, when they all of a sudden realized I am white and would cry as soon as they spotted me, especially if I was wearing sunglasses. These two were tough, they were like this for nearly a year vs the usual few months, but happily, we're on great terms these days.

Baba was trained as a *sangoma* and an *inyanga*, two different traditional healer roles, and had been a great *gobela*, or teacher, of many *thwasas*, or apprentices, along the way. He was well-known and well-respected in both the community at large and the regional healers' collective and beloved by many. Baba told me early on that I was already *sangoma*, as he was, that I didn't really need to *thwasa* (a word used both as a noun and a verb having to do with *sangoma* training) but that he would teach me about local medicinal plants and other *muthi*, or medicine, and teach me how to throw bones, something I'd been fascinated with for all my life.

From the beginning, he was much more sure than I was of my skills, and had no question about my abilities to help people on their life journeys. I learned from him every time I visited, despite the fact that I had only minimal (though very deep and traditional) isiZulu and he understood only very minimal English. I never heard him say anything but "light" in my language, though he threw in a bit of Afrikaans routinely, since he would have been made to study that at school and use it in his work in the mines as a younger man. I sat on a grass mat literally at his feet, and also visited other *sangomas* both locally and in Swaziland to broaden my knowledge of the vast number of ways traditional healers work. I'm so glad, given all that would come, that I spent as much time as possible at home with Baba in those years.

The other half of my week, at that point, was focused on Jabu and our joint project. We fell into a pattern, Jabu and I. He'd be at Kube three days each week in order to first do tryouts and then practice sessions for the youth choir we'd dreamt of separately and now were creating together. Our two damaged souls, both wanting to build the relationship and family we'd each dreamt of, struggled against our histories and our desires.

There were two sayings I heard a lot growing up, having to do with wishes. One, if I dared to wish aloud for anything, would come from my mother. "If wishes were horses, beggars would ride." I didn't really understand that at all – it seemed a good thing, beggars riding – but I knew it meant I should not dare to wish for anything. Enough said, I should just shut up and deal with whatever cards I was dealt. And the other was to be careful what I wished for, something I'd heard outside of home, which made much more sense but since I wasn't to wish for anything, didn't seem to really pertain to me at the time. That latter could have been my theme song for my relationship with Jabu.

It was, in so many ways, a cautionary tale. These couple years were full of ups and downs, highs and lows. One day we'd be in the studio in Durban, having driven down with thirty-some choir members to record beautiful music in perfect harmony, and the next we'd be shouting at each other, ending with me driving the three and a half hours back to the bush alone and in tears. Months later, we'd buy cows together – a very significant thing in the Zulu culture, choosing each one carefully and dreaming of the farm we'd build together on land we'd purchased on the picturesque Inanda Dam - and then he'd disappear without a word for weeks.

One year, Jabu surprised me with a lovely birthday dinner and a table full of friends, where he gave me the traditional gifts to formally begin to make me his *makoti* (bride). A few weeks later, he threatened to kill me, his kids, and himself because he'd decided – for no good reason – that I was cheating on him with a business associate he'd introduced me to several months earlier. At this point, one of the darkest times of my relationship with Jabu, when he'd suddenly become someone I didn't know and was making threats that were so serious I had to seek help, I was advised that I must have a bodyguard.

An acquaintance who knows about these things made a phone call. Before I knew it, I was back in Durban, in the local Woolworth's shopping center parking lot, sitting outside at my favorite healthy café and surrounded by about ten seriously muscled Zulu guys in paramilitary uniforms. They introduced me to their boss, who I only know to this day as "Chief." Still in a state of shock and very concerned about Jabu and his kids, I was able to register Chief's shock at hearing I needed to be protected from a local favorite son, this beloved gospel singer, yet also I could see that he'd learned that anyone is capable of violence.

The Chief is a soldier still, though I believe he's been out of the military for quite some time, and his training kicked into high gear quickly. He decided I needed the best, and had someone contact the man who often protected him – "He's young, but he's very, very good, the best I have."

A little while later, a good-looking, strong young guy showed up in street clothes and was greeted happily by the whole cadre of armed men. I thought at first that this was someone they'd just happened to run into, but no – this was the guy, Musa. Introductions were made, Musa was given his orders, and then we were on the way home with him following me on the familiar backstreets. I kept shaking my head on the way, unsure of how all this had happened, if it was genuinely possible that the man I loved had put me in the position of needing protection, and yet I didn't know that man who'd shown up that stormy night at Kube Yini threatening me. And so here I was. With a full-time, live-in bodyguard. For the next couple months, I'd been told. At least.

I valued my privacy and quiet time so much that I couldn't imagine how this was going to go. Despite having been shaken to the core the night before and still being in shock, my thoughts were of the more mundane: What did this Musa person eat? Were there clean sheets on the sofa bed in the home office? Could I sneak out and be by myself once in a while? And how was I going to see Jabu?

Then I remembered what had happened, and that this man I loved was so out of control that it was truly better for him if I kept myself away from him. That it was important to keep him safe. This was my old pattern showing up again, and it's not uncommon in domestic violence situations, for the abused to protect the abuser. In this case, keeping him safe kept me safe, too, so it was all for the best.

And so I began to settle into this new way of life, being protected in a way I'd never been taken care of before. Musa was, and is, very dedicated to what he does, so I only had to deal with my own discomfort and my grief over the whole situation. It was a relief to be able to sleep at night without being on guard, to know that I was safe, to be able to rest.

I didn't realize that the hard work of getting long-term protection still lay ahead. Musa and I spent hours and hours – days and days, really – sitting on hard wooden benches in the domestic court and in the Inanda police station, trying to get a protection order written and then served. It was an education in and of itself for both of us – watching young women with tiny babies in big piles of blankets trying to fill out forms so that there would be some hope of getting a support order served against the fathers of their children, seeing other women hiding black eyes behind huge sunglasses. And here I was, with all the privileges and knowledge accumulated over fifty-some years, in that exact same place.

I knew that a huge part of my goal was to get Jabu help – that the man he'd been that night he threatened to kill us both, to kill the kids, wasn't the man he truly is – and yet I wasn't any different than the dozens of women who camped out in those hot, stuffy passages every day. Being white didn't protect me, and I think my presence there opened the eyes of quite a few people.

It didn't help me get the help I needed either. The very police who were meant to protect me and my rights stood in the way of even getting the order of protection served, over and over. Musa and I witnessed so much refusal of help and degradation of those in need, it made me realize just how fortunate I am, over and over, to have his company and the resources to pay for that kind of assistance – and to be able to leave South Africa entirely if I wanted to.

I didn't want to. Not at all. In a strange way, all of this made me more determined than ever to stay. And through all of this mess, Musa and I bonded in a way that even we don't fully understand. He became a bodyguard because of one great loss – and I'm guessing many other ones, too – in his life. Much like Michael Oher, whose story was chronicled in the movie *Blind Side,* he likely has a very high Protective Instincts score. I'd always wanted a son and always felt like I'd have one, sooner or later, and while I didn't raise him, most of the time you'd never know it. Over those first few months of being together 24/7 and long conversations in the car and on those courtroom benches, we slowly integrated into each other's lives. It was, as it had been with others here in South Africa, as if we were just catching up on what we already somehow knew.

That first morning after I met Musa, he asked very apologetically if we could go downtown to pick up something from his wife at her office. It turned out that the Chief hadn't let him know a thing about his new assignment, and he needed clothes and things. I liked Suzi immediately. No question – she was and is a strong, kind young woman who is both no-nonsense and a whole lot of fun. I couldn't possibly have known that day how important both of them would become to me.

Musa and I had a lot to deal with those first few weeks, of course, but once the order of protection was in place and the police were eventually convinced to serve it, things calmed down and I began to heal. One day I realized that

Musa hadn't seen his kids more than briefly, once or twice, in those first weeks. He couldn't leave me alone, and I wasn't coherent enough to think of it. So I invited them to come meet us for lunch.

That was the day I met the girls who would come to be my granddaughters, Gia and Grace. They were four and a half and eighteen months old at the time, beautiful girls both shy and exuberant and so happy to see their daddy – as was Suzi. And the softer side of Musa came out too. I know it must sound strange, this way our family formed, yet if you believe everything happens for a reason, well – there you go. For me, it has to do with ancestors and reuniting of those I've known before on a soul level. No matter how you see it, it is a gift.

Jabu and I stayed apart for a while, but I was still deeply enmeshed with him. He wanted to go to therapy together, and at the time I did too. He'd made what seemed like a true effort, standing up in court and asked only that the protection order be amended rather than cancelled so that I felt safe enough for us to go to therapy and fix things. I truly believed we still had a future together, that we'd be good.

My optimism was short-lived. Despite the promise to go into therapy, Jabu stopped showing up after the first few sessions. Not long after that, we were on stage at the ICC – Durban's convention center. Months of work on both our parts had helped Jabu win the coveted Best Gospel Singer award. It was a glorious night, but the next morning after requesting I take many photos of him with his award, he disappeared again as he had done in the past before we began counseling, and he never attended another session.

We kept trying. We would make pacts to stop our legendary fights, realizing the damage we were doing to each other and everyone around us, but while those pacts helped calm the chaos, our problems didn't disappear. As great as our passion and our devotion to each other were, so were the old patterns and behaviors. They weren't going to go away without a great deal of the therapy he'd already bailed on.

At the bottom of it all were our individual issues. We'd both been through a great deal of trauma in our hellish childhoods, but I'd sought out help along the way, and he hadn't had that kind of grace. Worse, I'd fallen back into my old pattern of not speaking up for myself, something I'd learned with my parents. I rarely emphasized what I needed, focusing on his needs and that of the family. I took his mother grocery shopping every month, did whatever I could to encourage better relationships between him and his children, and even backed the building of a home ostensibly for him and his children, though his "ex" and mother of his youngest daughter considered it hers, both publicly displaying it and refusing to leave despite his lack of interest.

We both found solace in creativity and yet in the end, his need to constantly disappear and my abandonment issues made it impossible to be in relationship with each other, though God knows we kept trying. Jabu was one of my greatest teachers, and I wouldn't have the love I now have in my life without all that I learned in our time together. I saw, in these few years, that being a good person doesn't mean that only good will happen to you, that you'll live your life surrounded by unicorns and rainbows. Shadow and light, they are always both present in this thing we call being human.

My relationship with Jabu wasn't my only challenge. My work in the community caused a great deal of jealousy amongst the local *indunas,* or governors, within Ngwenya – and it would eventually become impossible for me to support this settlement I'd come to love so much. The Fouries, the original white South African "family" friends I had in KZN, would use me in ways that were incomprehensible to me, reinforcing those old predictions my mother had instilled in me, that I would die alone and broke. It was an awful situation that forced me to take legal action, but since the whole thing has not yet been resolved, I feel it's better not to dive more fully into it here. It's been a big lesson, that those whom call you family easily may not be the ones to trust with your love, energy, and money. No matter what color their skin is.

The doors kept shutting and the nos kept coming. I fronted a considerable sum to an American woman who'd been living in the Middle East to come and help with the admin for my foundation. I even bought another cabin at Kube Yini and a *bakkie* for her use, only to have her leave two weeks later without meeting with me and refusing to speak about what caused this change of heart. I repeated aloud far more often than seemed reasonable that I was not an ATM, and yet I was constantly asked for money, and it was assumed that I'd take care of people I didn't even know.

I'd learn that traditionally, African people – those with darker skin anyway – see money, as well as time and other resources, very differently. Those who have are expected to take care of those who do not, so in an odd way, being leaned on was part of being fully accepted within the Zulu community. I have yet to find an understanding of this from those outside the Zulu culture, but I do see that all of this was teaching – that I needed to work these old demons out, and for that I am quite grateful.

I take full responsibility for all my decisions, of course. I am the one who centered my life – my time, love, and resources – on those who couldn't or wouldn't love me. In trying to fill the deficit left by the way I was raised, I wasn't able to discern who I should choose to help, how to close the gap between feeling needed and feeling unloved and unwanted. I didn't even see, for the longest time, that I could choose at all, really. I just fell into relationships of different sorts with whoever showed up along the way.

It would take years of practice and learning via trial and error before I'd come to, as the Shaker song says, the place just right. Until I would find my heart's delight. And what happened between then and now, what broke us in the end? Well, it very nearly killed me.

Twenty-Two

In December of 2018, my Zulu father Baba Gumede unexpectedly passed away. I was away on one of the mandated trips I had to take beyond bordering countries every three months in order to renew my holiday visa while I waited what would be over three years for my permanent residency to be approved.

When Musa picked me at the airport in Durban, three hours away from home, he told me that Baba had been ill and had gone to the clinic a few days earlier for the first time in his life. He said Baba had been given medicine for blood pressure, he thought, and was doing better, that none of them had wanted to worry me while I was away and that Baba knew that for immigration reasons, I could not have cut my trip short. This is typical of Zulu men, of course, deciding things for you without your input, but there was nothing that could be done about it at that point. We tried to call Baba, and Mama answered his phone, saying that they'd call me back. They were in a taxi on the way to the hospital. Baba wasn't feeling any better, she said, and looked worse to her.

Tired from my travels, I fell asleep early that night, not having heard from Mama, though the phone network at home didn't work well in the evenings so I wasn't surprised. I had a dream of going to see my Zulu father and seeing a huge crowd, as I approached, following a small white *bakkie* up the hill. When I got there, the sea of people parted to let me into the yard. I was wearing traditional clothing in the dream, and speaking isiZulu to everyone, asking what was going on. No one said anything. The door to my father's rondavel was closed. I was led by the hand up the steep hill to the house my parents lived in, only to find Baba in a casket, my uncles propelling me forward to sit next to him.

I wrote this off, when I woke in the wee hours, to anxiety and being travel weary, to guilt at not being there when my beloved father, who always was there for me, needed me most.

The next morning, Siyanda called, and we caught up on all that had happened with work matters in Ngwenya, something he was supervising since I was in Durban full time now and there wasn't much going on. He'd heard – nothing is private in Ngwenya – that Baba had been at the clinic but had heard nothing further. He said he'd check later in the day with Mama for me – I wasn't fluent enough to speak with her on the phone myself yet. I told him I'd come up the following day, that I didn't think Baba had ever gone to the clinic in his life, to say nothing of the hospital, and we agreed he'd go visit with me, making plans to meet at the guesthouse midday. I happily unpacked that morning. Jabu was coming back from a gig north of Durban, and I was looking forward to seeing him before I went home to visit my parents.

Then Siyanda called again, less than an hour later. Someone from home had called him, he said, and asked me to sit down.

I knew. I'd known something wasn't right.

He said he was so sorry to tell me that Baba had died the night before. I collapsed on the floor. I have no idea what I said, but I didn't recognize the noises that would come out of me in the next couple hours. My world had imploded, despite all I'd been through in my life, like it never had before.

I thanked Siyanda and told him I'd be home the next day. He asked me to wait and recover from the shock a bit, and said he'd speak to Jabu and be sure he could drive me up. I don't remember much after that until I realized that Jabu was quite late in arriving home, something that was not at all unusual. I called him, something I typically wouldn't have done, knowing full well he'd come when he was ready. At first he made his typical excuses, but he stopped when he heard in my voice that I was not ok. He was never reliable, but he was always sensitive to these things, more than most.

I didn't want to tell him on the phone. I asked him to come by, but he had to take musicians home first, and so he demanded I let him know what was going on. I got the words out somehow for the first time, that Baba had died, and he literally screamed, "No, no" over and over. My father, once quite a ladies man who had been very happily married to Mama for nearly fifty years, had apparently promised him he'd teach him how to be a good man and a good husband, and the first I heard of it was that day. Jabu pulled over and called me back, asking a million questions I couldn't answer. But he didn't come home, even though he had to drive right past our exit to get all the guys downtown. He didn't even call to check on me.

I would find my own way home the next day, arriving midday and making my way up to my parent's house just as I had in the dream. The door to Baba's rondavel was closed. Two of the goats were curled up on the steps, looking as dejected as the dogs lying close by. Even the peacocks were dragging their feet rather than strutting as usual. It was hot, as is typical in December, though the drought had ended so the land was greener than I'd ever seen it.

I entered the house, leaving my shoes outside in a pile much larger than usual, and saw that everything had been moved around to accommodate this mourning period. Mama was dressed in traditional blue mourning clothes, but I couldn't see them as she was, even in the heat, under those fleece blankets in a pile, resembling a mountain on top of the usual mattress with all the aunties and uncles sitting around the perimeter of the room.

It's custom for only very close family members to sit on or next to the mattress with the matriarch in mourning, and as close as I'd become, I was very unsure of my status now that Baba had left us. Much to my surprise, a space was cleared for me to Mama's right, and I was motioned to sit right next to her. I heard a faint "Nomadlozi," and she reached out her hand for mine. My heart broke again, and I used the little isiZulu I had – *ngiyaxolisa kakhulu*, Mama, *ngiyakuthanda*, meaning I am so sorry, Mama, I love you – over and over, tears spilling down my face as I climbed up on the mattress so we could lean on each other.

Mama and Baba had done everything together. They had the kind of partnership Jabu and I wanted for ourselves. I admired that so much, and I couldn't imagine her on her own even as strong as she is, since typically widows never remarry in the Zulu culture. My brother Mandla came in and told me that the elders asked that I come back the next morning at ten o'clock for a meeting to plan the funeral, which I readily agreed to, of course. The usual plastic tub and dishtowel were brought, signaling that food was on its way. While it's incredibly impolite, I just couldn't eat, which was met with consoling cries of *"ah bakithi"* and *"shem,"* everyone nodding and understanding I was deeply grieving.

I made my way home to Kube Yini, stopping to watch a huge bull elephant who stared at me for a long while then lowered his head – much lower than usual – as if to say he understood too. When I arrived home, I called Jabu, whom I hadn't heard from since twenty-four hours earlier when I told him the news and told him not to come. Not to bother calling, not to come to the funeral, that if he couldn't come and comfort me when my father died, then he had no business seeing me again. I just couldn't fathom the lack of empathy, though I'd later see that he was, as usual, focused on his own loss and paralyzed by it, unable to be there for me. I knew clearly, even in my grief and not for the first time, that he just wasn't capable of being the partner I needed – or that my father had wanted for me.

I fell asleep on the couch, stripped down to a camisole in the heat and trying to catch any breeze I could under the ceiling fans in the lounge at my place at Kube. I dreamt that Baba and I were walking in the woods, his very favorite thing to do. He was teaching me which plant had which medicinal property, and telling me old Zulu myths and legends, pointing out the caves in the mountainside above us. He said that he knew he'd always told me that no one would ever harm me as long as he was alive, and while he was so sorry to leave so soon after we found each other, he now could protect me – all of us – even better from where he was, and let out one of his signature deep, rolling laughs. It was comforting, when I woke up, to realize I still had this strong connection with him. I'd had visits from dear friends and loved ones who had passed away my whole life, but this had an even deeper connection and vibration than usual. I slept until the dawn sky woke me up, prayed and bathed, and headed home to Baba and Mama's again.

The setup was just the same as the day before but with every elder in the family present, along with my siblings. I made all my greetings, then sat next to Mama again as we, I thought, waited for the meeting to begin. It was then that my mother grasped my hand from under the covers, her hand cold even in the summer temperatures, and said, in the same thready voice I'd never heard before yesterday's visit, *"Ngiyafunda uJabu, Nomadlozi. Ngiyacela, sisi."* She wanted Jabu, please, please.

I let out a big sigh and told her that he was very upset by the news but that he hadn't come home since I'd arrived back in Durban. And that I would not forgive him for not being there for her, and for me. She repeated herself, shaking her head negatively under the blankets quite vigorously. I questioned Mandla – was she saying she wanted him to be at the funeral? My brother nodded and added that she wanted him to sing, that as her future son-in-law to be – he'd told my parents he wanted to marry me a couple months prior – he must be there and he must sing.

I told my brother, who cracked a smile at my insistence I'd never see Jabu again and clearly didn't believe it, that I had just told him off the day before. Mandla told me that

I'd better call him. So I had to eat crow and call Jabu then and there, in front of the elders. He picked up my call as he nearly always did and listened to me, but didn't make a commitment. It seemed to satisfy the family, though, and so I sat back and waited for the meeting to begin, only to have my brother explain that they were waiting for me to start, as the eldest child.

Mandla is the next eldest, and I assumed as the oldest son (and because of my own self-doubt about belonging) that he would be in charge. But no, apparently my father realized on Sunday that he was dying and refused all IVs and medication, saying that he'd rather die without all that *umlumgu* medicine in him. He further said that I should be in charge of the funeral planning. That I was the eldest child, that my existence had been prophesied by his own grandfather long ago and all the elders were aware of this. And that most importantly, I shared his belief system – traditional all the way, with our good friend Jesus added in the mix, too, though none of that official church nonsense.

I sort of gulped down my amazement at this development and stepped into my role with no previous experience, though I was informed that there were parts of the service that we'd turn over to all the *sangomas* who would be present that day. We made a sort of schedule, an order of service. I wrote it all out in English so someone could translate it into isiZulu and have programs made. It was an intense few hours. The *gogo* who drank quart bottles of beer was keeping a close eye on me the whole time from her mat across the room. That day, I knew I needed to join them for lunch, and was able to eat a bit before making my way back to Kube Yini for the night. I'd like to have stayed at home, but it was unbearably hot, and all the beds and floor spaces were full of relatives.

The rest of the week went by in a blur, though I worked on a painting that now hangs in our lounge in the magic forest, one I call "Waiting for Baba." It depicts me, Mama, and my sisters sitting and watching across the land below home, my father's favorite view. I didn't hear from Jabu, other than once when he sent a message, just checking on me. When I asked if he was coming to the funeral, he said that he had a lot of performances over the weekend. I continued to dream that my father was with me and that got me through, though every time I went home and saw that closed door and the mourning animals, it cut deep.

There was, the afternoon before the actual funeral, the bringing home of the body. Just as in the dream the night he died, I, as the eldest, did follow the *bakkie* holding his casket home, then was able to view his body. He looked so tiny in the surprisingly ornate casket, his beautiful head peeking out of the white satin cushioning it. Malume, my father's elder brother and the one I knew best, took the bracelet that matched mine, which I'd brought, assuring me he'd put it on Baba's wrist when they were readying his body for burial, as a symbol of all of us children being with him. And that he'd leave the string one I'd brought him from Greece on too, that Baba treasured that as a connection with me.

That week let me see just how much I did belong, for the first time, in a way that was undeniable both to me and to the larger community. Even in my grief, it meant so much. I could feel the warmth of my father's smile on me. "Light, Nomadlozi, light."

Finally the day of the funeral arrived. I made the trek back, muscle memory likely driving me more than anything else. I was enfolded the minute I arrived, and Sandile, my shy youngest brother, led me to Baba's rondavel, now a hive of activity. My niece, Nozipho, the eldest granddaughter, helped me to choose the right pieces to wear from Baba's collection hung around the room, and before I knew it, I was fully decked out in traditional ceremonial pieces: feathers, beads, and shells galore. It felt better than I can convey in words. I won't go into the traditional and *sangoma*-led parts of the celebration of my father's life that took place over those days, as they are sacred and just beyond words, but I did know beyond a shadow of a doubt that this is exactly where I am supposed to be deep in my soul.

For the actual funeral, I wore more typical mourning clothes. I was more covered than I liked to be in the heat, my head wrapped with my feet bare, as is respectful. In the back of my mind, I was wondering if Jabu would show up, not wanting Mama to be disappointed when she was already dealing with so much. I'd tracked his phone earlier, something I rarely did. He was driving north, but whether he was coming home, I didn't know.

I was to read a poem that meant a lot to me, something by Rumi, and would stand next to Nozipho while she read one she'd written for her beloved *mkhulu*. I had also been asked to say a few words about Baba if I was able – my sisters were sure that I could. As the chairs filled and people gathered outside the big white tent used for funerals and weddings, it was standing room only. As I sat down next to my sisters on the mats, having set Musa up to fulfil Mama's request that he emcee the event, I saw Jabu's burnt orange Ford Ranger coming up the hill. He had, I'd find out later, left one event an hour away and would need to leave before the burial itself, but he was there, along with his two back-up singers, whom I was close to. The gathering crowd was very excited, Mama nodding at me from her mat in the center of it all.

They were seated, and the service began. It all went by in a blur. Nozipho and I managed fairly well, literally holding each other up while speaking from our hearts. Many songs were sung, including "It's a Wonderful Day," of course, and many tributes were made. Then Jabu sang a couple of his well-known songs before speaking of Baba – and of me too – very lovingly, blessing us all. Once he was done, though the service was not quite over, the three of them stood and left.

I hadn't cried too much during the week and had mostly held my tears in check over the service, but that this man who I loved so much and had devoted so much of me to for quite some time now was leaving without even speaking to me privately? It was more than I could take. I burst out in tears, my sisters on either side of me shaking their heads and staring at him in disbelief as he walked down to the *bakkie*. They helped me quiet myself, leaning into me and holding me in more ways than one, and we got through the rest of the service.

We all walked, en masse, to the other side of the yard for the burial. It had been cloudy and a bit cooler early on, but now the sun came out in a big way. Typically, I'd stay under an umbrella, but I was pulled forward to the side of the gaping hole in the ground, where my brother Mandla patted the ground next to him, indicating I should sit. Mama was seated with the aunties, who were covering the new widow with umbrellas.

The casket was brought forth and Baba's body was removed and then rolled up in blankets. A couple of my cousins stood on the wood logs at the bottom, having lowered themselves into the hole, and took both his body and many of his prized possessions into the grave. My nephew and another cousin then began to hack up his casket, after carefully removing all the metal fittings, and placed the pieces of it in the grave, too, a Shembe practice believed to prevent foul play later against the deceased or their family.

I was consulted all along the way by the men doing the work, and I nodded and pointed to what should be placed where while Mandla and I dodged the occasional flying casket shard. I have no idea how I knew what to do, but I did, without hesitation. Mandla would question me afterward, asking if Baba had taught me, to which I replied, "Not while he was alive," which made Mandla break out in a wide grin. He admitted he was glad I knew because he didn't and then he pointed out to me that the male peacock was standing on top of the chicken coop behind Mama and the aunts. The bird had been surprisingly silent all day, but now he was twirling in a circle with his feathers on full display. A final tribute to the man we all loved immeasurably, and always will.

When Baba used to tell me, "Light, Nomadlozi, light," he'd meant "right," as in "ok, we are done with that, what's next?" or "yes, my girl, you finally understand!" What he said, though, was a reminder to me always and forever to remember the light in everything. As someone who grew up steeped in negativity, fear, and anxiety, there is no greater gift. As an adult who does somewhat consistently do the work, personally and professionally, of shedding the layers to find the truth, to recall the reason we all came to this earth – there's no more valuable directive. And often, when I begin to lose my way or wander off my path a bit, I'll hear him say just that to me, somewhere in the ethers.

I heard him say this just this morning, and it rousted me out of bed just in time to see a pink ball of light rising over smoky fog laying just above the ocean. *Ngiyabonga kakhulu, Baba wami.* Thank you very much, my father.

I thought about two things. Rejection. And gifts. And the intersection between the two. As I watched the sun rise higher in the sky through the still-misty cloud layers, it was spilling literally golden light in a streaky path over the inky ocean waves. Those dark blue waters can be treacherous – deep, full of quick currents and undertow, home to sharks and more. And yet the light just dances on them, high-lighting the foamy crests of waves, playing and sparkling here and there, beginning to illuminate the shadows as all of it makes contact with the sandy shore.

My life has been like that. Darker to begin with, but nowadays, more and more light finds its way into my land-scape. I wonder how much of that is because I've literally chosen, day after day, year after year, to look for what is light, the positive in even the most difficult scenarios. The shiny side of the coin, no matter how tarnished the other side is. Decades of mindfulness training, coaching, therapy, painting, and time in the company of those who know this way has helped. So much.

Yet I still sometimes hear the old negative voices telling me that I'm out of my mind, that I should be more careful, that I should be afraid – very afraid. And while I know very well that living a life of fear does not work for me on any level – mind, body, or soul – it is easy to fall back into that quicksand of "what I should do/who I should be" instead of the free-spirited, wholly human being I know I am. It's all too tempting to take on this life as a series of exams to be passed – multiple choice/fill-in-the-blank vs. essay and free writing – rather than the amazing experiment it can be. Like getting sober, it's a process of recovery and best done one day at a time.

Some of the people I have loved most in this lifetime are the ones who have rejected me most strongly. The list, of course, begins with my biological mother. While she may have, in actuality, been rejecting herself using me as a reflection of her inner turmoil, the fact remains that the woman who gave birth to me never saw me as good enough for her, as right for her, and believed me to be "a miserable excuse for a human being." So maybe I've spent my life trying to be a good person, trying to learn the rules to this game, the rules she never taught me. Not to get her approval, I don't believe that is possible, yet to prove her wrong. To earn my place on this planet, which I now understand is my birthright and the birthright of every single one of us born into this world. In many ways, there's a lot of good in her setting me up to believe I had to work on myself, that no one would love me as I was, as cruel as that is to tell a child – or an adult, for that matter. In any case, like Rumpelstiltskin, I turned it into gold. Subconsciously, of course – I'm only seeing all this from the lens of my much older eyes now.

The next rejection was Lina. I lost my daughter in choosing to live in South Africa. I don't know if she'll ever understand how hard I tried to stay, for so long, in a life that didn't fit me, to be a good mother to her. Losing her was something I'd been afraid of for years, ever since my disengaging from my biological mother. I worried that the universe would somehow pay me back by taking my daughter. Shades of Snow White, perhaps, I don't know. There's a lot of life in those fairy tales, isn't there? Maybe one day, she'll read this book and understand, leaving us with a much happier ending.

And there's Jabu – we would try one last time, in the winter of 2020, to make things work between us. After a couple of months, I decided that I needed to allow myself to have the kind of life and love that would serve me and my calling far better than this relationship ever had. By then, it wasn't a hard decision at all, just a closing of one door and an opening of another, with far greater gifts to come.

Twenty-Three

He was the very best gift I never knew I wanted.

Sure, I'd always wanted a son, to raise a boy. I had nephews I adored and then Musa, a grown son who meant the world to me, but I never had the opportunity to bring up a son in this world, to help create a good man – or to buy all the blue baby clothes I could lay my hands on, or those little, tiny work boots.

Jabu had introduced me to his many children over the first year we were together. I was happy to get to know and spend time with them. Several of them had lost their mothers, so there seemed to be space for me. They all called me Ma, as Bu often did, a term of respect and family. A few of them visited me frequently, spending the night, and I went often enough to see the youngest boy, Mpho, who stayed with Jabu's uncle and his wife in the next township.

One of his daughters, Nomvelo, had been struggling for some time. She had a toddler daughter who lived with and was essentially being raised by her mother, Beauty, since Nomvelo was still in school when she gave birth. She was attending university halfway between Durban and Kube Yini, and while on a weekend getaway to Kube with Bu's mother and other relatives, we stopped to see her. It was our first in-person meeting after having talked on the phone for months. From the minute she climbed in the car, it felt right to be with her.

Things would get intense quickly. Nomvelo had endured no small amount of trauma in her life, and at that point, Beauty was past wanting to deal with it. I met up with Beauty one night outside Nomvelo's school residence in the midst of a crisis, and she told me she had given up on her daughter. She said she understood I had experience in dealing with trauma and emotional issues and she was more than happy for Nomvelo to come stay with me. That ended up being exactly what transpired. Nomvelo took the second bedroom in the flat Jabu and I had rented as we renovated a townhouse I'd bought in Salt Rock.

Things were good with Jabu and me, at that point. Nomvelo was very happy to see her father in a loving relationship, to experience a side of him she'd never seen. She would go back to school but return to stay with us whenever she was on break, even when our relationship was faltering, as it did often. In time, she convinced me – and then asked me to convince her parents – to allow her to take a year off school at the end of 2018. I could see that she could be a real asset to Jabu's career, our production company, and the youth projects I wanted to create, so I was happy to do that.

When Nomvelo turned out to be pregnant the following year, I was initially very happy about it – I loved her as a daughter and adored her completely so why wouldn't I be? She, as sometimes happens, was not, and was planning on giving the baby up for adoption. In fact, she told no one about it, and I was apparently the only one who was willing to query her when it finally became obvious a couple months before she was due. Her biological mother had even asked me if I thought she was pregnant, not wanting to upset Nomvelo by questioning her. Their relationship, as I was told by both of them, was not one that allowed for open communication and Beauty, her mother, felt that I was far better at discussing things with her than she was.

The story Nomvelo told me after I put my hand on her belly covered by yet another oversized soccer jersey was one that happens far too often. She was left alone with a guy at a party and she didn't say no, so it wouldn't be rape, as was the case with her first pregnancy. Not an uncommon thing for survivors who haven't had help to recover, and so I believed her – though most of her family did not once they were told. And she didn't tell even her best friends – not while she was pregnant and not after her son was born, allowing them to believe he was my child with her father.

That day, though, I took a deep breath and, without hesitating for a moment, gave her the option of continuing to live with me, with the baby. Jabu and I were in the process of moving to a bigger house anyway, and there would be space and help available. And of course, given my own gang rape experience and the subsequent pregnancy, I knew the pain of going through all of this alone. I certainly didn't want a repeat of that for this girl I adored.

I made it clear she would be the baby's mother, I'd just house and feed them and of course help care for the baby, too. I told Nomvelo that I would completely understand if she needed to give the child up for adoption, yet she did have this option too – I wouldn't take sole care of this baby the way her other mother had with her daughter, yet she wouldn't be alone with him either.

She thanked me and asked for time to think about it, said that she appreciated the offer. We both shed a few tears, and she said she was relieved to have someone know, that she'd been keeping it to herself for so long. She didn't know the father well, just from around school, and when she'd told him very early in the pregnancy, he'd just shrugged it off. As the months passed and the pregnancy progressed, she hadn't heard anything further from him, so it was all up to her.

I assured her she wasn't alone. We'd already been through a great deal together, and I hoped she would know that. She had been calling me Mama for quite some time by then. But I don't think she ever really understood how deeply I loved her. In the end, I'm sure she did not.

A couple days later, Nomvelo told me that she'd given it a lot of thought and that she felt she must give the child up for adoption, that she'd spoken with a woman she liked who was with a local agency. I accepted this, understanding all too well the situation she was in from my own experience. I wanted her to do what she needed to do in order to heal from earlier trauma in her life, and knew that adding an unwanted baby was likely not going to help. She asked me if I'd still be there when the baby was born and help her get through the delivery and handing the child over to the agency. Knowing my own limits, I replied that I was happy to be there for her, but that I wouldn't be able to see the baby at all. She seemed to understand.

The next several weeks went by quickly – I continued to encourage her to tell her other parents and eventually said I would need to confirm to her "other mother" that she was, indeed, pregnant and due sometime in the next couple months. Her father and I were struggling with our relationship at this point, and I had hoped she would tell him herself, but she stayed in her room the few times he was home. The one time she did spend an afternoon with him, for his birthday, he didn't seem to notice her swollen body and so that conversation never happened between the two of them. Jabu had not been coming home much, so I hadn't had the opportunity either.

I was incredibly uncomfortable with the whole situation. Nomvelo was staying down at her other mother's for a while, hopefully getting a prenatal checkup at the local hospital where she'd delivered her first child, not far from their home. She'd agreed, knowing it would make things much easier when the baby came. Antenatal care is very important to the medical system here in South Africa and not following those guidelines can lead to being refused hospital admission. While Nomvelo understood that on an intellectual level, she was clearly still in denial/disbelief, so I just continued to remind her as she always had an excuse when I was available to take her. As fate would have it, it never happened.

She let me know on a Monday morning that she was in labor. I'd thought she had more time, but apparently was further along than our first conversation indicated. We kept in touch, since Beauty was out of town working, and when Nomvelo called the next morning to say that she was getting really tired, I knew it was time to go.

It was my Zulu father's birthday, which explained some dreams I'd had the night before. He'd passed away just four months earlier, to the day, and I dreamt of him handing me a baby all bundled up, Zulu style, in a blue blanket. He told me this was the greatest gift he could give me and that he'd be with me as I raised this boy, which confused me as that was not the plan at the time. Then I woke up to the message from Nomvelo – not at all a coincidence in my mind. Musa drove me as quickly as he could, the hour-plus drive seeming longer than usual.

When we arrived at Beauty's house, Nomvelo was alone. She seemed quite focused on packing her bag, stopping and leaning against the wall for each contraction – only a few minutes apart now. Her belly had dropped since I'd seen her a week before, and she was quite calm. I asked if she wanted me to call the adoption lady for her so that she could meet us at the hospital and my knees went a bit weak when she said no. I caught my breath and asked if she'd spoken to her already. Another no, so I asked what she wanted to do.

With seemingly great clarity, she turned and asked if the offer I'd made for them to live with me (or us, if her dad and I managed to work things out, which was the plan at that point) was still good. Given the dreams I'd had the night before, I wasn't too surprised, and was very sure that the answer was yes. No question. We'd be moving into the new house in a matter of months, and there was space. My granddaughters Gia and Grace would be there, too, so it was already designed to be a kid-friendly home.

My concern at this point, though, was mainly to get her to a hospital before I ended up delivering this child myself. So off we went to the same small hospital nearby where she'd delivered her daughter a year and a half before. The lack of antenatal care was a big weight on my mind. It turned out I wasn't wrong to be worried.

When we arrived and went in the urgent care doors, a nice old baba immediately fetched a wheelchair for Nomvelo and chatted with her while I dealt with the sister behind the window regarding insurance and other formalities. The obstetrician who'd delivered her first baby was called. At first, she refused to admit Nomvelo as she hadn't seen her during this pregnancy and because she hadn't had antenatal care, of course. But the critical care doc on duty could see that the labor was fairly far along and so decided to examine her.

She still didn't look very pregnant, and they were sure it was a preterm delivery, though we both assured them that her due date had already passed. Nomvelo stayed calm – almost too calm, quite removed from the situation. She did confirm that I was her mother, allowing me to sign paperwork, but wasn't completely there, which I found understandable.

The staff wasn't sure, though. I let them know that this pregnancy had come about in a traumatic way, asking them to be a bit careful. Some were able to do that, and some –including her doctor, as things proceeded – were not. I found myself wishing, not for the first time, that all medical professionals were given really comprehensive trauma training – clearly this place had not had any, and I felt for all those who try to get help only to be met by less than compassionate professionals who are likely trying to deal with their own issues as well as the things they see and hear each day. As it was, given the obvious differences in our skin color, they were skeptical of this idea that I was her mother and unsure of what was going on. At twenty-two years old, Nomvelo could speak for herself, of course, yet she was not doing a whole lot of talking.

After the examination, things proceeded quickly. Her former obstetrician begrudgingly agreed to take the case. Nomvelo was wheeled upstairs to Maternity, and we had some quiet time during the lulls between contractions to talk about baby names and whether the baby was a boy or a girl. I was convinced he was a boy after my dreams, and she didn't argue, though she did shoot down many of my name suggestions.

By the time we came up with his name, Lesedi, which means "light," she was pretty fully dilated once the doctor came in to check. The doctor, an Indian woman in her forties, was clearly a rule follower, and was openly questioning both her decision to take on this delivery (because if things went south, it would be a black mark on her record) and whether Nomvelo and the baby would live (she clearly didn't think both would make it). I questioned her saying that in front of her young patient, and we continued our conversation out in the hallway at my request. She went on about my role, about the lack of antenatal care — even after I reminded her about the trauma and that I'd tried hard to get her seen, about these girls who keep getting themselves pregnant. The depth of negativity was pretty stunning, and I suggested that perhaps we should just get the baby born and then deal with whatever the results were as opposed to conjuring up every possible bad outcome.

At that point, she stalked off and starting making calls and giving orders, and the room filled quickly with nurses. Nomvelo's water hadn't broken, and she took care of that, accelerating both the labor and the nasty comments from the doctor because there was an infection and meconium in the fluid, which meant the baby was possibly in some distress. She shouted at Nomvelo about all of it, who was pushing with all her might.

I climbed up on the table, holding her back, wiping her face and whispering to her not to listen to all the negativity, to just focus on imagining the baby making his way easily. She'd calm for a minute or two, but the mood in the room was really charged and hostile, and it wasn't easy to find a still point. Just then, the doctor said that if she wouldn't push – though she clearly was – that she'd have to do a caesarean section. She tried to challenge Nomvelo that way but it only caused further distress, of course, and the doc began to say again that they would both die if she didn't try harder.

In the midst of all this, I was asked to go down to the office – a few stories below – in order to pay 10,000 *rand* for the surgery, that they couldn't prep the theater without that payment. I didn't want to leave her, but was told I didn't have a choice. While we'd let Beauty know when we left for the hospital, she wasn't yet there, and I knew that Jabu wouldn't be any help. Off I went to deal with all the paperwork.

The doctor's office hadn't sent them what they needed so it took maybe a half hour, which seemed like an eternity. While I sat and waited for the billing to be sorted out, I wondered how on earth I wound up sitting there, how my life got this complicated. I loved Nomvelo with all my heart, but our relationship was not easy. I'd failed with Lina in such a huge way, and I was determined to do better this time. I loved Jabu deeply, but also knew that unless things changed soon, we would not stay together despite all his predictions of us dying in our old age, just days apart. Yet here I was. This baby was coming, and I couldn't really deal with anything but getting him here as safely as possible and helping Nomvelo get through it all with as little further trauma as possible. I stood up straight, completed paperwork in hand, and got on the lift ready to face whatever came.

When I entered the delivery room again, it looked like a war zone. Nomvelo had pulled her IV out, spurting blood everywhere, and the nurses and doctor were scolding her like a child, asking her what kind of mother she would be. The doctor – who apparently still thought this baby was being born prematurely – was going on about it being such a small baby, that certainly she could get it pushed out.

Nomvelo reached for me, sobbing, "Mama, they are being so mean to me. And I can't push anymore, I just can't." I got back on the bed with her and said loudly enough for all to hear that she was right, they were being incredibly mean, which doesn't help anything. That they were the least compassionate, worst trained group of medical professionals I'd ever seen. Very loudly. They all heard me, and there was absolute silence in the room until one of the nurses said quietly that they weren't trying to be mean, that they just wanted her to get the baby out. The room took its mood though, from the doctor, and she continued to be both incredibly negative and unkind.

There was nothing I could do about that. The doctor asked me to go outside to the nurse's station and sign yet more paperwork, following me to say again that she didn't think they'd make it, especially the baby. I asked her if she had reason, and she could only cite the infection and meconium, using extremely shaming language. I told her that they would be fine – I knew they would be – and that he was strong, referring to the baby as a boy. She questioned how I knew – asking for the umpteenth time if there had been a scan. I told her no, but I just knew.

She stared at my *sangoma* bracelets, the beaded ones that I'd been wearing for some time now and the *isiphandla* one, made of goat skin for me when I completed my *thwasa* training, and then, seeing the look on my face, dropped the arguing and said she was having the theater prepped, that I could see the nurse for scrubs and to get changed because things would go quickly now.

I made sure that Nomvelo knew what was going on, walking with her on the stretcher to the operating room area and keeping her company while she rested a bit in pre-op. The anesthesiologist came by. The pediatrician, who also treated her and her older daughter, arrived – a kind-eyed, very calm Indian man whose presence was welcomed by us both – Nomvelo was so happy to see a friendly face. Two nurses came by – one to supervise her being wheeled into the theater and the other to take me to get changed in what must have been a staff locker room.

I have a selfie I took, all masked and hatted and scrubbed, which captures all I was feeling beautifully. My expression is pure "I have no idea what's ahead, but here we go!' I was excited to meet this new person, glad to be there for my daughter, and still not thinking about much beyond the next half hour while realizing I had nothing for a baby at home. When I came back into the pre-op area, there was no one there. I managed to find a nurse who went to check and sure enough, the obstetrician had decided I couldn't be in the theater as it was an emergency caesarian. What had changed, I didn't understand. Perhaps it was out of spite for challenging her. There was nothing I could do but pray for them both.

Time dragged as it does in hospital waiting areas. I knew I needed to update Beauty, Nomvelo's mother. She was concerned, of course, yet happy the surgeon was someone she knew. I questioned whether she'd let Jabu know, and she said she'd leave telling "your man" up to me, that she didn't see how he had any say in the matter. That she was working. I realized I had no choice – his daughter was in surgery, after all, so I called Jabu to update him.

He'd had, of course, no idea about any of this – that his daughter was pregnant, that we were at the hospital, that his seventh grandchild was about to be born. He was happy to hear from me after we'd had no contact for a few weeks, until he understood why I was calling – and went from disbelief to rage pretty quickly. His anger was targeted at the man who'd impregnated his little girl, then at her for falling pregnant again. For some reason I don't fully comprehend, having one baby out of wedlock is sort of okay in modern Zulu culture. Not ideal, of course, but not at all unusual either. The shame is put on the girl, as is common elsewhere, but by the time the baby comes into the world, it's all not such a big deal.

A second child, though – especially not by the same father – is a huge, huge thing. The shame felt by the family is palpable, and I know that this was exactly what Nomvelo had been trying to avoid by putting the baby up for adoption. Her father was livid. And a lot of the anger was quickly pointed at me. He didn't want to hear why I hadn't told him – though given the fact that he really hadn't been home, to speak of, in the last couple months made it difficult. I hadn't wanted to tell him on the phone, and had really encouraged Nomvelo to have that conversation but I could see now why she'd avoided it. The fact that they'd spent an entire afternoon together just several weeks prior, just the two of them, and he hadn't noticed was incomprehensible to me, yet denial is surely one of the strongest drugs, isn't it?

So here I was, standing alone having just fought all these battles to ensure both Nomvelo and the baby were as safe as possible, having negotiated with the very unhappy doctor and the hospital, in scrubs in the middle of an empty waiting area, being screamed at by the man I loved but who couldn't show up and be a father or a partner. It was a lot, and the exhaustion hit me all at once. I slumped down on the floor, took off the mask and cap, and rested my back against the wall. I was doing my best yet had no idea what was to come.

Bowing my head, I prayed. About all of it, to God and all our ancestors and to my Zulu father, who I was still a bit lost without. For this girl who was being cut open to deliver a child she didn't really want. For the baby, coming into the world at a time that was challenging already without having the family cards stacked against him, for the man who so desperately wanted to be close to his children and to build a family with me but who didn't begin to understand what love really is. For me – for the strength and wisdom to deal with whatever was ahead because I was already feeling mightily stretched by this life I'd chosen.

An unusual noise pulled me out of my deep practice, and I opened my eyes to see the pediatrician I'd met earlier, his eyes twinkling above his mask. He asked me if I'd like to meet my new grandson, and I was on my feet in an instant. The orderly pushed the cart closer to me – the plexiglass top revealing a pile of white blankets on top of a tiny white mattress. And in the middle of that pile was our boy, swathed in more white blankets, his eyes wide open. As I greeted him in isiZulu and told him that I was his Gogo, he looked at me as if he knew me. "Finally, someone I know!"

He was, the doctor told me, perfect. He was huge, weighing over four kilograms – so much for the staff's belief that he was a preemie, and had a full head of hair. He was so beautiful, and the doctor seemed optimistic, that he'd need to be on antibiotics given the meconium, but otherwise he didn't expect any issues. His Apgar scores were high, and he was just as strong as I'd seen in my dreams.

There were tears in my eyes as they rolled him away to the nursery for a full exam, and I slumped on the floor again, so relieved to know they were both fine. What a day it had been, and it hit me again that it was Baba's birthday. I couldn't imagine a better gift. He had been right about that.

Twenty-Four

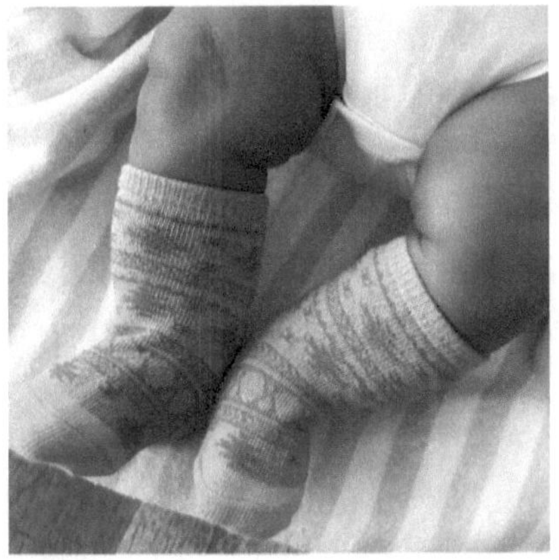

When I'd offered to help Nomvelo, I expected that she would be Lesedi's mother and I'd be his other grand-mother, with them living in my house with my support. That changed almost immediately after he was born. Nom-velo stayed in the hospital to recover from her surgery and Lesedi to recover from jaundice, and I commuted back and forth each day, trying to encourage a bond that didn't seem to be happening.

Nomvelo refused to breastfeed, saying that she really wanted me to be the baby's mother. Apparently Lesedi's eyes resembled his father's, and this bothered her. She had trouble connecting with him from day one. Instead, she took on a role more like an older sister, sitting at the side of his cot but not interacting.

I didn't agree or disagree with her request, wanting to give her time to bond with him and recover from the traumatic birth experience. Beauty agreed, saying it was all up to me but that she could not take on another baby as she had asserted the whole time we'd known Nomvelo was pregnant. The nurses worked with me, and eventually I taught Nomvelo to breastfeed, which finally earned me the nurses' respect as her mother and their willingness to express concern that Nomvelo had not connected with her son at all.

That disconnect continued once we got home. While Nomvelo would breastfeed as required, she was struggling to produce enough milk so we supplemented with a bottle, which she often wanted me to give him. She began to ask me, quite often, if I would be his mama, saying that she was happy to be his *sis omdala*, or older sister. I hoped this would change with time. It didn't.

And so I became his main caregiver from pretty much the beginning. I was clearly his primary attachment any-way, and even at a young age, he would bellow if I came home and didn't come greet him immediately, like a little Zulu man. While Lesedi was the light of our family for everyone, I was his mama, and everyone, including Beauty, saw this clearly. She visited regularly, bringing Nomvelo's daughter, and witnessed all of this from the early days.

Jabu and I found our way back to each other again when Lesedi was a couple months old. He was happy to raise Lesedi together, as our son, at his suggestion. I caught the two of them deep in conversation one night, Jabu explaining to him that none of this was Lesedi's fault, that he had the best mama now and that all would be well. He did apologize to me, too, as he always did, for his anger, citing his disappointment. Now, he said, he could see that this child was a gift, the son we had always wanted.

The next six months went by in a flurry of sweet moments, nappies, and naps. I was staying primarily in the Durban area at that point, at Jabu's request, and hoping to pursue work in a way the leadership of Ngwenya was not allowing any longer up north in the bush. Bu and I had found a nice three-bedroom townhome in a little beach town called Salt Rock, just north of the popular Ballito area on the Dolphin Coast, and moved there while I started searching for a more permanent home.

The townhouse was in a small, gated community, but as much as Jabu, my brother, and the rest of the family seemed to think that was where, as a white woman in South Africa, I needed to be, it turned out not to be for me. The woman next door, who we shared a wall with, made it crystal clear every single day that she didn't approve of our family in any way shape or form, screwing up her face and huffing at us every time our paths crossed. Which was all too often, since she seemed to blame us for any and all issues in her home. Jabu, used to this, was extra charming to her, but my response was to park our combi van outside for weeks – the one that had been branded with two- meter high photos of Jabu for the Crown Gospel Award campaign. She didn't appreciate that at all, surprisingly.

Beyond all that, as really I've accepted those kinds of things as par for the course here, I really felt the need to have both a freestanding house and land, away from the busy tourist weekends and holidays on the north coast. I knew it was time for me to build a proper ancestor house, as well, and it would take a certain sort of property to do that. It's traditional, in family homesteads, for the elders to have small round houses in which to pray and connect with their ancestors. You can find them in the city and suburbs, too, but not as often, as there's less space. I was looking for a plot big enough to allow for a nice one so that I could also conduct my *sangoma* sessions in it, as is the norm.

I had found the perfect place back at the end of 2018, and a good thing too, since it now it seemed Nomvelo and Lesedi were going to live with me for the foreseeable future. She wanted to take time off school and explore working on her father's career as well as other PR and marketing work. I had become very close to Bu's other kids as well as Musa, Suzi, Gia, and Grace, who'd begun to call me Gogo. While it may seem odd from a Western perspective, we really had become a family. In South Africa, the concept of family is both more loose and more broad. Both Musa and Suzi had lost their mothers at a young age, and I'd always felt I was meant to have more children, so we just fit together. There's nothing legally binding us, yet the ties of the heart are far stronger. My granddaughters were clearly going to need to go to progressive schools – they were growing up fast and were just so bright. The idea of living with extended family really appealed to me, and the new place would allow for all this and more.

The home I found was in a great little beach town not far from King Shaka airport, so therefore quite close to Jabu's home in Inanda too. The house was on a bluff high above the Indian Ocean and just off the local highway, which reminded me of the Pacific Coast Highway I loved in California. It had a swimming pool and all the bells and whistles I knew Jabu would love. It was, in a lot of ways, my last big effort at creating a home he could stay in permanently. I see now that there is no way any house would do that.

The sale went through quickly, but the house needed a great deal of work. All the exterior walls were cracked – they'd never been waterproofed properly – so we had to have the plaster completely removed and then get everything sealed, replastered, and painted again. We also wanted to renovate what had been staff housing into a proper flat for Suzi, Musa, and the girls so they'd have their own space, and the ancestor house I'd wanted needed to be built too. After much debating and dealing with my own feelings about spending so much money just on me, we also added a beautiful and very spacious art studio where I could paint, write, and see clients, something I never regretted once. Much of this book was written in the wee hours, watching the sun rise over the Indian Ocean in that space before everyone woke up and things got busy. Of course, doing all of this while welcoming a newborn added up to quite a circus, yet I loved the metaphor of taking the house down to the bones and creating a home tailored to our family. With the help of the trusted contractors who had renovated our place in Salt Rock, it all got done in time.

We moved in when Lesedi was less than three months old – luckily, he was pretty easygoing from day one. By this point, Jabu was once again not around, and by the time we'd moved, I'd lost hope of us being together in any meaningful way. I made the little lounge outside what was now my bedroom into a nursery and left the huge second closet empty, a daily reminder of our failure to fix what we'd hoped would soon be a solid marriage.

Still, I had this baby I adored, the older kids and my granddaughters, a place to practice spiritually both personally and professionally for the first time, a studio to create in, and that glorious view – plus the sea breezes. We swam most days, ate dinner as a family, and were constantly entertained by the three littles in the house. You would think everyone would be happy, yet something I still don't understand was going on.

Things between me and Nomvelo had begun to break down, and I couldn't seem to mend them more than temporarily. Beauty and I discussed it, wondering if perhaps Nomvelo was pregnant again. Her moods were unpredictable, and her attitude toward me changed with the wind – one minute sharp-edged and resentful, and then the next wanting just to be next to me. With the lack of sleep and the stress of moving and renovation along with missing her father almost more than I could cope with, I could empathize but not really improve things.

And then, in the space of a few weeks, my whole world began to come crashing down. Nomvelo left in the middle of the night one night, with no communication. The next evening, she messaged Suzi, I think, to say she was on her way back, and I asked her to not come until we'd met and talked. The discord between us was affecting the entire family, and we needed to clear the air.

We met at the Starbucks in the local mall, a place we'd often gone together as a treat, a girl's outing. As we spoke, it was clear to me that something had really changed. There was a deep resentment within her, which made no sense to me as I'd done all I could to support her in every way since the day we met, especially over the six months since Lesedi was born.

Our conversation was unrevealing. While she came back home after that, things did not return to normal again. There are traditional rites that are carried out in Zulu families when a baby is born, and while I had taken him home to Mama, the two of them falling into mutual adoration on first sight, and we'd introduced him to our ancestors in an informal way, he still had to be introduced to Nomvelo's ancestors prior to us completing the process. I'd spoken with Beauty about it, as she and her mother would need to do this as his elders, and even taken her home to discuss the whole process with Mama so that everything was openly communicated and done properly, with respect to both families. Still, she kept putting it off until I gently

insisted as he was turning six months old. We finally settled on a Sunday afternoon in October of 2019.

It was a beautiful day, and Musa and I loaded up the car
and got Lesedi ready to go. Nomvelo had told me that she
wouldn't attend despite my encouragement, and I'd been
assured it wouldn't be a problem. Just as we were to get the
baby settled in his car seat, however, she came out holding
him, all dressed and ready to come with us. I immediately
felt very unsettled in a way that I didn't understand, a sense
of foreboding running through my body. The mood in the
car between the three of us for the long ride was odd, and I
just prayed that everything would go well.

The air was charged from the time we arrived at
Beauty's home. She was not there and Nomvelo left me
and the baby with her *gogo,* who I'd never met and didn't
speak English, for a long time– when I queried her about
it later, she said that I was meant to meet her grandmother at her birthday party eleven months before, but
I hadn't come to the party for some reason neither of us
could recall. Eventually Beauty arrived and made preparations in her bedroom, inviting me to join them as her
mother lit the candles, burned *imphepho,* and spoke to her
ancestors, introducing Lesedi as their son. There was, to
my fairly decent understanding of ceremonial isiZulu, no
mention of Lesedi being in my care and joining our clan
as well, which Beauty and I had discussed with my mother
at home and again just that week. My heart sank further,
and Musa raised his eyebrow at me, also questioning, so I
knew I was correct in thinking this was not going accord-
ing to our agreement.

We all gathered in their lounge afterward, empty except for a few chairs and a mattress on the floor as they were moving house soon, the *gogo* staying in the kitchen. When I questioned Beauty, she fumbled and mumbled, saying that that all would come later. I was feeling literally as if I couldn't breathe, so I started to go outside and collect my thoughts, only to have Nomvelo tell me, in front of everyone and quite sharply, that I couldn't just get up and leave when things didn't go my way. That's when I knew that she had really turned against me, as she had always shown me respect until recently. We sat there for a while longer, the others making polite conversation while I fought back tears and tried to focus on Lesedi. We gathered our things and got ready to leave, the kids going out first so I spoke with Beauty briefly who saw that I was very upset.

I can't remember the excuses she made, other than saying that she was afraid her ancestors would be angry with her if she did what we'd agreed to, and that I didn't think I was going to adopt Lesedi formally, did I? This, of course, was exactly what Nomvelo had asked me to do, had gone to the lawyer's with me to initiate, and I'd agreed to. I had been supporting Nomvelo in every way for years now and had handled all the baby's expenses, so I asked her what exactly she'd told her mother my role was. She answered that she'd said I was taking care of the baby for them. And that's when my world collapsed. That, and when the *gogo* walked us to the car and thanked me for being her angel.

I cried off and on the whole way home, unable to speak at all, and went to my ancestor house when we arrived, praying for wisdom to deal with this impossible situation.

Nomvelo stayed clear of me from then on, really, we didn't ever discuss it. I kept Lesedi close to me, and I spoke with a few trusted friends about the whole mess, then Mama suggested I come home so we could sort it out together. I called Jabu and reported the whole situation to him, as he knew we were to do the ceremony, but he couldn't take part as he'd never paid damages to Beauty's family for impregnating her with Nomvelo out of wedlock – for this reason, Beauty always said he had no claim to Lesedi.

I packed things up a day or two later to make the long drive home and took Lesedi with me, knowing what was to come, what I had to do, deep down. I spent a few afternoons at home with Mama discussing all of it, and she gently but clearly helped me to understand that this would never stop. That the ancestral business wouldn't get straight, that Beauty wasn't understanding what we'd explained or more likely, didn't want to. That there would always be drama, and that while I'd done a good thing it wasn't at all appreciated. Jabu, of course, had said he'd intervene but did not and had gone missing again – and really, given the history, he didn't have any rights and neither did I, legally, though we'd begun the process.

I asked Musa to let Nomvelo and her sister friend, who had done nothing wrong but was also living with us, know that I needed them to move out while I was gone. I wasn't up to being there for that, it would have been impossibly difficult. I could see the trust between us had been broken completely. I had no idea if this had been the plan from the beginning or if Nomvelo had had some sort of breakdown, but it didn't matter. I couldn't negotiate my way clear on this one, since I no longer trusted any of the players, and it would be a long time before I trusted anyone new again. This really marked my exit from the Ndlovu family at large, although Jabu and I would try again briefly the following year.

I spent a few more days just soaking in Lesedi and his beautiful light, waking early each morning with him sleeping next to me as he had his whole life, in the Zulu way. Playing and jargoning back and forth with him and his delightful babbles and giggles. Taking him out into the bush and watching his eyes grow large as giraffe peered inside the Discovery windows. It was both a very sad and sort of magical few days, and it gave me time to accept the inevitable more fully. Though I won't lie – even now, writing about all of this, the tears fall. Still.

My brother Sandile came back to Umdloti with me and Lesedi and was, in his strong yet very silent way, a great support. The day after we arrived back, having spent most of the night watching Lesedi sleep, I called on my ancestors to bless him and keep him safe always. We took a long bath, and I fed him all his favorite foods as he smiled and chattered away, happily oblivious to the change that was to come. I put together a few of his clothes – he was outgrowing them all quickly anyway – and toys along with a supply of nappies and formula. As I carried him to the garage where Musa and Sandile had the car ready to go to Beauty's house, my knees started to buckle underneath me, the grief setting in. Our gardener took him from my arms, to say goodbye, and I burst into tears, waiting only to see him safely in the car seat then went in the house and collapsed.

I don't remember the rest of that day, not at all. I know Suzi checked on me, and I eventually found my way up to my room and just stayed under the covers. Musa came to tell me that they had given him to Nomvelo, since she was there and Beauty was not. Eventually, I slept, dreaming of Lesedi as a young boy over and over, only to wake up each time realizing that I'd had to do the unimaginable. I'd given up my son, this boy who I loved so very much. Just as my parents had asked me, when I was four and a half years old, to decide which sister they should give away, I'd had to make a decision that no one should ever, ever have to make.

As usual, I turned off my phone that night, only to wake up the next morning to messages from Beauty and Nomvelo. They said, over time, that of course I could still see Lesedi, that I could even have him live with me but that we'd have to negotiate about that. There would have to be agreements. I replied that I loved Lesedi – despite Nomvelo's accusations that I had never loved him – and would be happy to be his mother, but that at this point, given all the bad vibes and broken trust, it would have to be a closed adoption, which they refused completely.

This conversation would go on for days. They would not meet with my lawyer but only with me, trying to cajole me, which I really couldn't do. I needed someone to transcribe our conversations so that my words would not be twisted as they had been for months now. The message that finished it all for me, though, was one from Beauty asking me to be the good sister she knew me to be and to send along all of

Lesedi's things, spelling out each item. His clothing, toys, books, cot, travel cot, car seat, high chair, pram – all of it. Salt in the wound, for sure, and proof, perhaps, that this had always been the plan.

It would take a long, long time to recover from this one, and truthfully, that is still happening in different ways. Yet I don't regret my decision. It's clear this would have happened eventually, and my life would have been filled with drama until it did. And it would have caused irreparable damage to Lesedi – much like what happened to Jabu, his grandfather, whose family history was full of trauma that affected him greatly still. I was trying to help this Ndlovu son grow straight and true and to never doubt that he was loved or lovable, unlike his *mkhulu*. But sometimes, even the best intended plans just don't work out.

A day or two after we gave Lesedi to Beauty, I saw an Instagram post on Nomvelo's feed. She was standing proudly on a set of steps, wearing clothes and shoes we'd chosen together and that I'd bought for her. I wondered how it felt for her to wear them, given all that had transpired. To this day, her father posts photos of vehicles, his home – featuring my artwork, and similarly, wearing clothing we found together – all gifts from me or purchased for our future together. And I see how different our values truly are. How lucky I am to know that life isn't about things. I hope that Lesedi somehow knows the difference, as he grows. And I wish I'd sent this part of the letter I wrote, a month or two after he'd gone, to him:

Even if I never get to see you again, Lesedi, even though this has been so painful, I wouldn't trade a minute of it. Not for anything in the world. And I truly hope I've done the right thing – it would be unbearable for us both if they were to take you away when you're three years old, or five, or ten. Better, I'm advised, to do this now, so that you won't remember me. Which breaks my heart, as I will never forget you.

You are a gift. To me, to our whole family, to whoever gets to raise you. We named you well – you are such a bright light and I hope no one ever puts that light out, that you bring so much good to the world purely by being who you are. Your eyes hold the wisdom of the ages and yet you are so astonished and delighted by the smallest things like watching your hands gently wave in the air. As young as you are now, you're so aware of everything that goes on – you would shout when you heard my voice when I arrived home, and do this funny little dance when you saw me approach, along with that incredibly charming smile you will always have. I will miss you, always, and send you my love as you grow and thrive and become the man I know you came to be. Maybe someday, our paths will cross again under better circumstances. For now, I'll trust that the ancestors will watch over you and keep you well.

Ngiyakuthanda kakhulu,
Mama

Twenty-Five

Having lost Lesedi – along with most of what I considered my family – I was a bit lost too. Jabu, despite promises to help, had not intervened on my behalf, and so I finally saw that there was nothing left of our partnership. I didn't feel I could trust any of the Ndlovus anymore, really. The pain was just too great to try to sort out whom I might be able to stay in relationship with, so I blocked all of them from my life.

Left alone to process the pain, I once again dove into all the tools I'd gathered along the way. I spent a lot of time tending to my broken heart as well as examining the choices I'd made in primary relationships throughout my life. More learning, more insights, of course – and more therapy too. I immersed myself more fully in traditional practices, wanting to comprehend my history of failed relationships in ways which would allow me to change my patterns and hopefully avoid this kind of pain in the future. I spent a lot of my days in my new ancestor house, the door of the rondavel open to the sea breezes and my dogs coming to check on me occasionally. I began daily practice of *phala*, or prayer, in those first days after Lesedi left us, a habit which continues to this day. Over time, I started to see things that had repeated in cycles – all the way back to my childhood.

While I was considerably healthier than I had been a decade earlier, the emotional pain also manifested in my body. I began to see the physical patterns more clearly – this wasn't the first time a broken heart felt like a broken back, for example. Back when I lived in the US, even though I had access to amazing healthcare, I really struggled. I had been diagnosed with myriad autoimmune illnesses over twenty years, and had undergone a battery of treatments for what was finally determined, as previously mentioned, to be a long-term, deeply seated case of Lyme disease. And I'm still not sure that's what it really was, though an amazing team of alternative physicians and practitioners helped me to recover enough to come to SA, for which I'll always be grateful.

I do know that a childhood full of trauma and abuse can lead to long-term medical issues, both physical and mental. Research supports that. And a body under constant stress will obviously struggle. I hated being seen as sick and all the judgment that went along with it, and had long had the sense that something else was behind all the dis-ease. From the bouts of bronchitis and pneumonia in childhood through adulthood to the chronic depression and anxiety to decades of intense pain and being told I'd end up in a wheelchair, illness was part of my life – until I found my way home.

Interestingly, this is not an unusual history amongst the *sangomas* and *inyangas* I know here. In fact, Baba Credo Mutwa – a gifted writer, healer, and teacher along with *sanusi,* or keeper of Zulu traditions and lore – had fallen ill in similar ways, and he wasn't the only one whose story resembled my own when it came to health or lack thereof.

Growing up in America without the benefit of this cultural understanding, I was raised as most were at that time to respect doctors and see them as somehow above other humans. To believe that only they could diagnose and treat the sick, and that they, and their companion, the pharmaceutical industry, always knew exactly what was wrong and how to fix it. While in South Africa, it's likely I would have been identified as a *sangoma* or medium as a child given my abilities, in the US it was all seen as a problem – both the physical health issues and the extreme sensitivity and ability to see beyond what most could access.

What I see now is that there are healers and those who would do harm, with a huge spectrum of everything in between, everywhere. There are those who study the allopathic medicine system and all its intricacies long and hard, and those who decide to use it to mask the sicknesses inside themselves. Both of whom will go out in the world and call themselves doctors.

There are those who will travel the world to learn from yoga masters and the ancient teachings over a lifetime, and those who will take a 500-hour course and call their own starved and surgically manipulated bodies the results of "a lifetime of practice." Those who learn the age-old secrets of herbal medicine at the feet of those whose elders imparted the knowledge to them, taking in every bit of the ways so many plants can heal, and those who package who knows what in fancy labeling, whether pharmaceutical or new age, and charge a fortune for it. There are plenty of less than moral traditional healers here in South Africa, for sure. It is perhaps the human way to try to help others and also, in some, to profit from the vulnerable.

I see now that doctors and the whole spectrum of healers with which we are more familiar are human beings, just like us. Physicians believe that they should have the answers, that they should be able to fix people, and will often push the boundaries of the Hippocratic Oath and its promise to do no harm far beyond what is safe for the patient rather than admit that their abilities do not allow them to find the solution for this particular problem. I see that people dealing with illness are taught to identify as the patient, to talk about "their" cancer or "their" diabetes or "their" psychosis as if it were a permanent part of them, a fifth limb.

What I know now – and yes, this is just my opinion, yet it's hard-earned and learned from a great deal of experience – is that our bodies will find equilibrium if we allow them to, if we learn to listen to what they are telling us.

The summer before I came to South Africa, I spent a week or so at Kripalu, the Western Massachusetts yoga center my teacher Jonathan Foust helped create, in a workshop with Dr. Bessel van der Kolk and his now wife, Licia Sky. Van der Kolk is the author of a book that changed my life completely, *The Body Keeps the Score*, as well as the founder of the Trauma Research Foundation. At the time, I hesitated to sign up because I'd decided not to pursue becoming a therapist – and Bessel himself would tell me over that week that I should never pursue that kind of training, that my inside knowledge was far more valuable and might be lost in the process. So I thought it wasn't for me, a lay person, until my friend Sarah, who I'd later meet at Phinda on that first visit, said she was interested and we decided to go together.

What I learned there, in such a whole body sort of way, was that there is really nothing wrong with me. I'd done years and years of therapy to understand intellectually that I wasn't all the horrible things I'd been taught as a child, yet what I didn't fully learn is how deeply my experiences of trauma and abuse lived in my body – using illness and pain to speak to me, to show me what so needed to be healed. Life-changing does not begin to describe it.

It would take years of reflection and finding ways of listening and moving and healing in order to move out of what had become deep patterns of pain and dysfunction, all here on this land that seems to hold so much magic for me and is said to be the birthplace of mankind. I needed to come home and collect the parts of myself that had been missing for so long – parts that had literally been beaten out of me in the earliest years of my life and denied by the society I grew up in, never understood and often maligned.

In an odd way, for me, the differences between conventional Western medicine and centuries old traditional healing methodology echo the differences between Western – specifically American – sociological practices and those here in South Africa. After some time here, I began to see that even in this place halfway across the world, still seen by many as "deepest, darkest Africa," western ways have begun to change what was once so magical.

This showed up in a funny way the other day, reminding me of something that happened in those first months I was in South Africa, when people began to see that I was not going to come back to the US anytime soon. I received several messages from concerned friends, both virtual and people I'd spent time with regularly, asking if I was ok, if I had brought enough with me. Did I have everything I needed? When I assured them I was fine, and asked what they thought I might need, one of the answers – across the board – was toothbrushes. Did I have enough toothbrushes?

As dedicated as I am to dental health, I found it a funny thing for them to be concerned about, so I took my newly minted knowledge of the bush and put it to use. I snapped a branch off a dry quarry shrub and whittled off the bark on one end, as Dingane had taught me, then chewed on it until it formed a collection of bristles, sort of like a little broom. Then I mixed a bit of ash and water in the palm of my hand and held the stick toothbrush next to it, took a photo, and sent it to my concerned friends with a note reassuring them that I was just fine.

The funny part is this: that four years later, I opened up my Instagram feed to see a photo of a very similar stick in an advertisement for a fancy online health shop in the UK. This "natural toothbrush chew stick – tooth-cleaning twig" can now be yours, in sets of twelve, for a mere forty dollars. Or I'd be happy to go find you some, if you'd like. That kind of contribution would feed a lot of people here.

I've long held the belief that Africa, generally, and South Africa, specifically, has great gifts to share with the world – in complete opposition to the popular belief of many "first world" countries that they must come save the poor Africans. Save us from what, exactly? Over the past four centuries, Western countries and, more recently, China, have taken much away from this continent, in terms of material goods. Even worse, they've significantly chipped away at the tribal cultures that once guided life here, in between intertribal disputes over land.

The way I tell a brief history of South Africa to visitors is this: The Dutch explorers decided that they needed a stopover for their trade in India and points beyond, and settled on Cape Town as the right place to set up shop. They needed plenty of laborers as they "improved" things to the point of filling in the land itself, so they tried to enslave the "natives," the Khoisan. The natives weren't easily tamed, since they were Nomadic hunter/gatherers who tended to see a *kraal* full of sheep as a handy butchery nicely provided by these white people who had shown up. So instead, the interlopers imported their labor force from the southeast of Africa, Malaysia, and India, creating a unique population base.

In time, the British decided what the Dutch had done was very good, indeed, and so proceeded to fight for and win Cape Town, forcing the Dutch to move further into the interior of South Africa. Eventually they founded a gold rush town they named Johannesburg, which went on to grow mightily into the business center of the country. The British decided, after the city had taken root, that they'd very much like to have Johannesburg too, thanks ever so much, and fought for that spot as well, winning it from what were called the Boers at that point, now known as the Afrikaans. These hardy settlers, great farmers, would move further west and northwest, eventually settling in places now known as the provinces of Free State, Mpumalanga, Limpopo, and KwaZulu-Natal.

This land was, at one point, part of the great migration path down the eastern part of the African continent. The prey animals like wildebeest, zebra, and antelope would migrate, eating the grasses in season, then moving to the next area as the weather changed, with the predators following them along the way. Tribal people would follow, too, and there were many villages in which to stay and trade along the way, forming communities dependent on the migration itself.

When the farmers began to erect fences for their livestock and farming, this of course interrupted the migration, causing communities to fracture and fall apart too.
In addition, the cattle and other domestic animals eat the
grass roots and all, unlike the wild animals who leave the
roots intact to grow again, over time decimating the natural landscape and changing conditions for the human
inhabitants as well.

In the late twentieth century, conservationists began to
buy back the farmland, creating reserves that bring things
back to their original state and then returning the animals to places like Kruger and Hluhluwe-Imfolozi on a
national and provincial level and Munyawana and Phinda
in the private sector. All of it was and is focused on tourism, which, in turn, can benefit the local tribal communities over time.

This is obviously not a complete history, yet you get the
idea. Between colonization and later, the apartheid era, the
traditions, rights, and very lives of the various tribal people – too many tribes to list – have been affected on every
level. And then there were the missionaries. In my mind,
churches have always been about controlling the masses,
and therefore represent a fear-based practice, though obviously they provide a sense of safety and comfort for many,
along with doing good work. Surely, the white settlers, new
to deepest, darkest Africa and the powers she holds, were
frightened on a regular basis – the wild animals unlike any
they had known, the massive storms that blow across the
land, the caramel- to ebony-skinned people who held such
wisdom and perhaps what seemed like savage ways.

The newly transplanted souls must have taken great comfort in their well-worn bibles and the words they had studied since childhood. Perhaps it felt safer to try to stuff all of Africa's wildness, knowing, and glory into the square box of Christianity and to assume that, somehow, the native people would be better off following the ways that brought the European settlers such great solace. Maybe they meant well. Surely they did?

I grew up in a small Finnish Lutheran church on the Cape, and it was certainly a refuge for me as a child. Then I went on to find a church home in Lincoln Park Presbyterian Church, a very mission-driven church in Chicago with both local and international mission projects. I don't have anything against church, per se, yet when the entity that is created to foster belonging turns into a harsh taskmaster that creates shame and feelings of inequality and worth-lessness within their flock, I see that as both a huge prob-lem and a crime against humanity.

I'm sure the early missionaries who came to Africa and South Africa may have had good intentions, yet what they did was decide that they knew better what was right in this wild land than the indigenous people who'd been here since time began knew for themselves. They also used the Bible to convince those this land belonged to that these new white-skinned people had a right to take the land away, use them as cheap labor, and treat them overall as if they were young children. All of this set up a system that made it easy for things like land confiscation and apartheid, and raised generations of whites to feel they were superior to those who should have inherited this country.

In providing only minimal and far inferior education to the black population, they created a modern-day population ill-equipped to take over lodges returned to the tribal councils through land reclamation. Far worse, though, is that so many black Africans have moved away from African traditional practices. While there are some hybrid churches, like the Shembe one here in KwaZulu-Natal, which allow for parishioners to continue long-held ancestral traditions (along with more controversial practices like polygamy), many black South Africans have been raised in more Western churches, creating a huge rift within themselves as they try to somehow fit generations of African into a much more constrained European way of being.

One of the gifts I firmly believe that South Africa, and Africa generally, has to offer is this beautiful way of both respecting their ancestors and including them in their day-to-day lives, in the very structure of their families. This business of being human is not easy – and white people worldwide are pretty much led to believe that they are on their own, creating a kind of fierce independence that allows them to do things like explore the world and assume that their way will work for everyone. Many, of course, have a strong faith in God, which serves them well personally and brings comfort to what can be seen as a challenging existence, religion giving them a framework to structure their lives on. That is, in many ways, a beautiful coping mechanism yet for many, church is a once a week gig.

The spiritual (not religious) movement has in more recent times allowed people to bring the sacred into the everyday, giving them a way to move in the world without as much fear, or at least ways of managing it. Tara Brach, the beloved Buddhist teacher I've had the good fortune to spend time with, tells a little story about the fear and anxiety she (and I) see as a big part of this being human. She paints a picture of two prehistoric lizard-type creatures, out one afternoon. One sits himself upon a large flat rock, settles into lotus position and begins to "om" himself into a calm and peaceful place. The other scurries about, checking the position of the sun as a way of telling time, announcing in a high-pitched voice that it is about that time of the afternoon when the pterodactyls swoop down, looking for snacks each day. You can guess which one gets eaten first. Tara makes the point that we are, given the sitting lizard's sure demise, descended from the anxious, careful ones, and therefore this fear we have inside of us is understandable.

Having grown up in a house that felt like an emotional minefield, with outbursts of anger and fury a regular thing and fear of much in the outside world served as part of the daily menu, I was a pretty frantic lizard as a child. I felt I had to be, in order to survive, in order to even begin to protect my younger siblings. While both school and church were refuges of a sort, the undertone of my life was this fear of being seen as less than, as not normal, as unlovable and unworthy. Certainly not good enough to warrant any kind of life of my own, any wanting or desires – all of which led to believing the programming I received, that I was here to take care of other, more worthwhile people so that they could have easier, better lives. None of it made sense, any more than my very white skin and long straight hair, not really.

When I think about my loved ones and those I meet so often here in KwaZulu-Natal, lovely people in black bodies with tightly curled hair or shaven heads, I realize that they grew up in a similar yet different way. By virtue of the color of their skin and whether or not their hair could hold a pencil, they were born into a society that told them they were not as good, not as worthy, and certainly shouldn't have dreams of becoming more than a support to the lives of others – others who were born into a different body and a different set of expectations.

There's a conversation I've had, more times than I can count, in rural homes sitting on the floor on woven palm mats, waving flies away and watching young toddlers crawl on and off the laps of their grandmothers. These are amazingly strong women who have seen much in their lifetimes, the ones who are often the rock of their families for decades on end. They tell me about apartheid ending and how they gave birth to or perhaps helped another mama to bring a child into the world, and they held that child up to the sky, telling the gathered family members that this child, born into freedom, would have a different life, that they could be anything they wanted to be, that they would not be held back or subjected to cruelty and punishment based on their skin color alone.

Only to find that this whole new world was not much different. Yes, there was more freedom of movement, that sort of thing. But the fact remained that being black in South Africa means you are seen as a second-class citizen. At best. And this happens everywhere, I know, to some of us. Maybe it happened to you.

In the end, this conditioning has taught me a great deal, and there have been valuable gifts woven in the ropes of these beliefs that bound me up for so long. If I hadn't had this experience of growing up being forced to be something other than who I truly am, I don't know if I would have taken the leap of finding out who I was capable of being, and likely not the physical leap of coming home to South Africa. And I really doubt I'd have the most important relationships I have, the greatest gift I can imagine.

From early childhood and perhaps from that deep feeling of not belonging, I have had an incredibly close, rich, beautiful knowing that my ancestors are with me, other than when I got lost trying to be "normal." In the Western world, this aspect of being human is mostly not discussed – certainly not back in the 1960s. While I could (and probably will) write a whole book on the subject, I cannot tell my own story, or that of the Zulu family and friends I've introduced you to here, without recognizing *amadlozi*. The ancestors. Those who came before us. Those on whose shoulders we rise. Those whose DNA and hopes and dreams we carry forward.

Everyone has their own point of view on exactly what an ancestor is. There are the literal ones, those whose lives grew the family trees we were born of. There are cultural ancestors, ones whose words and images, centuries later, strike a strong chord inside our hearts. Van Gogh, Rumi, Hafiz, and O'Keeffe especially are with me in this way, along with others. There are those who appear in our dreams, who show us our path and accompany us, who protect us in ways we cannot possibly comprehend. Like our internal images of God, they differ from person to person and from time to time. Call them angels, guides, companions, what have you – they are the ones who carry us forward, and I do not think I would be here without the beautifully strong ribbons of connections they have woven together under me, creating a supportive foundation for me to move from.

In the African traditional world, there is an incredible structure of tools, ceremony, and practices that have been in place since the beginning of time, seemingly, and that have been criticized and even demonized since colonization began in an effort to bring these "savages" into the fold of Christianity. Thankfully, some of the churches here in South Africa have softened their more Western programming to allow for both. And who can't use as much support as they can get? I don't see a conflict between the two.

The thing about ancestor and traditional African practice, in particular, is this: it acknowledges the sovereignty of both lineage and individuals. It encourages each of us to become all we can be, to fulfill our potential and to bring all our gifts into play for the good of our own lives, our families, our society, and the human race. In choosing to be who we are rather than who we are told to be, we honor those who came before us and clear the way for those who will come after us. It honors who God intended us to be.

Certainly I would never have found my way home without these practices and the presence of my ancestors, and I'm not sure I would have recovered from losing families and children along the way without them, either. And so with respect and gratitude, I will follow their call for the rest of my life. *Thokoza.* Just as a plant grows best in the soil for which it was intended, I have begun to thrive here in ways I've never felt before – at the point in my life where I expected to slow down and retire. I'm often accused of aging backwards as the effects of the magic of belonging begin to show physically, and my body heals from all those years of dis-ease.

Do I wish I'd figured this out earlier? Or been more receptive to the call earlier, less limited by all those beliefs I internalized? Do I wish I'd been seen at an early age and guided in the traditional ways? Yes, some days. Of course. Yet I know, for the most part, that everything does indeed happen when it is time, and I am so very grateful to be right where I am, right now.

Twenty-Six

I wondered many times over the years about that Future Self visualization I'd done as part of my coaching training – especially after arriving in South Africa and in my struggles to gain permanent residency. In my dream-like state, that place in the magical forest had seemed so real – and I was still quite convinced that it was in the Pacific Northwest of the United States or maybe on the Sunshine Coast of British Columbia. So I questioned whether, given how difficult it is to become a South African citizen, perhaps I would ultimately move back – something I really couldn't comprehend fully or imagine at all.

Even as I wondered, I continued to live and plan "as if." As if I were able to stay in this country I loved so much, as if I truly did belong here even in the eyes of the government. I'd bought and renovated the house in Umdloti, thinking I'd stay there. There were those magnificent views of the Indian Ocean, the sound of the sea lulling me to sleep each night. I loved it and the artsy little town, and yet I'd built that home for me and Jabu and his kids, and he and his children were gone. There were so many memories of Lesedi there, in particular.

It was also not entirely comfortable. Umdloti is a predominantly white community, and most black people only come in to work for the day to support the lifestyle many enjoy. I wondered if I would ever go to the grocery store with my Musa, my son, without the cashier telling him as he loaded items onto the counter to wait, that she was helping "madam," only to be rather speechless when he answered her in isiZulu, *"Ngi no Mama"* – I'm with my mother. It was all fine, even beautiful, but not really home. I missed the bush, too, yet it was getting harder and harder to make time to spend at Kube Yini.

In the early days of the pandemic, I spent many hours online poring over ads for farms an hour or so inland in the rolling hills of the Midlands. I'd grown up on a small farm, and I still loved visiting them, drinking in the open space and the animals, the gardens, and the dirt roads. I thought I'd buy a place not far from Durban and maybe build a small house, somewhere I could stay a couple nights a week to let the dogs run and spend time in the beautiful area called One Thousand Hills – for good reason.

Once the restrictions loosened up, I found my way to visit one farm, I loved the land itself, despite the fact that it had a couple houses already built on it. But it was a bit more than I'd imagined, at least to start. Negotiations with the owners proved tricky, and it just didn't feel right, though I met a lovely estate agent through the process. I chatted with her about my dreams and sent her a batch of ads, telling her which ones I was interested in.

I also questioned my sanity – not for the first or last time – because really, I'd just finished renovating this gorgeous home on the coast. But it also made a lot of financial sense. Moving inland meant much better pricing and, given the way the world was going, stashing away some extra funds was looking like a wise move. It was a time when nothing really made sense anyway, so off I went to look at a place that was completely different than what I'd dreamt of, at least recently.

It wasn't until well after I'd bought this place that I understood what it really was. From the beginning it was obvious it was a treasure: a great investment and the perfect location, fifteen hectares of virgin indigenous forest only ten minutes from a great town with everything we'd need, a short distance from family. I figured that Baba Gumede had somehow led me to it, given his love of forest and the fact that the house had been built from the stone on the land.

But what I didn't remember, until the night of my birthday in 2020, was that it is the home of my future self. It is exactly what I saw in that visioning session, all those years ago, sitting in my suburban DC La-Z-Boy chair and looking out at the few trees across the way. I knew when I walked into this home that it was special – I loved every detail. Yet it took me a while to see just what a gift it is. There's a dam, down the lane and through the woods, which we will repair and fill with water and hope to see what I now recognize as storks swimming contentedly with their young. We'll build a beautiful labyrinth, and my family and I will sit out on that deck, watching the stars. Even my hair is cooperating, the white swirling in amongst the blonde, and the artwork is ready to hang.

This being human, this living as a soul in a body of flesh and bones – it has its challenges. It does. And yet aren't we lucky to be here at all? Aren't we?

I'm so glad and so grateful for all of it, and for the opportunity to share my stories and to help others create their own. I hope you'll stay, too, even in the hard times, and weave your own tales of wonder. I hope you find a deep sense of belonging and know you are loved. Because you are. We all are.

The invitation is to step into it all, one day at a time, and to find joy in all that you can.

To love and be loved. It's that simple.

Welcome home.

Twenty-Seven

In the end, after all of these bumpy, curvy, dusty roads I've travelled over the last several years (and before that too) what have I learned?

That a place can call to you and bring you a great distance only to challenge you mentally, physically, and spiritually in ways well beyond your imagination, all while whispering so strongly that this is home?

That someone – a grown man, a mostly grown person who calls you mama, or anyone really – can show up in your life and become so close to you that you forget to guard your heart, and then leave you without explanation, unclear as to their motives and whether there was truth in any part of the relationship?

That the innate gifts you have will bring you just as much challenge as they will bring you joy, often much more, yet that they truly do define you and infiltrate whatever you choose to do with your days whether you acknowledge them or not?

Yes to all of that and then some.

And yet they've taught me, too, that I am far, far stronger than I know or will admit to knowing. That while I often feel like that little girl who was told she'd die alone and broke, there is and always has been a spectacularly powerful and wise old woman within me too. She has brought me through experiences that many could not survive and allowed me to tell the tales, to inspire others to stay and not define themselves by the external events inflicted on them. To tell the stories and yet not become limited by them. She has allowed me to witness the journeys of brave souls and to welcome new ones to the world, to help many find their own inner resources and others to grow in what can only be considered hostile conditions. I like to think that she has been with me as I've written this book – the good, the ugly, the amazing, and the crazymaking– cajoling me to share openly and deeply from my heart when really it would be far easier to erect very, very thick walls around all of my internal world, put on a very good disguise, and walk around pretending to be that elusive thing called "normal."

The biggest lesson I've learned – the one that I possibly came to this Earth in order to master – is the concept of truly not caring what anyone else thinks of me. And that, in turn, means being exactly who I am. This is far more challenging than it sounds. As I've learned along the way, sometimes those we love most – my daughter Lena, for example – aren't able to cope with this sort of change. In becoming myself and reorienting everything as a result, I've lost her and much more. In any case, if I've helped her and others embrace themselves and their true identity much earlier than I embraced mine, that is worth a lot.

The greatest gift of this lesson is that it brought me a love that I've never known in the form of a wonderful soul my granddaughters affectionately call "The Fireman." Shenge is really truly a fire fighter, yes, and yet his very being is also just that stereotype. He's the guy who is there when you need him, even when you don't know you need him, and the girls adore him as much as I do. While we aren't your standard couple in terms of race, age, and societal norms, our hearts are aligned in ways beyond understanding, and I consider myself most blessed to have found this man who is both a grounding metronome in my life and a catalyst for so much good in my days. Who knows how we found each other, though we suspect our fathers have been pull- ing some strings up in heaven or wherever they are. We are just happy to have created a family and a life that works beautifully for us.

It hasn't always been this easy or this good, and I'm surprised to this day that we were able to meet and fall in love. If not for the whisperings of my ancestors, I never would have agreed to our first date, but somehow that happened quite quickly. And as I carefully stepped through the very muddy parking lot, he met me halfway and opened his arms in a big hug. Somehow, I just knew I was safe. And home. That feeling has never changed. The man makes me smile, just by being who he is, and he smiles a lot when I'm close by too. I don't know how to convey how very odd that is, for me. An entirely new feeling, to feel better with a new person in my life, rather than on high alert.

As an adult who carries a diagnosis of Post-Traumatic Stress Disorder, I've worked hard to understand and heal from my trauma history. When I first began learning about the clinical explanations for behaviors that had long mystified me, PTSD was most often characterized by the "fight, flight, freeze" responses, and while I'm not a fan of labels, it was enormously helpful to have terms that somewhat normalized or maybe even legitimized what I'd been doing for so long. Flight was my clear specialty – whenever anything got too tough whether it be a relationship or a school assignment, I'd just run away. Literally, if possible, and in my mind if not. I wonder how many fellow bookworms did their best to fall deeply into the pages of a book as a refuge. Until injuries in my teens and early twenties prevented it, I was at my very happiest running and continue to in my dreams decades after my physical body began refusing to go along for the ride.

Fight wasn't really an option for me, growing up, and so I never went that route, thankfully. But freezing? Yes please. I was a champion disassociator, and I imagine I've spent years of my life separating myself from what was going on around me. Learning to manage triggers helped, and after a couple decades of educated practice, that's all a thing of the past.

It's only been recently that I've learned about another coping mechanism. The one thing that I had no idea I was doing, no clue as to it being a trauma response, no real awareness of it at all. The fourth "f" – fawning. The one that has likely really shaped my life in ways that have taken decades to shed.

It is, in essence, feeling that you must earn your right to be here on this Earth by catering to the needs of others. By putting everyone else (and this, in my case, means everyone – those close to me, complete strangers, and everyone in between) before meeting your own needs.

Apparently the idea is that in doing all you can to make yourself invaluable to others, you feel somehow that you are protecting yourself from further trauma. I've spent my life doing just that. That's the short story, anyway, which will have to suffice here and hopefully explains to us both why I've lived my life the way I have. I like to say – and it's quite true – that I have no regrets. And yet I can't fathom how different things would have been if it hadn't taken me so long to figure all this out. Still, as the work of a lifetime, it's not a bad use of several decades to have shirked off the cloak of unworthiness, shame, and self-hatred to follow a path of calling, exploration, and compassion. And the difference in how I live now, the freedom I experience and the connection I feel to those who have come before me and to those still to come, is not quantifiable.

Had I, for example, not spent three days a week sitting in my doctor's office with an IV drip in my arm, dreaming of the day when my body wouldn't be in pain 24/7, I'd never have had hours and hours sitting still and picturing a life in South Africa when that calling returned after many years of trying to forget about it. Had I not spent so much time with my former partner's children, I might not have understood that the best way to help young women and children thrive is to teach Zulu men to become modern day warriors, putting their offspring above all and using the fighting spirit of their ancestors in as many ways as possible to make things better for their people today. Had I not experienced my own body being violated and abused, how would I be able to sit and listen to the stories of others in such an open way, allowing them to shed the baggage they've carried for so long so that they can create a new story, a new way of living?

There's much in this world of ours that I do not understand, that I will never comprehend. Watching American politics from afar is beyond confusing, and it's painful to watch the country I was raised in go backward so rapidly in terms of human rights alone. All across the globe, it seems the cruel, the narcissistic, and the power hungry are winning. And all I know to do is to share my stories and the practices I've picked up along the way, to help those who crave a better world to connect to their ancestors and their roots so that they can branch out and blossom and bring good to us all. I'm not sure, in my lifetime, that I'll see the change that so many of us desire, yet I can surely plant seeds that will grow long after my bones turn back into earth.

I can stay, thanks to all I've learned along the way. I can love, thanks to those who love me – sharp edges, messy moments, and all. I can live my life with the man who holds my heart and our beautiful family we've woven together. And I can hope, thanks to all the beauty that still exists in so many ways all around me and in those spirits I'm privileged to connect with every day.

Most delightfully of all, as this book goes out into the world, The Fireman and I will stand together on the wooden deck outside our house that looks out over the magic forest one morning, in front of our family. We will make our vows to each other and in the eyes of the ancestors, become husband and wife, having found enough hope and even more love in these crazy, chaotic times to begin again, with each other. To create the next stories, to fill each other and the world around us with light and good.

Perhaps all of this is what storytellers mean when they say, "And she lived happily ever after."

The end.

GLOSSARY

Amadlozi – the ancestors
Baba – father or older man
Bhuti – brother or contemporary male
Gogo – grandmother or elder woman
Ikhaya – home
Imoto – automobile
Indoda – husband
Indodana – son
Intombazane – girl
Inyanga – traditional healer, in a physical sense
Makoti – bride
Mama – mother or older woman
Mamezala – mother-in-law
Mfana – boy
Mkhulu – grandfather or elder man
Ndodakazi – daughter
Qaphela – beware, a warning
Sangoma – traditional healer, in a psychic/emotional sense
Sbari – brother-in-law
Sisi – sister or contemporary female
Skwiza – sister-in-law
Thokoza/thokozani – a traditional way of greeting, thanking,
    addressing ancestors
uBabezala – father-in-law
Ubizo – calling
Umfana wami – my son
Umlungu – white person
Umuntu – person

This book has been a lifetime in the making – and it has sometimes seemed that it's taken another lifetime to write, yet here we are. While I'm grateful for the company of far too many to mention by name throughout this process, there are a few I'd like to thank publicly here.

Maggie McReynolds and Sky Kier at Un-Settling Books, you have been beyond patient and extraordinarily kind for this journey much longer than any of us anticipated, and I appreciate you both so much. And I'm very much looking forward to extending your knowledge of all things Zulu with the next book!

Nona Jordan, my dear friend who spent four years here in Africa, thank you for our early morning calls, for our bush adventures in Zambia, and, most of all, for our ongoing conversations about life, love, and this book.

The group of lovely individuals who have been in various renditions of my Being Me communities over the years. We have laughed and cried and walked the path together since well before I left the US, and as lonely as those first months in South Africa were, your daily presence in my life was a lifeline through everything.

Wendi MaDumakude, you and our girls have been the brightest light I could ever ask for, and such loyal and supportive companions as I've written and written. Thanks for using your indoor voices while I wrote (and napped!) and for the constant encouragement. For refusing to allow me to give up, even when I really wanted to do so.

My ancestors, the beautiful crew of souls who have carried me through a rather unusual and sometimes very challenging life, and for the calling they have issued so loudly, so strongly – if not always as clearly as I'd like.

Indoda wami, my husband – you too. Always. Your gentle encouragement and unending patience have made these last months of writing, rewriting, and editing possible. This book may never have reached the world without your ever so subtle pushes across the finish line.

And my father, Baba Gumede. You showed me, for those three precious years we had together, how to be *umuntu* rather than just an *umlungu.* How to be true to my soul, my ancestors, and my calling. Even now, you are the greatest teacher I've known.

Ngiyabonga kini nonke kakhulu – thank you all, very much.

Umuntu, ngumuntu, ngabantu.

Now living happily ever after in her magic forest, Christa Gumede Buthelezi uses words, creativity, and traditional Zulu ways to invite people to become who they truly are rather than who they were told to be. In *Ubizo: A Story of Finding Home*, she shares her personal experiences of doing just that, from her childhood in the US to her current life outside Durban, KwaZulu-Natal, where she lives with her husband, children, and grandchildren along with a pack of three somewhat domesticated dogs and a whole lot of birds and monkeys.

While you may not be able to visit with Christa in person, she has several online homes where you can connect. For those of you who travel, look for updates on in-person retreats and workshops in the magic forest.

WEBSITE: thisbeinghuman.co
INSTAGRAM: instagram.com/_nomadlozi_
FACEBOOK: facebook.com/ubizobook
TIKTOK: @christakhulula

SCAN THE QR CODE TO VISIT MY WEBSITE

Thank you for reading! As a first-time author, I welcome your thoughts. The very best way to support the book is to leave a review on Amazon or elsewhere online – your encouragement means the world to me. And feel free to invite friends to read UBIZO as well! I'm happy to meet with your book group via Zoom.

Following is an excerpt from
Christa Gumede Buthelezi's novel in progress,
Chicken Goat Cow: Tales of a White Sangoma

Follow the writing journey at
http://www.thisbeinghuman.co

Chapter One

I began to stir, that morning, in an oversize, luxurious bed made up with fine Egyptian cotton sheets and comfy goose down pillows. Something had begun to wake me, yet I clung to sleep like a young child, stretching my legs under the weight of the warm duvet. Through closed eyes, I could sense a bit of light in the room, yet it seemed far too early to rouse myself. I began to run through the opulent hotel's room service menu in my mind.

My imaginings of a perfectly poached egg on wilted spinach with the Barcleigh's well-executed Hollandaise sauce and my favorite gluten-free seeded bread, all served on fine porcelain with a crystal bowl of berries and clotted cream, were interrupted rather abruptly by an insistent tapping on the window. I rolled over and covered my head with a pillow, musing about whether to have coffee or Earl Grey. I was sure it was only a pigeon out on my balcony overlooking the private walled gardens of this posh London neighborhood.

Just as I began to drift back into sleep, it started again – this *tshook, tshook* sound, sharper this time. Clearly this pigeon had been joined by friends. I began to wake more fully, only to find myself registering the heat in the room, the bright sunlight coming through the window, and, as my feet hit the ground, the soft, slick feeling of the cow dung-polished floor.

I quickly realized that I was no longer living that life, the life I'd lived for decades of privilege and international travel – and, quite frankly, of being both bored and spoiled simultaneously. No, I was not in London anymore. I was at home.

Home, the very traditional and sprawling collection of block and zinc-roofed rondavels and rectangular houses painted a bright aqua hue, where most of my Zulu family resides and traditional spiritual consultations have been conducted for many years now, first by my father alone and now also by my brother and me. And there were no pigeons, of course, only a small flock of insistent hens and chicks looking for the special seed I kept for them as a treat. Furthermore, there was no room service, and judging from the angle of the sun and the rising heat, I had clearly overslept.

I rose quickly, wrapped myself in a big towel, picked up the heavy five-liter plastic jug of water I'd collected from the Jojo tank the night before, and went around the side of my little two-room house to where there was some semblance of privacy. There, I shooed a couple of spiders from the plastic tub I kept on hand, then filled it and quickly scrubbed myself with a face cloth, as I'd been taught, from head to toe.

Carefully stepping on the largest stones so as not to muddy my feet, I made my way back inside, my body easily drying in the sun as I did so. Then I rubbed coconut oil onto every bit of my skin I could reach. This was my concession to protecting my skin, Zulu style, without using the ubiquitous Vaseline. I had my limits, after all.

A quick glance out my back window proved my fears right – the day's clients had already begun to gather under the huge sausage tree uBaba had planted as a young man. I pulled on a simple sundress and slipped on my slops – what I'd grown up calling flip-flops. Then I wrapped my hair in a scarf, twisted my *ibhayi* around my waist, and headed outside, blinking at the sun's strength. December had proven to be even hotter than usual. We were much busier than usual, too, as everyone was beginning to return to their traditional homes for the festive season.

I headed away from the waiting crowd, though, knowing that there wouldn't be time for lunch and needing something in my belly for the day ahead. The thin, aluminum pot lids askew on the makeshift counter inside the family "kitchen" showed me that my nieces and nephews had made off with the curry from the night before, so I settled for a cup of tea and the crusts of the *phuthu* we'd made the previous day. The maize meal crumbled as I wolfed it down. I was sure I'd already been spotted and would be expected momentarily to begin the day's consultations.

As I picked my way up the gravelly hill, I saw her. The very young mama sitting on a big rock, a bit removed from the others, wearing clothing that had once fit but now gaped across her milk-filled breasts. Her baby's neck barely held up his head, his muscle tone clearly not developing the way it should. This child, much wanted after the tragic death of his father, was clearly not thriving. And it would be my job to figure out why.

I took a big breath, adjusted my *doek*, and walked up to the bench, greeting the old men there warmly and respect-fully – "*Thokozani, ninjani?*" They smiled broadly, show-ing off patterns of missing teeth and blackened gums from years of snuff indulging, and I could sense the long sto-ries about to erupt, all of them vying to get my attention first. I interrupted gently, saying, "*Ngiyaxolisa – sorry, sorry Mkhulu*" and pointing at the baby. "*Indodana yethu,* our son, he isn't right. I must tend to him first. Sorry, sorry."

Their necks collectively swiveled first to see the boy and then back to nod at each other quite seriously. They all mumbled their agreement. "*Yebo ma, ah bakithi.* You must."

I gathered up the child and the usual overkill of velour blankets swaddling him, even in this heat. With my free arm, I helped the young mother to her feet. She, too, was rather listless and weak, and I wondered what was at the bottom of all this dis-ease. I guided her down one set of steps and then up to the door of my father's rondavel, his office. As he was away tending to *sangoma* business, I'd been using his workspace.

It was my very favorite place to be these days. While a far cry from the gleaming, polished rooms I'd frequented in America and the UK, the large, round space was full of *muthi* and magic, and I felt stronger there than anywhere else. My gifts had been part of my life for as long as I could remember, yet surrounded by a lifetime of gourds and jars containing herbs, stacks of ceremonial costumes and strings of beads made by my parents, and all manner of feathers and quills, I knew undeniably that I was exactly what everyone called me – the white *sangoma*.